THE WANDERER'S CURSE

THE WANDERER'S CURSE

a memoir

JENNIFER HOPE CHOI

W. W. NORTON & COMPANY

Independent Publishers Since 1923

For information about permission to reproduce selections from this book, write to Permissions, W. W. Norton & Company, Inc., 500 Fifth Avenue, New York, NY 10110

For information about special discounts for bulk purchases, please contact W. W. Norton Special Sales at specialsales@wwnorton.com or 800-233-4830

Manufacturing by Lake Book Manufacturing
Book design by Marysarah Quinn
Production manager: Lauren Abbate

ISBN 978-1-324-03551-0

W. W. Norton & Company, Inc., 500 Fifth Avenue, New York, NY 10110
www.wwnorton.com

W. W. Norton & Company Ltd., 15 Carlisle Street, London W1D 3BS

1 2 3 4 5 6 7 8 9 0

For 할머니, 할아버지,
and 엄마

Running away, without telling anyone, seemed necessary.

—AGNÈS VARDA, *LES PLAGES D'AGNÈS*

echo

THERESA HAK KYUNG CHA

the in-between-time: from when a sound is made
to when it returns as an echo
no one knows if it was heard,
when it was heard
when it would be heard
if ever at all
but it continues on and on and on
maybe thousand years

someone's memory

tale

legend

poem

dream

CONTENTS

THE WANDERER'S CURSE

PROLOGUE

I HEARD THE SHRIEKING ALL the way inside the house. However improbable for an entirely gated city in southern California, I thought surely a wild animal must be somewhere nearby, lost or imperiled. The voice held a distinctly metallic treble, almost elegiac, and I imagined the body containing it perplexed by these manicured streets, darting across the golf carts–only lane, eyes scanning for rough grass strips, wooded glens, any bit of open country, only to find a blank horizon blunted by an electronic boom barrier gate.

Then I stepped outside and saw her: my wisp-thin mother, wielding a pair of four-foot-long hedge clippers, wailing beneath an overgrown tree. They looked gigantic in her small arms, like those jumbo-sized scissors used in ribbon cutting ceremonies. Except there was nothing celebratory about the moment. With each snip Umma wept and howled louder, jerking the shears shut, bobbing her head elastically forward and back. She did not appear in control of her body, which moved in an odd staccato, like a marionette—ungainly yet entranced.

Puzzled by the sight of her, I asked, "Don't you . . . have a gardener?" But she ignored me.

When I was a child, I often found my mother yanking weeds from the front lawn with exacting force, for full afternoons in 100-degree heat or casually on her way to the mailbox. This was different. I understood as soon as I saw how the tree's sharp branches tumbled down, dragging gashes across her skin.

"*Umma, please, don't,*" I said, conjuring the few Korean words I could speak.

She paused, but not on account of me. It was a scorcher that day, high nineties, parched and unremitting. For a moment she stood still, eyeing the cuts on her arms and the fallen debris scattered at her feet. Then she raised the clippers and continued snipping and screaming and weeping, powered by that mysterious force tugging so madly at her strings.

Earlier that day I'd flown in from Manhattan, where I'd recently finished college. I was twenty-one, still radiating a new grad glow. At the airport, I searched for the woman I'd known growing up: our aloof ricewinner, taskmaster, and domestic dictator, who wore beige sweater sets from a store called Petite Sophisticate, who sported a sensible, chin-length perm she blow-dried straight, who rarely, if ever, smiled.

That was before our family went kablooey. This was her after: standing at the Arrivals gate, same slight frame, barely clearing five feet. But the rest of her appeared to be trapped in some frantic state of repair. She'd dyed her gray hair orange, teased and pinned it up with glitter-spangled butterfly clips. She'd swapped her sweater set for a sequined bolero and wore flared blue jeans she'd plucked from the children's age 10 to 11 sale rack. "They only $7.99!" she bragged. "How can you beat that?!" She was smiling deliriously, as if to distract me from something. Then I saw it in her eyes, as I would that afternoon beneath the tree: terror, at her own unraveling and closer, a barely tamped but quaking loneliness.

One year later, I received a call from my mother. It was July in New York City. The garbage on the streets, ripe from the hot concrete, oozed an unspeakable odor, and I was in a mood. I'd been puttering around since graduation, hoping a career path might materialize between Craigslist gigs and 2-4-1 happy hours. That night, I'd have to return to my post as bar wench at a Lower East Side German biergarten. Until then I'd planned to lie motionless in bed, staring out to a brick wall through a window screen caked with alley dust, imagining instead the ocean's lap-ping tide or tree leaves quivering through cool gusts of wind. I wanted to hear, too, a silence so pure and quiet that it might transfer a similar stillness on my mind. Instead the din inside me seemed to slosh around, spilling out messy-like beyond my body and into what remained out of view: yowling feral cats and from the synagogue next-door, voices wafting over, a shapeless lament.

When my mother called me, I answered to engage in another unknowable scene. Who was she today? And would this version of her behave as if we were no longer estranged?

After brief greetings, she asked me: "What do you think of Alaska?"

"As in . . . *Alaska* Alaska?"

"Yeh," she said. "What do you think of your mom living in Alaska?"

I thought of the day I caught her bleeding and screeching in her front yard. Then, like an avalanche, I pictured igloos, lumberjacks, roving packs of wolves, virgin snow, towering pines, Jack London, mush! mush! Until Christopher McCandless slid in with his rusting blue bus, along with the Grizzly Man and his grizzlies—adventurers whose lives and quests had been annihilated out in the Last Frontier.

What did I think of my mother in Alaska? I didn't know what to think. I couldn't answer her question, couldn't recognize our likeness either, how both of us seemed caught in some half-baked, hopeful loop, determined to hit the reset button, as if it could be so easy to wake up suddenly changed or cured, someone else, somewhere new. I didn't know how this would only be the beginning of a greater wandering, for both of us—a series of peregrinations that, no matter how far we tried to get away, somehow brought us back to the truth of ourselves. To each other.

It would take a while. For starters, I didn't actually think she'd go to Alaska. (Did they even have kimchi up there?) So I hung up the phone, fell back asleep. Within a week, my mother was stowing a rice cooker, a television, and two suitcases into her truck. Molder, her Korean Jindo dog, sat shotgun, and together they hit the road. Eight hours to Sacramento, California. Thirteen hours to Bellingham, Washington. Thirty-six hours on a cargo ferry streaming through the Pacific, until at last the reward: a view of sun-dappled waves, the sway of lush green trees, off a path once forged by fortune-seekers in search of discovery and gold.

She called me upon her arrival too. "In Alaska," she said, "even the weeds is beautiful."

And off my mother went, into the wild.

PART
ONE

ROWLAND HEIGHTS HOUSE
2,650 sq. ft., 4BR, 3BA

From Redfin.com:

"BEAUTIFUL COMMUNITY HOME BUILT IN 1998.
PRIDE OF OWNERSHIP, VERY PRIVATE, GREAT QUIET
NEIGHBORHOOD. 20 FT HIGH CEILING IN LR. MAPLE
HARDWOOD FLOOR, FORMAL DINING, SPACIOUS
FAMILY ROOM W/ FIREPLACE. 1 BEDROOM SUITE
DOWNSTAIRS, MASTER SUITES W/ WALK-IN CLOSET,
BALCONY W/ VIEWS TO HILLS, CITY LIGHTS, VALLEY
& MOUNTAIN VIEWS. BERBER CARPET, 2-CAR AT-
TACHED GARAGE. 2 SUITES, 1 DOWN & 1 UP. BACK-
YARD FOR ENTERTAINING. HARD TO FIND HOME
WITH GREAT PRICING."

Points of Origin

FIRST YOU SHOULD KNOW: I was born with a blue butt. So was my mother. Thirty-two years and many thousands of miles of land, sky, and sea separated her creation from mine, yet we emerged the same— mad for first breaths, ten-fingered, ten-toed, chick-like tufts of black hair nested atop our soft skulls and, incredibly, a wavy-bordered blue spot not unlike Rorschach's inkblots blooming across our tiny bums. Blue like ice-cold lips, blue like the ocean at midnight, Picasso's most melancholic bluest of blues.

By the time I learned about my blueness, it was already gone. The spot disappeared sometime after my fourth birthday. I have tried to recall that other version of me. In perhaps my earliest butt-related memory, I am taking a shower with my mother: The water beat down on my shoulders thunderously. I was sullen about something, slid open the glass door to escape Umma, and she smacked my bottom. I remember crying in the showy way children do when they're old enough to know better, then peering behind me, seeking proof of my mother's betrayal. But I saw nothing but plain tush. I was neither red nor blue. We stood as nude as newborns, unshy in our nakedness, water cascading across my mother's towering body as she fumed and I wept in her shadow.

My sister, Laurie, born seven years before me, retained her blueness well through kindergarten. We know this because Laurie's teacher mistook the marking for an enormous bruise and confronted my mother at an emergency conference. When Umma told me this story, more than a decade had passed but the encounter still annoyed her—not for the absurdity of the accusation so much as for the teacher's ignorance. "We are Korean," my mother explained incredulously, as if forced to qualify that the grass was green or that birds could fly. "We are all born this way."

I didn't believe her until I saw one for myself. I was about twelve when my aunt gave birth to a boy; while changing his diaper, she plucked the baby up by the ankles, and there it was, a bona fide blue butt in the flesh. My mother pursed her lips at me, as if to say, *See? Told you.* But I was too distracted by the striking shade of blue before me—not happy or cheery but deeply dark hued. A kind of sorrowful inheritance. Confirming its realness did not sate a bigger question that had begun to prickle within me, about provenance and place. Rarely did Umma speak about where she came from, the home she left at twenty-three, who she was there as a child and adolescent. Without knowing her origin, what did blueness mean for me?

Science says melanin-containing cells trapped within the dermis during fetal development cause our unique coloring. The birthmark, known as the Mongolian spot, is commonly found on the bums of East Asian newborns and dissipates, in most instances, by age six. According to Korean folklore, our coloration derives from Samshin Halmoni, Grandmother Spirit, a deity who slaps us to life when we are born, leaving behind the blue spot. In other interpretations Samshin Halmoni beats the baby blue until it is forced from the womb. Some of us will never know we arrive to the world this way, backsides budding with the artifice of trauma by some magic in our chemistry. Then one day we awaken, an inherent part of ourselves dissolved from the body, spirited away.

My mother didn't relay these details (I had to root around, looking for answers on my own). The one time I asked Umma why we were born blue, she said, "Because we have Mongolian blood," then promptly walked away, leaving me to steep in the utter mystery of her frankness. That was how it was with her, ever a trail of contextless, unimpeachable absolutes I was to accrue and accept without inquiry. Whatever autobiographical scraps I managed to scrounge together did not coalesce into a full portrait. As I grew older, I assumed such obfuscation pertained to her generally withholding nature, or because she valued the tidiness of stoicism. It did not occur to me these omissions related to a grander evasion: an attempt to get as far away from home, and the life she'd lived there, as possible. Aside from blueness, what else had carried over from her to me, and what did she hope might permanently dissipate with distance and time?

Perhaps none of my business, to have her whole past unspooled before me, as if anyone is owed that level of exposure. But when I stood weeping in the shower, in her shadow, I could not see myself apart from her. I was looking to my mother then as any child does, to see who I could, and should, become.

It may seem conceptually obvious to note but, back then, Umma was around my age now, late thirties, which is to say that as a kid I had assumed being an adult, an "old" one at that, meant you had arrived at certain precious knowledge about life and self's greatest enigmas. I thought I knew everything . . . at seventeen, then twenty-five, then thirty-three until, eventually, I realized I didn't know jack shit the whole time and maybe *that* humbling culmination was the whole point.

Here is what I'd sussed out, by the time I got to high school, circa 1998:

Umma was the Boss Bitch, the Decider, our Head Honcho, who held every account and paid every bill working morning and night shifts as an open-heart-surgery nurse. To her coworkers and the outside world, she went by Chris, short for Christine—the name she'd adopted in America. A staunch pragmatist, she packed my sack lunch salads with 200 ccs of ranch dressing in urine sample containers. ("So what?" she'd defend. "They're sterile.") In her free time, she noshed on squid jerky while watching *Unsolved Mysteries* after Sunday service. She could be quite ruthless, as if for sport. I once saw her haggle a Rip Curl T-shirt down 100 pesos from a toothless vendor on Rosarito Beach, just for the thrill of the deal. On the rare occasions we dined at American restaurants, she could eviscerate a server solely through her body language: crossed arms, perma-scowl, and pushed-aside plate, her eyes aflame, as if pleased by how skillfully she could spoil the meal for everyone.

Perhaps she reserved a specific ire for her own family. Nothing could be clean enough, neat enough, good enough. Any infraction, however minor—say, a single roasted sesame seed accidentally skittering onto the floor—merited thorough excoriation. She called us stupid so frequently our idiocy earned a shorthand, in both noun and adjective form: "What are you, stu?!" or "How could you be so stu, Stu?!" or nearly breathless with rage, "Aigoo . . . *STU!!!*" Although maybe we deserved it. If we helped with house chores, she'd yank the sponge or vacuum from our hands, and, infuriated, carry out the task herself. She often accused us of "do-da jobs," meaning you do the work but all "do-da, do-da!" half-heartedly and half-well. I don't think this was entirely fair or accurate of her to have claimed. But as my mother became increasingly impossible to please, we felt relieved once she stripped us of our duties. It was easier, acquiescing to her potent will.

And what incredible energy the woman expended to keep her world looking perfectly in order. She controlled every inch of her domain: the edict of coasters beneath room temp glasses, just in case; the perfect fan of *Better Homes & Gardens* issues splayed on the Pine-Sol'd coffee table; the immaculately wrapped fake presents staged beneath the Christmas tree come December; no trust for mops, brooms, or dishwashers, cleaning most things by hand or down on her haunches until appropriately "spick-and-span."

You could see such exactitude even in her handwriting, the ringlet curl of her cursive Cs identical and uniform in each printing. This made her signature impossible to forge on my missing homework referrals. Which was the only thing I could rely on my father for—his easily replicable, Richter scale scrawl. I could also ask for his autograph in-person and, with his eyes glued to the television, I'd place the pen in his hand, position the tip on the line and say, "Go," and he'd sign without so much as a glance. I could've contracted him into drug muling out of Juárez, and he would've been none the wiser. That was his way, playing life all loose.

My father. The squat mechanic with bald legs but a head of plentiful Lego man–like black hair he kept combed and parted to the side. Six days a week he worked at his smog check shop called Best Transmission. Though he held no executive power at home, the free agency seemed to suit him just fine. During the day he managed the shop, where he kept a stack of business cards with his American name. (When he used to pump gas at a Mobil station, people started calling him whatever was stitched on his work shirts, *Jim* stuck, and he never objected.) At night he strode around our house in white BVDs and an undershirt, a Tecate ever-glued to his engine oil–stained hands, looking pretty damn carefree. He was a simple man of simple pleasures. I never saw him read a book besides the Bible. He liked to hoot at the TV whenever Tiger Woods drained a putt or Jack Nicklaus nailed a double-bogey. He spoke Spanish fluently too. When Laurie asked him to sing "La Bamba," he'd serenade us with a hip-sway, and we'd groove along to the trill of his rolled Rs. This was my father at his best. It's how I wish I could remember him.

How did Laurie put it? "There was always something weird between you two. An awkwardness." To the rest of the world, he was the happy-go-lucky guy, the funny dad at church and a proud alto in the choir. Privately, I didn't get him, and he didn't get me—a girl, teen, then young woman, bearing his stocky legs and leaf-shaped mouth but all the while a stranger.

Beneath the ho-hum exterior, there was something dangerously capricious about his nature. The very whiff of possibility that the course of his life might instantly change at any given moment left him chronically unpinned to reality. I watched him invest his time and money in dozens of get-rich-quick schemes. I'd heard the stories in passing, too, of when he used to be a coffee shop short-order cook, a pizzaiolo, a suitcase salesman at swap meets, a commodities trader on the Pacific Stock Exchange, and so on. He seemed fueled by the transformative, untapped power of his own potential. In his mind, he was perpetually one shot away from deserved glory, big or small. For instance, he once hired a Chinese Olympic Ping-Pong player to stack his odds at winning our annual church picnic tournament. But like cramming for an exam, he started training right before the match (which ended tragically for him in a draw).

My father applied this foolhardy optimism to our relationship on one occasion. When I turned twelve, he bought me a set of miniature golf clubs and recounted a story about a Korean girl who'd recently received a full-ride golf scholarship to UCLA. It wasn't too late, he attested. If I put in the work, I could be the next golf prodigy—maybe even a golf legend! He said this with a peculiar gusto, like an Amway evangelist seeking new disciples. "Full-ride," he repeated. "They even paid for her underwear."

Maybe, in me, he glimpsed his own future: our unstoppable alliance on the course, a rhapsody of matching pastel polo tees, flickering flashbulbs, aces in every hole. But this vision did not fit with our existing dynamic. My father didn't typically perform bold gestures in the spirit of bonding. He was not malicious but absentminded—the type of man who disappeared the day before I was born, such that my mother drove herself to the hospital while in labor. He materialized in time for my birth, so the story goes, but with no explanation.

Shortcomings like these I'd learned to attribute to his overall opacity. My father was born in a unified Korea—a concept so remote to me now, as if he'd survived a myth, stepped out beyond the page, to enter the world I knew: sleepy suburbs, Happy Meals, Saturday morning cartoons. I didn't learn Korean, his native tongue, nor Spanish, his love language. And though he spoke English too, I suspect he grasped far less than what I'd assumed as a child, for we never managed to truly understand each other.

On the other hand, he lacked basic follow-through, as with those golf clubs, for at no point did he teach me how to use them. I suppose he assumed I'd learn through osmosis. I'd seen him practice his golf stroke countless times before, wiggling his hips, planting and replanting his feet on the living room carpet. He'd draw back his invisible five-iron with slow, calculated precision, mounting tension palpable, like an arrow poised for release. Once he hit the invisible ball, he watched it sail beyond the bounds of our kitchen, garden, driveway—a success in an imagined distance.

I did not become a golf star, nor did I find out if the recipient of underwear scholarship lore became one either (if, in fact, she ever existed in the first place). My father was on to something though. By the mid-2010s, Korean young women topped LPGA rankings and would soon altogether dominate the sport. The trend had something to do with Korean persistence. From an early age, Korean children are taught the importance of repetition in pursuit of perfection. According to the *Journal of Sport & Social Issues*, Korean players practice longer and harder than any of their counterparts, first to arrive at and last to leave the driving range. Which is to say you don't have to be born a "natural" in order to flourish. Some relationships require, above all else, tenacity over time.

We had our moments. For five Valentine's Days in a row, I bought my father a half-pound Hershey's kiss. It was satisfying to see him consume the whole thing, usually in one sitting. The wordless exchange helped verify some symbiosis between us, however rare or imperfect the act.

When I went to college, I didn't hear much about my parents' lives as empty nesters. They were so different, so poorly matched. Yet I came to believe they'd learned to love each other, the way arranged marriages are said to progress—in adequate, indefinite cohabitation. Such is the ignorance of awayness.

*   *   *

SHIT WENT SIDEWAYS my sophomore year, in 2004. One spring afternoon, my father phoned my sister, who phoned me, to say Umma had lost her marbles. She hadn't eaten for days, couldn't stop crying. "She's drinkin' lots of wine," he told Laurie. "From the *box*!"

Our father seldom admitted to the state of his own limitations. Yet here he was, flummoxed by our mother's sudden sea change. I called her. Between wails, she alluded to my father's infidelity.

For all his faults, my father did not strike me as the cheating type. Duplicity appeared beyond his means. Back in the '90s, when Laurie wanted to travel to Europe to visit a boy she loved, Dad snuck into her bedroom, took her plane ticket, and buried it under a rock in the back-yard. His caveman-ish subterfuge did not last long. The next day, he returned the ticket to Laurie, declaring his disapproval, which was his way of acknowledging he did not ultimately wield the power to circumvent the truth; he could not stop her.

According to my sister, our father adamantly denied the existence of a mistress. Why, then, was our mother starved and drunk? Umma had withered down to ninety pounds, her whole body a wound. She'd abandoned her stalwart trifecta: She did not attend church, she did not clean, she did not eat. No one anticipated such a turn (then again, did any of us really know her anyway?). We weren't the "family meeting" kind. But, seeing no other alternative, Laurie and I flew home to southern California.

* * *

WELL, IT WAS UMMA'S HOME, not ours, not really. By then our family had already lived in six places, nine more before I was born. My mother had a knack for exiting these spaces with remarkable pragmatism. No tears or wistful glances back before the trailer gate rolled shut, carting our ephemera to the next house and the next. When she stated, "We're moving," we moved. She chose where. No one usually bothered to ask why.

The three-bedroom with the prolific lemon tree or the condo near the Jazzercise studio I can glimpse in swatches of time (fallen coins rolling into gaps of the hardwood floor; my tiny hand skimming the stubble of a burnt sienna–colored carpet). But the first house I can vividly remember was the bungalow on a cul-de-sac's crook in El Monte, California. The town's name comes from a translation of archaic Spanish, meaning "the wooded place," deemed so in the eighteenth century by passing missionaries and early explorers. Back then thickets of cattails, wispy willows, watercress, alders, and grapevines spindled through the low-altitude land between the Rio Hondo and the San Gabriel River, before California was even California. Remnants of this past had disappeared by the time my family arrived, and no trace of us would linger after.

The Arcadia house came next, where we lived the longest—my childhood home. It was painted periwinkle and located forty minutes east of Los Angeles, beside a Ralphs supermarket. From our curb, we could see a set of desiccated foothills crouched behind the Scottish Highlands–themed middle school, whose marching band bagpipes keened in the early mornings. Arcadia was a buttoned-up place ("City of Homes") named after a region in Greece once immortalized by Virgil as an imaginary, idyllic paradise. Peacocks did often roam the streets—pesky little buggers who squawked and shat on multimillion-dollar neo-Tudor rooftops in the rich part, Upper Rancho, miles away from anywhere we could afford.

Then, without warning, Umma sold the Arcadia house for a cookie-cutter two-story three highways away in a neighborhood called Rowland Heights. The new place boasted her desired components: vaulted ceilings, French doors, Berber carpeting, a two-car garage, a brand-spanking-new dishwasher she planned on using strictly as a drying rack, all situated on a rustic, European-sounding street. Local highlights included Asian-centric strip malls outfitted with Korean supermarkets, KBBQ restaurants, boba cafés, a BCD Tofu House. "What else do you need?" Umma said.

I needed her to wait—less than a year, until I left for college. Without a driver's license, my father would have to shuttle me to and from school. The extended commutes would add up to days, weeks, months, no conversation, no radio, just us in one of his jalopies from the shop, hurtling past the fragments of city in-betweenness, simmering in our unbearable silence. Umma didn't care. These were necessary casualties in the unknowable course she'd steered us on. A part of me never forgave her, even though I should have seen it coming.

House-hunting roused my mother's spirits in ways nothing else could. Every time she passed an Open House sign staked into a lawn or posted on a street corner, a compulsion overtook her and like Sleeping Beauty drawn to the spinning wheel's spindle, she diverted her course for that sharp, bright light, and nothing could stop her. She U-turned her way into driveways festooned with rainbow bunting and balloons. She paced empty kitchens, dining, living, and primary bedrooms, assessing sunrooms and linen closets. Did the house have central heat and air? Was there an EIK or HWFs? Was it W/D ready? Before I could drive, I learned what a "half bath" meant and the difference between high and low pile carpet. Other mothers, white mothers, spent afternoons with girlfriends for tea or wine. On her days off, Umma toured properties with her Korean real estate agent. They chatted about starting prices, amenities, and charming street names, because Umma's singular wish at the time was to find her perfect home.

Maybe, then, there was a blueness to her the whole time—a pulsing, unseeable reminder to belong some place, the right place, and how arriving there might at last slake the urgency of her restless ways. By intervention day, in Umma's dream house, we thought all that which we could not see might air out—a straightforward task, like opening a window in a smoke-filled room. Simple enough.

. . .

WE HAD OPTED FOR a daytime confrontation. I was hungry. While waiting for a mysterious fifth person to join us, I inspected the fridge. Its shelves—ordinarily packed with banchan or hot dog stir-fry or an earthen pot of leftover mung bean stew—were empty, save for a lone Tupperware of kimchi. The rice cooker sat idle on the kitchen countertop. Beside it loomed a near empty box of Franzia wine, its iconic tipped glass barely containing a merlot tsunami.

The secret guest, a Korean man, finally arrived, wedging himself between my sister and me on the couch. He introduced himself as my parents' newly installed pastor, from their Korean Presbyterian church. Never saw the guy before, never even caught his name.

While I had attended the same church as a kid, I had since fallen out with God. Anyway, what business did this random dude have in our private turmoil? I made my distaste for the pastor's presence known, in the effortless way one resumes old habits among kin. And once again I was the youngest sibling, mercurial and willful; Laurie the eldest, out of necessity palliative, practical. I ignored the pastor's overly familiar small talk, his questions about my college classes or Laurie's job in D.C.—rookie moves in my book, as if he were courting our favor before opening gambits.

Sometimes silence is the wiser play. My mother understood as much. She sat in an armchair, postured like a skittish cat, keenly aware of the encroaching forces who'd backed her into a corner. She was always small but armored with a merciless disposition, from afar all clenched fists and furrowed brow. Up close, I could see how she was held together with tender, graceful lines, like the silhouettes of her precious Lladró figurines. It did not occur to me she could be just as easily broken.

A coffee table divided Umma from my father, who sat in a matching armchair, leaning back, his bare feet crossed at the ankles. The demeanor of the absolved.

"So," my sister ventured. "What happened?"

The pastor cleared his throat, called my mother in Korean by her church name, "*Elder Choi.*" "It's time to be reasonable," he said. "For your children."

A stillness settled over us, disrupted only by Umma's resonant panting. She could no longer cry. Trembling and hyperventilating, she looked alive and dead at the same time.

I turned to my father and asked point-blank: "Are you having an affair? That's why she's not eating."

He waved his hand in Umma's direction, exasperated, as if to say, *Who do you believe? Just look at her.* "It's in her head," he shouted. "I told her I wasn't, but she won't listen."

"Umma, did you hear him?" Laurie asked.

"He's telling the truth," I said.

Of course, he wasn't. The pastor knew that as well. So did everyone at church: David's mom, Linda's dad, all the parents, their kids, the choir director. Gossip had spread as far east as Manhattan, where a former youth group friend even caught wind before I did. The other Elders had seen my father with a woman from the choir, carousing around the San Gabriel Valley, in front of BCD Tofu House, holding hands. No one said a word, just carried on whispering, staring piteously with their quiet knowledge, when my mother served post-service bibimbap, when she sang in the Praise Team. Here, now, we were trying to convince

Umma she'd lost what little she had left: her mind. And she took it, staring off beyond us, eyes fixed to some avenue unfurling in the distance. The afternoon sun began to waver, sending lapis-hued shadows across her face—rendering Umma, for a moment, unrecognizable. Then the light changed again, spiriting that version of her away.

ALLEN/BROOME STREET
2BR, 1BA

new york > manhattan > housing > rooms & shares
$965 - ***********LES room for AUGUST 1ST--untilities included
Reply to: hous-185902978@craigslist.org
Date: 2006-07-24, 10:28PM EDT

Hello there,

I have a room for rent that is pretty much amazing. I can send you pictures if you would like to know more. I spent a lot of time and effort fixing the place up and i love it. hope you do too.

looking for a CLEAN, responsible roommate who will pay on time . . .

fits a queen size bed . . . room gets nice sunlight. also a/c that cools down the whole apartment . . . .Close to grocery, laundry mat, trains: F, V, B, D, 6, J, M, Z, and plenty of restaurants and fantastic bars.

The apartment has a common space and brand new kitchen appliances. The kitchen is a great size, perfect if you like to cook, like me. New bathroom as well. i work a lot and am not home often. about me: i bartend in the neighborhood and am writing a book.

extremely comfortable full sized bed (not a even a year old), dresser, and wardrobe for sale at a reasonable price as well, so less for you to move!

email soon please--would love to meet up and show you the place.

many thanks and best of luck on your search.

JC

The Smelliest Street in Manhattan

IN 2005, I MOVED to the smelliest street in Manhattan. This is not hyperbole. *New York* magazine would eventually crown Broome Street between Allen and Eldridge the stinkiest stretch in the city for its Summer Guide 2011 package. At the time of the article's publication, I no longer lived on the Lower East Side, but the details kicked up an ignominious whiff of the past I could not fully dodge, so it seemed, for long.

Passersby interviewed for the piece described the block's odor as on par with "the most disgusting subway smell," redolent like a "flushed-out catacomb," or as the writer put it, so "ripe and outlandish" it could make "a person feel perverted." The smell's composition also stumped two olfactory experts, including a former *New York Times* perfume critic, though their consensus circled around a baffling potpourri of cat urine, raw sewage, and live poultry.

Back in the early aughts, my neighbors and I didn't need professionals to confirm the obvious. We were quite familiar with the Broome Street Stench: a villainous funk that outmatched the most fetid storm drains at Chinatown fish stalls or the rankest heaps of hot garbage on August trash days in Alphabet City. The Stench's source could be traced to Hu Chou, whose generic warehouse belied what existed, putridly, out of view.

Curiously enough I do not recall smelling anything of note when first visiting the apartment building on the corner of Allen and Broome Streets, whose hulking brick side lay a few doors down from Hu Chou. Nor did I encounter the infamous woman living in Apartment 2B. Someone must have worked very hard to hide her, along with the potent, ammoniac scent emanating from her doorway.

Perhaps this clever person was Poney Zhang, the sprightly Chinese lady who represented property management. The day I toured Apartment 2A, Poney met me at the building's blood-red door. After exchanging greetings, she ushered us quickly through the "lobby" and up the stairs. Lobby is a generous term for what was essentially a dingy, dank section of black and white tile on which a row of trash cans stood, containing various stages of waste. Above the ill-fitting lids, a sign read in both English and Mandarin: NO SPITTING.

I considered the lobby the same way I considered the pocked stucco hallways or the fluorescent lights imbuing everything in a ghostly pallor: This place had character! Certainly any apartment worth its salt came with a slew of quirks. I'd lived in Manhattan for three years and was now twenty, signing my first lease; I didn't want any old place. The desire was so urgent it felt unequivocal. I needed a slice of New York that seemed to be disappearing. Making a number of concessions for the right match seemed completely within reason.

On the second floor, Poney swiftly opened a heavy red door and commanded, "Come Miss Choi! Come!" At the time I interpreted Poney's celerity as enthusiasm, but now I see. A matching red door across the hall, propped open by a long metal charley bar, revealed a sliver of neglect: rotten linoleum floor, peeling floral wallpaper, and a pile of junk stacked like abstract art, backlit by the light streaming in from Allen Street. Wrongfully, I'd assumed this apartment to be under construction. In no way could I have imagined that a human being resided within.

Her name, I would soon discover, was Agnes.

•　•　•

MY FIRST NIGHT in Apartment 2A, I awoke to a voice bellowing outside my door: "Get off me, I says! Get off me, you sonuvabitch. I says get off me!" I contemplated calling the police. But the ruckus continued in such a canned cadence, well into the wee hours, that I no longer believed the existence of any imminent threat—rather some nightmarish recollection played on loop from which the person could not seem to escape.

This, I'd soon learn, was one of Agnes's many idiosyncrasies. Later I'd eye her through my peephole enacting another. Every morning, she parked her wheelchair at her apartment's threshold a few feet from mine and sat there . . . waiting. The ignition of stovetop burners clicked incessantly in the abyss beyond her propped-open door. She wore cat-eye glasses. Her silver, center-parted bob conveyed a sense of girlishness while the large breasts resting atop her lap formed a fleshy slope, outlined clearly by the thinness of her housedress. Other times she wore nothing, wheeling past her open door buck naked while scooting a bleach-soaked mop across her kitchen floor, not neutralizing the overwhelming urine smell so much as garnishing it with a noxious topcoat.

Oh, these were not ideal circumstances in which to reside as a twentysomething. But I concluded I'd be spending almost no time indoors. My roommate, a perky blonde from Sag Harbor named Grace, moved in. We'd studied abroad together and happened to share the same reckless joy of mild promiscuity. In the mornings, we took turns playing a game called Whose Shoes? guessing, based on the style and size of footwear, the type of lover the other snuck in the night before. Sometimes we blew our meager wages from cleaning people's houses or cat sitting or cater waitering on shitty but strong well drinks at Odessa Bar on Avenue A only to splurge on short stacks with warm maple butter at Clinton St. Baking Company the next morning. Grace didn't mind the Broome Street Stench or Agnes, because when you're young and broke in the city, your inner negotiations lack rationale. A subtle glamouring ensues. You can no longer decipher what qualifies as "acceptable" living conditions so long as certain needs are met. You become blind to closet-bedrooms, rundown kitchens, and jerry-rigged bathrooms in favor of prime location, subway access, or cheap rent. And sometimes this glamouring lasts for far longer than it ought to.

It would be another decade and change before I could make this realization on my own. Back then I could not conceive of living anywhere else, in any other city, for the rest of my life. The business of adulthood was an opaque matter, problems for Future Me. I was cossetted by a breezy myopia then, the kind permissible only in youth. This immediacy, which pulsed with such unflagging promise, was so intoxicating I never imagined its inevitable end.

As far as I saw it, if Larry Clark could cast Rosario Dawson in *Kids* by spotting her perched on an East Village stoop, every waking moment offered the potential for a life-changing chance encounter. I didn't want to be an actress per se, but I did indulge in the fantasy of being "discovered." You could skip the messy legwork, rolling boulders up the wrong mountains year after year, because someone else recognized your undeniable talent. I didn't know what talent I possessed, but it was the not-knowing that thrummed with such ineffable possibility.

Which makes sense, considering how I'd landed in New York. I moved to the city from California at seventeen years old—a young seventeen at that. Ever the late bloomer, I looked all of thirteen, baby-faced, flat-chested, and still haunted with occasional blooms of cystic acne. I wasn't some whizz kid, just a November baby who enrolled in kindergarten on the early side, mostly so my mother could avoid the cost of daycare. I was aware even as a child how she was figuring it out as she went along, which frequently left me stranded in gaps of ambiguity. I was always fed and clothed, but who might drop me off or pick me up, how I'd get home, and to whose home (a neighbor's, a friend's, a babysitter's—sometimes before they got there themselves) remained constant uncertainties.

I devoted my last years on the West Coast to fanciful daydreams: how the Publishers Clearing House team with the giant check might bum-rush our front door. Or how I'd finally win a McDonald's Monopoly Dodge Viper, so I could pop a wheelie and flip double birds to the SAT prep academies where I'd vastly underperformed, or the low-rider Honda Civics kitted out with whale-tail spoilers, or the tacky McMansions and new money that never belonged to me anyway—Umma's frown growing fainter and fainter, only a Wile E. Coyote–esque plume of smoke left smoldering in my wake.

Alas, I needed an actionable plan. Our high school student body consisted of around 60 percent high-achieving Asian Americans. Ineptitude in math and science made me something of an anomaly, especially since this deficit did not sharpen my abilities in complementary subjects. I did get admitted into a couple Advanced Placement English classes, but I couldn't seem to stay awake reviewing the required materials. I did not grow up an avid reader. (It is very possible I did not read a book in its entirety until sophomore year of college.) I'd inherited my father's propensity for serial shortcutting, relying on whatever Spark Notes summaries I could rustle up for free online. I got busted once, when I described the plot of *Watership Down* for an oral book report based solely on a used edition's cover art and jacket copy. I did not learn my lesson. In another honors English class, I gave a presentation on *Madame Bovary* with a puppet show to Cyndi Lauper's "Girls Just Wanna Have Fun" blasting from a boombox. The performance yielded minimal context and maximal, if non-sequitur, entertainment value—enough, I'd hoped, to distract from the obvious: I had no idea what I was talking about.

Since I hadn't taken the prerequisite, I couldn't register for the one course that genuinely piqued my interests. TV and Film Production appealed to the wannabe filmmakers along with the alt kids, sometimes overlapping with the theater dorks, but mostly Star Wars and Beatles aficionados and a posse of burnout juvenile delinquents—social circles to which I did not belong. The fruits of their labor appeared weekly on the campus news show, broadcast during homeroom and on the local public access network. The resident film critic, a senior with a penchant for action flicks of the *Con Air* variety, would soon be vacating his position. To throw my hat in the ring as his successor, I decided to pen a letter on college-ruled notebook paper challenging him to a Siskel & Ebert–inspired on-air duel of wits.

He chose *15 Minutes*, a crime thriller flop starring Ed Burns and Robert De Niro. Much like the film, our conversation was forgettable. But my stunt worked. I stepped in the following year as critic and assumed the role with unabashed, extremely uncool sincerity. I was a self-proclaimed cinephile, you see, so this meteoric ascent corroborated an already burgeoning, unearned sense of intellectual superiority. I devoted my time to composing punchy scripts, using the class blue screen for low-budget effects (a camera-rumbling time machine, for example, to review *The Time Traveler's Wife*), and edited my segments on an early version of Adobe Premiere.

Was I annoying about the whole thing? Absolutely. Unlike my predecessor, I recommended foreign films like *Run Lola Run* and supplied Academy Awards predictions based on an official handbook I'd dog-eared and committed to memory. I dumped the previous one-to-five hot dog rating scale, delivering my verdict instead with a tongue pop and two finger-guns pointed to the screen, where a rainbow-colored letter grade would illuminate. ("I give this [points fingers] a B minus.") When my peers spotted me in the quad, they aped my moves. ("I give *you* . . . a C plus!") And like the precocious asshole I'd become, I counted down the days until I could hightail it out of town. Maybe I could eventually become a full-time critic, or a screenwriter, or at the very least get cast in a season of *The Real World*. Any iteration seemed equally conceivable, existing in concentric orbits. To find which story I'd actually live out, I needed to get my ass to New York. I can't explain why. It's a city with unusual gravitas and like many maudlin souls, it's where I believed I belonged.

Despite my uninspiring GPA, I decided film criticism could serve as a catalyst for my scattered ambitions. I set my sights on attending a university in Manhattan, often mocked as a landing pad for those rejected by the Ivies. The guidance counselor, a murine woman adept at razing fledgling ambitions, suggested I aim for more "realistic" schools; the UCs were out of the question, New York a pipe dream. I didn't have the numbers.

She didn't know about a loophole. I could apply for a film theory major at the university's arts school, by way of a ten-page portfolio paper. I chose to write mine on Italian Neorealism—a subject I had discussed once, with a campus security guard who occasionally tuned in to my movie reviews and professed his colorful, unsolicited opinions from the driver's seat of his golf cart. He had been taking film courses at a local community college. From our conversation, I stretched a few broad strokes into a verbose treatise and somehow, I got in.

A week before I departed for college, my mother sat me down and burst into tears, aberrating from her usual icy demeanor. She and my father hardly spoke to each other. It seemed equally probable the absence of children in the house could prompt a new era of marital civility or doom.

"You're gonna drink and have sex and do drugs!" she cried. This was not a warning so much as a dirge, preemptively mourning the loss of my innocence. It was a bizarre confession; in no other circumstance had she acknowledged my autonomy. I assured Umma she had nothing to worry about, then shed that exact progression of virginities soon, in relatively quick succession. I wasn't seeking rebellion. I wanted to live in New York because I'd fantasized the city could furnish me with an identity, setting me on the path to actualize whoever it was I was supposed to be, like a smooth stone skipping across the water toward a known glimmering place.

· · ·

When I first got to the city, I was Snow White in the magical forest except instead of affable animals, I flitted about, enamored with bodegas, bong shops, and buskers, under the sweet spell of Mamoun's falafel and Nuts 4 Nuts. At school, my mind was not particularly pliable to cinema studies compared to my classmates, who could easily debate the semiotic relationship between diegetic versus non-diegetic sound in early talkies—a topic that, at best, offered the ideal white noise and dim lighting for the most expensive naps I've ever enjoyed in my life.

By fall 2004, I was nineteen, failing a course on film comedy—ironic, seeing as how there appeared to be nothing remotely amusing in my life, on or off screen. It had been six months since the intervention; in that time the truth had surfaced about my father and his mistress. I had been the last to know.

It was an unseasonably frigid afternoon when I answered my mother's call. I was sitting at the entrance steps to the Ukrainian church on East Seventh Street. The trees around me looked sickly, hollow-trunked, spindly-branched, the whole block muted to gray scale. As we spoke my mind wandered to a scene from *Battleship Potemkin*. Sergei Eisenstein's 1925 silent film is regarded as a cinematic masterpiece, specifically for the iconic Odessa steps sequence, in which Cossack soldiers descend an infinite staircase, decimating a crowd of bystanders. A fallen boy is trampled; a runaway baby stroller tumbles precariously out of reach. No dialogue is spoken, yet what unfolds is utter calamity—a splicing of images and moments, to prolong the agony, to heighten the ruin, until reaching an indelible, vibrational point.

That day, I sensed Umma had started eating again. Over the phone she sounded newly nourished, like an unwatered plant whose roots had been freshly soaked; still wilted from neglect but hanging on, alive. "Did you speak to your father?" she asked.

My sister phoned immediately after, wondering the same: "Have you talked to Dad?"

I had, for a minute or so. Mostly silence. Since I'd moved across the country, he never called me. Not once. Occasionally I reached out to him, to pantomime the shape of kinship. Both of us seemed to understand what remained unspoken: After years of strained interactions, our distance at last felt comfortably capacious.

During his call, we cycled through the regular, empty prattle—weather, church news, and the topic as of late: Was Umma any better? Drinking? Crying? Maybe . . . yes . . . I dunno, he said. For some reason I felt compelled to add, "Well, we're all responsible for our own actions."

The quiet that descended then was not our usual kind. A microscopic chorus of reticence commenced: a switching of hands, a stiffening in posture, the inertia of a held breath. Rather than confess, as he had intended to do, he hung up. There was no memorable end to our final conversation. I can't recall now if he even said goodbye.

The swift dissolution of my parents' marriage thereafter came as no surprise. One assumes these types of separations have a more profound effect on small children, especially for those who've only imagined their parents as noble figures, devoid of flawed, interior lives. I was not so disillusioned, yet no amount of foresight or acceptance could have prepared me for the events that followed.

I couldn't recognize the difference between what my mother wanted and the limitations of what I could provide. Mostly she rang me and I stayed on the line as she wept, monitoring the subtle fluctuations in her grief—the hoarse expirations, the plaintive panting. I answered between classes, before and after shifts at my café job, bereft of any nuance (as if my counsel is what she'd been seeking). I was hyper aware of what possible outcomes might arise if I didn't pick up the phone. That year six students had committed suicide at my university. Many had jumped, two from the upper floors of the library, one from the art school's rooftop. Posters hung in hallways and on bathroom walls, nudging mental health resources, hotlines, and counseling options.

For immigrants my parents' age, divulging one's private affairs to a complete stranger and then getting charged for such a service is considered a laughable expenditure. My mother didn't strike me as a jumper (the woman hated a mess) but she was, if anything, resolute. Should she set herself on a task, she worked efficiently and with finality, no do-overs.

That was who she used to be, anyway. I wasn't quite sure anymore who she was now. Then, on one of our calls, my mother laid out something concrete, a timeline, how she might not live long enough to attend my graduation. I said what came to mind: "You need to speak to a doctor." I may have even begged. How hard could it be? She worked at a hospital.

This managed to snap Umma out of her trance. "Who do you think you're talking to?" she hissed with sudden, searing clarity. "I never should have raised you American. If you were a real Korean daughter, you would just sit there and listen. Like a wall."

Ah, there she was, the captious woman who raised me, exactly as I remembered. What on earth did it mean to be a *real* Korean daughter? Failing at being a good daughter, that I could grasp. The Korean part I couldn't square. Okay, I lacked traditional characteristics. For instance, I understood just enough Hangukmal to discern when church parents were criticizing my subpar Korean language skills. Fielding complaints from them was one thing. Hearing with such conviction, from my own mother, I was a categorical disappointment was another. It seemed unfair, to be chastised so definitively for an offense so abstract: a paucity of cultural identity.

Something strange happened to me then. I didn't realize I could flip on-to-off, like a switch, but it happened this way, instantly. I stopped answering her calls. I resolved to leave the country and applied to study abroad in Paris the next semester. Fall turned to winter. She kept calling, and I did not pick up. I needed more time, more space, more land and sky and sea between us, our continental drift.

Before my departure overseas, I boycotted Christmas, fortifying the choice by covering open holiday shifts at the café, Drink Me on East Sixth near Avenue B. "No time to fly home," I feigned. "Saving money for Paris." But in an unexpected dramatic overture, my mother booked a last-minute ticket to New York on Christmas Eve and holed up at the Waldorf Astoria. This shocked me. She did not splurge on lavish, impulsive expenses.

My sister took the train in from D.C., but when I did not appear at the hotel, my mother asked Laurie to visit the café. They sat on a reclaimed church pew lining the wall directly facing the service counter. My mother rested her head in her hands and watched me for hours. I felt oddly on display, as if she were monitoring my every move to inspect when I might falter. I had misread her entirely. She'd watched me with a fragile wonderment, as if I weren't spooning loose-leaf tea into sachets or topping up chipped teapots with boiling water or rearranging pastries in the glass case but conducting an elaborate symphony. Eyes alert and quivering, the way one looks when waking from a dream, she savored every detail, as if she knew she might lose me, and never see me again.

I shared a bed with my sister at the Waldorf that night, and on Christmas morning, we rose to find our mother had decked out the side table with festive dollar-store finds. Ratty tinsel. Red and green strawberry hard candies. She'd brought presents too. Ferrero Rocher almond nougat. Polyester socks. Cash tucked into gift bags embellished with jolly cartoon reindeer. "Just a little something," she said, in a near whisper. The sad scene rattled me, and though the day had only begun, I felt the urge to walk out of the room, through the lobby, passing beneath the teardrop chandeliers, hopping on the 6 at Grand Central to Astor Place, to trudge along East Seventh Street and up six steep flights until arriving at another depressive scene: my lofted twin bed in a windowless converted office. But I did not walk out. I said thank you. Ate a nougat. Wore the socks. The gift I gave her is that I stayed.

Was I selfish? Yes. Perhaps even cruel. But my mother's brittle state felt like yet another betrayal; the dissonance between who she used to be and who she was becoming disturbed me so deeply I couldn't bear to watch. Maybe because there was no room for what I'd lost. Though he continued communicating with Laurie, after that final phone conversation with my father, he and I never spoke again.

We had been here before, though I could not remember it. My parents had separated shortly after I was born. My father requested visitation with Laurie, but he did not ask for me. Three years later he returned to our lives, and I was none the wiser. Life repeats itself. The second time around, again he put up no fight to keep me, as if this was our only outcome, in this cycle or the next.

I heard his voice for the last time about a week after I turned twenty. He left a message on my phone. I remember listening to the recording many times, memorizing the long, repentant pauses between his words. ". . . I think it's late . . . but . . . happy birthday . . ."

The message reminded me of a game we used to play. I would ask my father, "How old am I?" and for years he'd answer, bewildered, "Thirteen?" I wanted to know why he couldn't remember, but rather than press him on the matter, I turned the question into a joke. "Ha! Thirteen?!" I'd say. Then I'd scoot over to my mother and we would tease him, because wasn't he just so clueless? Sometimes my father smiled nervously before guessing, so I'd help him with the answer. Or sometimes I would laugh in his face and then run away, while I imagine I remained in his mind an utter mystery.

* * *

TURNS OUT, MY FATHER hadn't been paying rent consistently for his business. My mother had cosigned the shop's lease, so to settle the ten years of outstanding debt, in 2005, Umma relinquished her dream home. She relocated to Canyon Lake, one of four entirely gated cities in California, plunked into an excessively brown, desiccated patch of Riverside County.

Depending on how you look at it, either I deserted my mother at the pinnacle of her despair or she had opted for necessary solitude, entombing herself from the outside world to enter a time of repair.

I needed time to repair too. In Paris, for every unsolicited Konichiwa and ching chang chong flung my way, you would have thought I was donning a goddamn rice paddy hat, peddling a rickshaw down the Champs Élysées. No, I was a different cliché: twenty, enduring what I imagined was a well-concealed internal crisis. In reality I was running around with Manic Panic red-dyed hair, mainlining Fiona Apple and Tom Waits albums, perpetually day drunk on three-euro bottles of wine.

After being an object of curiosity in France, I returned to New York dead set on living where people minded their own business. I'd heard from a former fling about the allures of Chinatown. He was white and British, and so it was likely a learned disposition for him to describe the neighborhood with such Orientalist excitement. He'd regaled me with apocryphal tales, alleging that an underground baby trade thrived out of sight or that the Triad governed the streets after dark. And, rather distastefully, he referred to the omnipotent, sour smell pervading below Canal as "mung."

The area enticed me for other reasons. My new block straddled two neighborhoods, and I could travel between them without interrogation. If I headed north, crossing Delancey Street and the traffic funneling onto the Williamsburg Bridge, I'd pass Precision Haircutz (a Dominican barber shop), the Church of Grace to Fujianese reborn in the old Allen Street Municipal Bathhouse, or the dilapidated bodega on Stanton whose awning advertised BEER – COFFEE – SANDWISH. From there, I'd stroll to my favorite downtown haunts: the Detroiters' dive, Motor City, for well whiskey and Vernors ginger ale, soul and rockabilly bops humming along the hubcap-lined walls. Or the vegetarian diner Kate's Joint on Avenue B, which sold my beloved unturkey club, served by a woefully hip, slow-footed wait staff. If I walked south and west, I'd hold my breath near Hu Chou and peek into the neighboring storefront—a makeshift rec room where Chinese folks watched soccer matches or costumed historical dramas, seated in rows of crammed folding chairs. I could then wander to the Hua Mei Garden on Forsyth Street. A group of elderly men gathered there in the early mornings, strung up their handcarved bamboo cages, silently admiring their songbirds who, unlike their owners, partook in hopeful chatter.

Further into Chinatown, if someone spoke to me in Cantonese, we could mutually shrug off the lingual divide. People seemed to understand the value of anonymity. You could see it with the empty MSG vats outside shops whose window signs touted, NO MSG. Or at my favorite market on Mott Street, which stocked a zoologic array of animal parts including a set of alligator feet splayed over a pail of ice. Chilling in a nearby fridge were stacks of raw, individually plastic-wrapped poultry, each curiously labeled "Patrick." I did not ask about Patrick, and no one asked about me.

During my perambulations, I noticed a distinct population of entrepreneurial elders. One old man, who worked in the crevice between two buildings from a cardboard box station, cobbled shoes. Another man with a similarly modest setup performed the single trade of watch battery replacement. Women, however, sold what looked like dried bean pods on street corners for ten cents a pop. Or they rummaged through garbage in search of aluminum cans and stowed their bounty in large bags, hung on the ends of horizontal shoulder poles—much like the pails on a milkmaid's yoke—then tottered across town to the recycling depository. I could not bear the sight of the oldest women, who reminded me of my grandmother, Halmoni. She'd been raised in a village doctor's family but fancied herself high-born and would rather commit seppuku than sift through someone's trash. The middle-aged women who frequented the bins hemming my stretch of Allen Street reminded me, painfully, of my mother. They foraged with a familiar resting scowl, an expression resigned to fate. I wondered who they returned to, whether a caring family awaited them or not.

. . .

FOR THOSE INITIAL MONTHS, I managed Agnes with alacrity, resolving to stay out of the apartment as much as possible. I lit pungent incense at my door to disguise the urine scent suffusing the hallway. I accommodated her near daily requests, usually for a carton of milk or a cup of coffee from Chinese Hispanic, the bodega near Hu Chou—services for which she tipped me, on occasion, a quarter. She made a show of this each time, pleased by her own generosity, and enclosed the coin in my hand, imparting, "For ya troubles."

So I had a kooky New York neighbor! Fine. I'd managed to score a rent-stabilized apartment, which meant my affordable monthly rate could only increase by a lean percentage every year. Residents of the building, predominantly the non-English-speaking Chinese, had been living in their tenement-style apartments for generations. These were rent-controlled—to me, the diamond-in-the-rough category of New York real estate (more or less fixed, inexpensive rent). The units were typically equipped with a free-standing bathtub beside the kitchen stove; in similar prewar buildings, one apartment on every floor did not usually contain a toilet, requiring the renter to access a private water closet down the hall outside their front door. No one in their right minds willingly relinquished these places but instead passed them down to younger family members, who then resorted to revamping on their own dime. With upkeep no longer contractually under management purview, once-sharp corners rounded beneath decades of slapdash repair—the passage of time compacted into paint and wallpaper, layers upon layers, like rings on a tree.

My apartment had been stripped and recently renovated. Nothing special: linoleum floors, a shower stall, a fresh paint job, walls for the newly divided two bedrooms. At some point it occurred to me that prior to my occupancy, someone must have died in Apartment 2A for such a rare vacancy to open. I began to worry if their ghost had stuck around in a perfunctory act of hazing. One night, my kitchen window collapsed with an alarming thud. No one could be found on the nearby landing, but on the window's screen, two tiny handprints lay outlined in dust.

On another night, my apartment's heavy fireproof door unhinged itself. The Chinese repairmen worked expeditiously on both tasks, as if haste might neutralize my concerns.

And I did have concerns. For an entire winter, I heard a series of ominous sounds coming from the unit above mine. It was as if someone was dropping bowling balls from the top of a ladder; between the thumps, a woman expelled blood-curdling screams. When my ceiling leaked a mysterious brown fluid, I knocked on the door upstairs. The entrance was festooned with crimson and gold Lunar New Year banners, which the fluorescent lights cast with a foreboding gloom. A Chinese man answered in an undershirt and slacks, a gravity-defying cigarette suspended from his lower lip. He stepped aside, as if expecting my arrival. I found no screaming lady, no bowling balls, merely a running bathtub filled to the brim with dried herbs and a brackish, muddy liquid. I shut off the faucet and never saw him again.

Agnes, on the other hand, made appearances daily, leaving nothing to mystery. A solitary woman of her age finds respite in routines, and her most memorable one involved a kind of echolocation. Craning her neck out of her door, she listened for footsteps from the nearby stairwell, a distance she must have memorized, for it did not seem she had been outside of her apartment for some time. Whenever a neighbor trudged up the stairs, she yelled, cantankerously, "Hey Mista! Wouldya take this down fah me? Wouldya take this down?" From her fingertips dangled a too-small black bodega bag teeming with garbage. Our neighbors' footsteps padded up or down the stairs without pause. So Agnes resorted to chucking her trash down the hallway before slinking back into her lonesome cave. I often came home to find her refuse strewn across our hallway: empty milk jugs, Table Talk miniature fruit pie boxes, crumpled napkins, paper coffee cups.

About eight months in, I started scheduling my exits, hopeful to dodge Agnes encounters entirely. What became taxing wasn't so much the persistent demand for my neighborly engagement or Samaritanism. Though it was not my responsibility to care for Agnes, the situation plied upon me an unmistakable guilt, whenever I said no, whenever I wanted to live my own life, whenever I walked away. Though I did not realize it then, I had been avoiding my mother with a similar vigilance.

It was the act of bearing constant witness to her incontrovertible desolation that weighed upon me most. Agnes endured a cycle of indignities, and these ordinary humiliations required a kind of grace. The vestiges of one's independence are sacrosanct, perhaps most when there's little else to salvage. I was not yet equipped to face such grim realizations. I rarely considered what she was like before 2005, when she was my age, or what it may have taken for her to leap to the other side, propelling her on this feral retreat from decorum. Whether she was shouting in her sleep or guarding her entryway, there was something terrifying about Agnes. Perhaps because she had nothing left to lose. A lip in the doorway did not allow her wheelchair beyond the realm of her apartment. She was the Ghost from Mothers Future, a warning sign presented in portrait. Framed by the doorway across the hall, I watched her pass the days, wondering if she did or didn't know she'd been marooned. Apart from the army of young roaches streaming out of her home, she was alone.

· · ·

To speak broadly, if monolithically, in Asian culture it is universally understood that abandoning your elders is a moral crime. I didn't grow up hearing the words "filial piety," but I saw the phrase enacted whenever Umma served food to Grandpa first, always passing the plate with two deferential hands. Or how we bowed to my grandma for New Year's Day blessings, as if in the presence of a deity. I had learned my Korean phrases phonetically, and perhaps because I did not speak much Hangukmal with my parents, it did not occur to me I ought to extend such specific acts of reverence to them as well.

Filial piety is a main tenet of Confucianism, an ancient Chinese moral and ethical code. The founding father of this belief system is the philosopher Confucius (551 to 479 BCE). As a teenager, I assumed Confucius was a caricature co-opted on innumerable occasions to relay a white person's interpretation of old country Oriental wisdom; a cunning but slanty-eyed, fortune cookie aphorism machine, à la Charlie Chan. But he was indeed a real person, whose values still inform East Asian cultural norms today.

Neo-Confucianism, which blends Buddhist and Taoist philosophies along with older Confucian teachings, initially came into popular favor during the tail end of Korea's Goryeo dynasty (918 to 1392). By King Sejong's influential rule (1418 to 1450), these beliefs had fully integrated into the common home but also extended into the public sphere. The tradition emphasizes patriarchal order; as children honored the head of their family, so too did a people unto a ruler, enshrining this ideology as a strong political and cultural influence in Korean society well beyond the end of dynastic rule. Family devotion was chief among the many principles, to an extent that superseded individual needs or desires. My mother and father were raised to honor such notions. Be good to your parents and your achievements will bring your household and lineage respect and fortune; obey your husband; welcome your elders into your home as adults; care for those who came before you . . . and so forth.

I hold an unwavering adoration for my grandparents. Well into their nineties now, they have endured the hero's journey endemic to their generation, surviving Japanese Imperialism, the Korean War, and their country's rapid ascent from developing nation to economic powerhouse. It isn't so much their eventual passing I find upsetting; death is an inescapable fact. I fear instead the loss of what they take with them, what cannot be pieced together from photos or soju-infused recollections: the memories, dreams, and personal minutiae that constitute a soul. Which is to say, what concerns me most is one's irrefutable obsolescence.

I would never know if Agnes had children, if she ever married, if these were desires she once clung to or not. Other than the occasional Meals on Wheels delivery, over the five years I lived on Allen and Broome, Agnes entertained only one sporadic visitor: her chain-smoking, tracksuit-wearing, Crown Victoria–driving nephew, Marty.

Marty owned a sub shop in Staten Island, which, I figured, operated as a money laundering front for the mob. Not once did I see Marty take Agnes outside. Nor did I see him supply fresh food or gifts or the coffee and milk she continually requested from neighbors. He stayed the duration of one Marlboro Red. On his way out, he'd say, "See ya later Aggie," and it is possible he was the only person left on the planet to know her by that name.

* * *

YOU HAVE PROBABLY HEARD the parable-like tale of the Inuit, leaving the elderly to die atop ice floes weaponless and alone. The tradition has entered the greater Euro-centric cultural consciousness, existing somewhere between fable and ethnography. Perhaps we cling to this story because it provides a dignified exit, sparing everyone the slow decline of the body, before senility or incontinence ravage whatever remains.

One of the last documented cases of elder abandonment among the Netsilik (Netsilingmiut) Inuit occurred in the 1920s, on King William Island in Northern Canada's Arctic Archipelago. Knud Rasmussen, a Greenlandic polar explorer and anthropologist of Danish-Inuit descent, lived with the Netsilik during his epic Fifth Thule Expedition and chronicled the long winter marches between hunting grounds. "I made exhaustive enquiries as to the treatment of the aged," Rasmussen wrote. Maybe he expected to witness an official rite of passage, watching a grandmother peacefully float into the sunset. He did not behold such an event. But, in a few instances, a woman who could not keep up with the pack slept on the ice, nearly freezing to death. A shaman named Samik expressed what Rasmussen hoped to observe acutely: "For our custom up here is that all old people who can do no more, and whom death will not take, help death to take them."

According to my grandpa, in Korea's olden days, when elders could no longer contribute to the household, families deserted them on deep late mountaintops. The practice, called goryeojang, sounded fishy to me, as melodramatic as any other Korean folktale, where daughters transformed into silkworms or lotus flowers in otherworldly acts of piety and faith. But goryeojang supposedly happened during the Goryeo dynasty, so we are told, prior to Confucianism's widespread dominance.

True or not, here is the version my grandfather extolled:

> A halmoni is served a final meal when she reaches the age of seventy.
> She eats her favorite foods as her grandson watches, perplexed. Why
> is Grandmother crying if she's eating the dishes she most adores?
> Later the boy's father prepares for the journey into the mountains
> and straps the halmoni into an A-frame carrier on his back. The son
> asks to tag along. The trio wind through a dense forest and wooded
> paths, up peak after peak until reaching a barren summit. The father
> unties his A-frame and leaves it behind with the old woman. As he
> begins the trek back down the mountain, he notices his son dragging
> along the A-frame. "Son, we don't need that anymore," the father
> says. "We've already left Grandmother behind." But the son replies,
> "I'll need this one day. How else will I carry *you* up the mountain?"
> The father, stunned by this revelation, rescues his mother, and all
> three return home.

When my grandpa finished this story, he chuckled, ever impressed
by the cleverness of the boy. He proceeded to draw a sketch of the
A-frame, known in Korean as a chigeh. He used an ink pen and in
short strokes recreated the frame's pointed shape, its braided ropes,
gesturing on his own body where the straps slung over the shoulders
like a backpack. He rendered with incredible detail the plies of the
rope, the knots in the wood. Grandpa's laugh faded as he sketched
the mountain, the sun, the sky, the old woman until, dotting the page
with his pen tip emphatically, he said, *"This is where they left you."*
An open grave.

The Japanese have their own version of this story called ubasute,
meaning "abandoning an old woman." The allegory begins with a similar pretense: After a farewell party, a son carries his mother deep into
the woods, so she will not find her way back to their village. As they
climb farther and higher beyond the forest, up the mountain, the son
notices his mother breaking off twigs from low-hanging branches, leaving a trail scattered behind them. He admonishes her for such conspicu-

ous indiscretion. But the mother corrects her son. The trail is for him, so he can easily find his way back. This is when the man changes his mind, and they descend the mountain together, mother and child.

. . .

I DON'T KNOW what exactly happened to Umma in 2005. But it was evident some sort of transfiguration had begun, out of her family's sight.

Before the divorce, Umma had only taken two big international trips in her life: when she moved to America from South Korea in 1976 and when she and I visited Madrid in 1998. For the latter, Laurie was studying abroad and we stayed with her over Christmas—a miserable two weeks consisting largely of our mother's endless grousing, due to the absence of kimchi in Spain. Nearly a decade had passed since then when Umma started traveling the world alone. I discovered her whereabouts solely through the notes she sent, from Buenos Aires, Amsterdam, Beijing, Paris. After visiting the enormous soapstone statue of Cristo Redentor in Rio, she proclaimed via email: "You can spread my ash on the Corcovado."

Her first postcard arrived on a rainy morning. To get to my mailbox, I'd held my breath while dodging the trash trail Agnes had chucked down our shared hall. A picture of the Fontana di Trevi practically glowed between the Con Ed bill and junk mail, its fluorescent green water speckled with spotlights. On the back, my mother had written from the Vatican: *Walked everywhere, got lost many times & all . . . had capuccino on street.*

A few weeks later, I found a new postcard, depicting a lush coastal town bordered with red flowers. *Mt. Etna was visible with smoke coming up,* she'd scribbled in Sicily. *After a day at sea, next stop is French Riviera.*

She dispatched the most curious message from Santorini:

I came down on a donkey. It was tough. By the time I got to the bottom of the steps, I was able to enjoy & had to get off the donkey. I sang & called you & your sister's name over & over. Can you imagine?

I couldn't. What would possess a woman to scream our names across the Mediterranean while riding on a donkey? In my sunless apartment, I examined the postcard's photo: the elegant masonry of a whitewashed plaster church, its crosses emboldened against a cobalt sea. Then I stashed my wine key in my pocket and headed to work at a nearby club, where I shilled Red Bull vodkas in a poorly rendered mock casino, before returning home—to the Broome Street Stench, and Agnes, and my scenic view of a brick wall—still wondering if what my mother wrote was true.

. . .

AGNES COULD DO NO MORE, yet death would not take her. In fact she often bucked her solitary fate by imploring that I visit.

"Won't ya come in? Come in!" she'd shout at the doorway. "Let me show you. I did this all on my own. Let me show you."

I'd enter the kitchen, roaches scurrying at my feet, blue flames haloing the stovetop. "It's lovely," I'd say.

Then, when she wasn't looking, I'd turn off her burners. "You shouldn't leave the stove on!" I'd say, which she ignored.

Next came sunlight, flooding through the curtainless windows. In her bedroom she had a cot, a blanket, peeling sun-bleached wallpaper, a rotary telephone, an AM/FM radio. "My people are *Basque!*" she'd say, dentures clacking. She owned no books. Displayed no family photos. "I worked for Columbia University for forty years!" She'd show me how she stowed her pocketbook beneath her pillow. "They're crooks!" she'd say. "The goddamn Chinese!" Then she'd take my hand, squeeze it, pull me close. Cataracts had eclipsed her eyes into a fog. Beaming, she'd whisper, "My, you're beautiful. Just beautiful!"

Time inside Apartment 2B may have stopped for Agnes, but my world carried on. I graduated college, celebrated birthdays, and started bartending (the same way I had maneuvered through high school—winging it). I adopted a cat, then another. Grace moved out, a new roommate moved in, then another. My mother continued sending postcards, occasionally phoning, and sometimes I answered (proof of life, for both of us). Whenever I reentered Agnes's home, though, she greeted me the same. "Let me show you! I did this all on my own. Let me show you . . ."

Then one week, her door stayed shut. I began to worry, so I called 311, and an operator connected me to Adult Protective Services. There had been a file on Agnes that closed in 2004, a year prior to my arrival. I re-opened the file and told the case worker about the open flames, the urine smell, the trash. They dispatched an aide. Months passed until the door opened again, propped by a brick on the floor. Chinese repairmen in paint-splattered jeans peeled the floral wallpaper from the walls and scraped away the cracked tiles. The apartment appeared the way I thought I'd found it on my first day, under construction. But now, Agnes was gone.

. . .

IN 2010, APARTMENT 2B got gut-renovated and two businessmen moved in for fifty times the rent Agnes had paid.

She continued visiting me in my sleep: Two different men carry her down the hallway and stairs. Her wheels glide beyond the building's blood-red door, through the archway, straight into the sunlight. "They got me outside!" she hollers. "But you. You never helped me!"

Even after I moved away to a tree-lined block in Brooklyn, her voice purled in and out of my dreams: "I worked for Columbia University for forty years!" "My people are Basque!" When I lived on Allen and Broome, I thought she'd repeated herself again and again due to lapses in her memory. But these declarations weren't for me. It was as if she spoke herself into the world each time, so as not to forget the life she used to live, who she used to be—an incantation against the imminent, to insist: *I exist, I exist.*

Before Agnes left, she did meet my mother. They held each other's hands, eyes fixed through matching vintage eyeglasses, beaming. "My, you're beautiful!" Agnes said. "You're beautiful," my mother echoed.

Umma would not end up like Aggie, but there had been one desolate moment after I'd stopped answering her calls in 2005. I wouldn't find out until many years later, on the eve of my thirtieth birthday, when the city's glamouring had started to fizzle.

"Could you ever imagine feeling so sad to end your life?" she said.

"I can't," I lied.

We retreated to our own thoughts for a moment, silent but not yet ready to hang up.

Then my mother told me how one night, shortly after I'd moved across from Agnes, she'd swallowed a fistful of pills and passed out in her closet. I wanted to ask countless questions, to climb back up the mountain, to reach her. But by then a new story had already begun to unfold between us. So I asked, "What happened?"

And her words hung in the air like birdsong: "I woke up."

Jen Choi, Jen Choi! 11-14-06
This is a same post card you sent to me
except the Blue dome.
Santorini is just so beautiful.
I came down on a donkey. It was tough.
By the time I reached the bottom of
the steps I was able to
enjoy & I had to get off
the donkey. I sang &
called you & your sister's
name over & over.
Can you imagine?
The next stop is Sicily.

miss Jen Choi

FWD

10002+303A

ROMA
Jen Choi, Jen Choi,
I'm having an amazing
time here in Rome
Walked everywhere, got
lost many times & all
had a capuccino on the street
Watching people walk by.
I'm mailing this from
Vatican.
off to cruise.
See you in Greek isle

miss Jen Choi

CITTA' DEL VATICANO

Escape Artists

CANYON LAKE HOUSE
1,752 sq. ft.: 4BR, 2BA

www.canyonlakeca.gov

Welcome to the City of Canyon Lake's website! Canyon
Lake is a unique master-planned community that was
developed by the Corona Land Company starting in 1968.
Incorporated on December 1, 1990, the City of Canyon
Lake's mission is to provide public services that sustain
and enhance the quality of life for our community.
. . . With a current population just over 11,000 residents,
this recreation oriented community also has the distinction of being a fully governed city.

Molder

M Y FIRST TRIP TO Canyon Lake, in the summer of 2006, I'd deemed something of an exploratory mission, to assess what had taken shape post my graduation, amid Umma's divorce. When I spotted her at the airport, decked out in a sequined bolero and children's jeans, I wasn't sure if I was looking at the Before or After of a tragic makeover. Or was she caught somewhere in the middle? The purse my mother clutched was made of a shiny holographic vinyl, its warped iridescence flashing a distress call. She looked at me wild-eyed, buzzing with an almost feral volatility.

Laurie arrived soon after and, like me, quietly noted our mother's troubling state. We drove around her new neighborhood, winding past the body of water for which the city is named. We watched as Umma's pumpkin-colored neighbors partook in a noisy sport called "sit-down hydrofoiling." They torqued through various loop-de-loops while being towed by speedboats blasting Limp Bizkit upon the manmade lake.

We did not spot any fellow yellow folk around. Umma now belonged to a mere 1.6 percent Asian population (fewer than 200 people), a drastic change from Rowland Heights where my parents had lived among nearly 30,000 Asians. Prior to her move, it is unlikely Umma considered what Edward Blakely, then dean at University of Southern California's School of Urban and Regional Planning, surmised of gated cityhood— that barricading one's domain was "the final act of secession from the wider community . . . a retreat from the civic system." Perhaps the only thing she acknowledged outright was how she liked the city's tagline: "Canyon Lake, a little bit of paradise."

At a stop sign, I noticed a lane allocated strictly for golf cart traffic. A man rocking aerodynamic Oakleys pulled up, a cartoonish inferno of decal flames searing the sides of his buggy. At the sight of him, my mother announced: "I'm thinking of buying a golf cart."

"You want one of *those*?" my sister blurted, flaring her nostrils as wide as dimes.

Umma nodded as the man veered off to join a group of dad-types also partial to hair gel and peroxide, milling about Canyon Lake's country club parking lot. It was as if a casting call for Guy Fieri look-alikes had broken for lunch.

"Oh, it's just a thing to have," Umma reasoned. This was a phrase that had in recent months entered into heavy circulation. The mother who raised us didn't buy things "just to have." Almost ascetic in nature, she had owned minimal belongings for vanity's sake. Even her knock-off Louis Vuitton fanny pack, which she'd purchased at a Korean grocery store in downtown LA, served a practical purpose. That was the old Umma, though. I wasn't sure what version of her had pecked out of the cocoon or how long her latest impulses might last.

Still, a golf cart? She was perhaps the only Korean on the planet to detest golf, perhaps in large part due to my father's avid interest in the sport. He spent every free moment, including Christmas mornings, at the driving range. Used to, anyway. What he partook in these days remained as mysterious as his exit from my life.

According to my mother, after she sold the Rowland Heights house to pay off his debts, Dad moved into a trailer parked behind a nearby Korean supermarket. Or at least that's what I recall her telling me. The notion seemed absurd, but then a detail emerged oddly viable enough to legitimize his situation: He'd joined an LA Fitness, to use the locker room for his morning shower and shave. Strange logic, to rent a trailer and join a gym instead of finding wheel-less shelter with a functioning commode, but that was him to a T.

I pictured my father standing at the shared mirror, morosely combing his definitive part. Or I saw him in his trailer, eating from a tin of mackerel pike, chopsticks scraping the metal ridges, the sharp fetor of canned fish suffusing the paper-thin linens. When I conjured these scenes, I did not pity him. I wondered instead what it might take for him to realize the permanence of all he'd lost.

Would he ever? Umma used to describe my father as a dansehpoh, meaning single-celled. This wasn't a knock on his intelligence but a way of distilling how he inhabited the world—so uncomplex as to seem primordial, thinking only within the realm of the encompassed self. A heedless way to carry on as a human, paying no mind to consequence, to simply drift.

Nearly two years into our fallout, I insisted our predicament did not trouble me. I was naïve enough to think our loss was really his loss, for he'd never find out who I'd grow up to become. The flipside was I'd never see him again either, but what other choice did I have? I suppose I could have been the virtuous one, continuing to reach out to a person who has not shown interest in maintaining a connection. It seemed smarter, relieving myself of expectations. So I resolved to treat his departure like an unsolved missing persons case, as if he'd taken a walk into the woods and never returned. This was much more bearable than the alternative: that he lived in the same old town, had resumed his same old life, undisturbed without me.

No remnants of his existence could be found at the Canyon Lake house. Plenty of unusually high-femme decor diversions had been left in his place. The lava lamp night light Umma installed in the living room glowed incandescent purple waves around the clock. She drank her favorite roasted corn tea from a red high heel–shaped mug, which stepped over the words *High Maintenance*. A feather-trimmed pillow hung on her bedroom door, *The princess is out* embroidered on one side in silver cursive, *Spoil Me* on the other. My grandparents, who were temporarily staying with Umma, seemed largely unfazed by their daughter's turnabout. Perhaps this is to be expected for people who have survived civil war and imperialist rule. Things could be worse.

And technically, Umma wasn't alone. She had moved there with her dog.

• • •

THE JINDO HAD first shown up three houses prior, in Arcadia. My uncle D supposedly purchased the puppy from a Korean middleman at an undisclosed location in K-town. He had a knack for procuring pure-breds that frequently "ran away" from his company. Umma didn't care much for pets (another mouth to feed and more shit to shovel) but for some reason, she took this one in. The breed, according to Uncle D, was pricey of course, the best of the best, a rarity in the States, but most importantly Korean and thus, without question, an exquisite specimen. The dog did not look especially exquisite when it appeared one day, sitting floppy-like in our backyard.

At the time I didn't know anything about Jindos. Had I asked my uncle, or really any Korean national between forty and sixty-five, they would've likely described the pinnacle of canine intelligence and dignity, the world's finest dog—largely unknown to most of the world.

Jindos are South Korea's fifty-third "Natural Monument," canonized between Ulleung chrysanthemums and five-ribbed thyme shrubs (#52) and a Confucian shrine's 400-year-old tree (#59). They marched in the 1988 Seoul Summer Olympics Opening Ceremony. And like members of a royal court, they have lived alongside several Korean leaders at the official presidential residence, known as the Blue House. During South Korea's implementation of the Sunshine Policy—a diplomacy effort initiated in 1998—President Kim Dae-jung gifted North Korea's Kim Jong-il a pair of Jindos as a kind of peace offering.

Which is to say Jindos are an emblem of Korean honor and identity. Koreans have weathered significant periods of cultural, geographic, and economic obliteration. Perhaps to be Korean, then, is to steadfastly endure and to take pride in the innate sensibility of perseverance. For example, countless cultural touchstones (including the Korean language itself) were either outlawed or destroyed throughout Japan's reign of imperial terror. Indigenous animals were among such casualties—except for the Jindo, so the story goes. Even an enemy could see: Here was a dog so extraordinary, it deserved to be spared from the darkest days in a nation's history. Imagine believing in such a possibility.

Though Jindos are considered native to Jindo Island, located off the southwest coast of the Korean Peninsula, theories persist on how the dogs got there. One speculation: They descend from an animal that washed ashore from a Chinese merchant's shipwreck sometime between 960 and 1270. It is also possible the Jindo is related to battle dogs brought over during the thirteenth-century Mongol invasions. Jindo Island had func-tioned then as a refuge for Korean rebellion troops. In the fourteenth century, military forces evacuated the island, leaving it empty—except for those dogs, who roamed alone there, wild, for nearly a century.

Prototypical Jindos are distinguished-looking creatures, bearing a golden pelage, sickle-shaped tail, and devious smile, sharing a likeness to their trendier domesticated peers—foxy like a Shiba Inu, lupine like an Akita. They are said to exhibit superior problem-solving skills and homing capabilities. Their extreme intelligence is known to both impress and alarm their owners. The dogs are master escape artists. They are capable of digging their way out of elaborately fenced backyards and can supposedly scale walls up to eight feet high. They jailbreak out of instinct, to explore their neighborhoods, expand their territory. And when they are not allowed to reside indoors with their humans, they jailbreak out of boredom.

But how did they get to the States? I suppose like many immigrant stories: because someone else brought them. According to one (albeit sketchy) blog, the first Jindo allegedly arrived more than a hundred years ago, when an American service member formerly stationed in Korea relocated to Hawaii with his dog in tow. Though the breed may have landed in the contiguous states as early as 1972, the 1980s wave of Korean immigration ushered in a simultaneous influx of pet Jindos, specifically in southern California, and probably under illegal auspices. Beefed-up restrictions protecting the breed's "authenticity" have since become so strict, these days it is challenging to export a "purebred" Jindo from South Korea and altogether impossible to remove certified Jindos from Jindo Island.

But we're talking about the '80s; you could just get away with stuff back then.

Regrettably, due to irresponsible breeding practices and owner ill-preparedness (Jindos require extensive training), the dogs began to surface in animal shelters. Lack of familiarity led to misidentification. Adopters, who assumed they'd welcomed, say, German shepherd/Husky mixes into their homes, frequently lacked the capacity for or interest in taming their mysterious strays. However, those who have the wherewithal are handsomely rewarded with an extraordinary protector and companion.

Dr. Phil McGraw (yes, *that* "Dr. Phil," of daytime American talk show fame) was up for the challenge. His darling Maggie had been rescued from Koreatown. In 2009, Maggie bit a family friend, which led to a personal injury lawsuit. Court documents obtained by tabloids stated the Jindo had an "unpredictable temperament," intimating Maggie had bitten others and had even murdered the McGraw family cat and rabbit. The McGraws eventually settled out of court, likely without any admission of wrongdoing. And, perhaps to Dr. Phil, his dog truly could do no wrong—Maggie, his shadow as he called her, who slept in his bed, accompanied him to work, traveled the world with him and his wife—a testament to the power a Jindo can hold on their humans.

The feeling is mutual. Jindos ordinarily attach to one person and one person alone. Despite sharing the free-roaming sensibilities of their primitive peer, the Australian dingo, Jindos have earned a reputation for an unparalleled allegiance to their first owners and do not acclimate well to multiple handlers. This proved problematic when the Korean American Federation of Los Angeles, in partnership with the South Korea–based Jindo Dog Promotion and Innovation Agency, waged a campaign to induct the breed into the LAPD canine force. Though they developed some skills useful in detective work, the dogs were easily distracted. As an officer described in the *Los Angeles*

Times, his pup trainee "just wanted to please me . . . If I wasn't there, she'd go off task." The program ultimately folded because "a good police dog does its work to stay on the hunt and stay focused to satisfy a drive, not to please its master." For owners and fans of the breed, this foray may have only confirmed the Jindo's most venerated trait: unquestionable loyalty.

• • •

THE JINDO UMMA got from Uncle D was a six-month-old female puppy with black fur, save for her tan belly, paws, cheeks, chest, and the two gingko bean–sized spots above her eyes that rendered her the inquisitive type. She looked Asian, which is strange to say of a dog. Yet it was undeniable in certain features (the eyes, the nose, the coat). Her left ear drooped downward though, unlike the proud, pointy ears Jindos are meant to possess—the flaw, my mother suspected, that led Uncle D to give the dog the boot.

I'd assumed we wouldn't keep her either. While I'd long begged for a pet, by the time this one appeared, I'd hooked onto another fantasy: moving as far away from home as possible. Umma didn't ask for my help anyway. She dutifully provided enough to sustain the Jindo's baseline needs, offering minimal outward affection (a familiar approach I'd experienced as a human under her care). Umma bought a doghouse, set food out on the back porch, and walked the puppy across the street for checkups at the neighborhood vet clinic, where no one had ever heard of the Jindo breed before. At no point was the dog allowed inside the house. And after a month, she still didn't have a name.

College departure dangled before me like a golden carrot, and I was fixed on a future elsewhere, leaving no room for new bonds. But to be called something is a gesture of permanence, which even I could see the dog deserved. I brainstormed one option.

Back then I'd acquired a near-fanatical fondness for the sci-fi series *The X-Files*. I was smitten with the protagonist, played by David Duchovny. Maybe it was his unflinching pursuit to make the unknown known (conspiracies, aliens). Or maybe it was the unassailable fact the man exuded sex (some people just do).

Mostly as a joke, I suggested my favorite character's name. It wasn't a word that rolled off the Korean tongue, a necessary component to consider in our family. And Mulder was a man, on a show about paranormal phenomena. I was sure my mother would veto the idea. She made a "huh" noise in the universal way one acknowledges and dismisses a mediocre suggestion.

The following week, I returned home from school to see a red heart-shaped tag hanging around the dog's neck. Punched definitively in metal were the words:

MOLDER
CHOI

"The way you spelled it," I said. "That didn't look weird?" Not exactly moldy and not quite a superlative mold, reminiscent of a middling kind of decay. How humiliating, I thought—for the dog.

Umma paused from sifting through bills in the kitchen. "But don't you think she looks just like a Fox Molder?" she asked, with surprising candor.

I quickly came to resent my suggestion. For reasons I cannot comprehend, my mother fervently opposed sending Molder to obedience school. Each time we opened the backyard gate, she bolted out like a bull at a rodeo. If we were unable to corral her into the garage, she promptly ran across the road and mocked us from the busy shopping center's sidewalk by performing a mischievous dance, stamping her feet into the pavement, swiveling her head side to side like Stevie Wonder. A real showboat. Every time I got close, she dashed away beyond my reach. It was worse when Umma doddered after her, calling in Korean, "*Moldaaahhh! Moldaaaahhh-yah! Ih-dee wah-bah Moldaaaahhh!*" which never worked.

By the time we got to Rowland Heights, a tangible alliance started to form, between Umma and Molder. I recognized their connection immediately.

Umma and I were at our closest when I was seven or eight years old. As her little lackey, I used to crouch by my sister's door, listening in on telephone conversations, to report back the juicy details: "She's gonna sneak out again!" Or "She says she's in love with Pat!" And Umma, folding the laundry or sitting on the toilet, would nod, give a *that'll be all* hand shoo, and I'd skip off, well pleased. My sister and father, who maintained a special bond of their own, had no doubts about my allegiance. When Dad came home with a new golf set or Laurie got another piercing, they pleaded, "Don't tell Mom." And I said, "Okay, okay." But I always did.

Umma and me, me and Umma. She trusted me in a way she trusted no one else. By that I mean she let me preen her almost nightly. At her bedside, my small hands would part her hair this way and that. When I found a patch of white hairs, by her request I'd pluck out the offending strands. Or we'd take turns lying down, gingerly cleaning each other's ears with a tiny wooden spoon. She looked innocent beneath the lamplight, momentarily unsullied by life's disappointments. It was as if that light held decoding powers. I could see her, the disappearing ink made visible—eyes wide, body curled, like me, a girl. I thought in those moments the impenetrable veneer dropped, and she'd let me in.

A child cannot, alone, sustain a mother's happiness, and there seemed to be no end to the source of her displeasure, which distended beyond my realm of understanding—perhaps beyond her own. I grew older. Our closeness waned. And since she represented my only immediate model of Korean womanhood, I assumed her cold, distant demeanor epitomized a greater archetype of Asian moms and by proxy Asian women. As if the events before I was born hadn't altered her outlook on life. I thought instead I was seeing her exist in a hardwired state: relentless, joyless, less.

Oh to raise a teenage daughter. No easy task with a know-it-all. But I also pity Younger Me, for what she did not know; for the ease with which she dispensed cruelty; for her tender, fractious mind. Stupid squabbles made cataclysmic and unforgivable: no sleepover parties, no rides to friends' houses, no Hamburger Helper; no access to the world Umma had dropped me into, and for what reason? I could think of only one. If she couldn't be happy, no one else could.

I suppose she had grown to despise me the way I despised her, because we came from each other. Bitch seeing bitch. And in the flurry of some petty argument, doors slamming, throats sore from our irascible volleys, I screamed—and really screamed, because I foolishly believed it: "I will *never* be like you." The words hung there, ringing, expanding. I wonder if she remembers that day because I can't forget it.

Of course she preferred the dog.

What an uncanny sensation, watching myself gradually displaced from Umma's life. Suddenly, when she shouted at me from across the room, it was no longer, "Jennipah!" but the accidental fusion, "Mold-Jenny!" One day I even caught her scooping my food with the same spoon she used to dish out Molder's meal. She preened the Jindo, cleaned her ears, brushed her coat. To make matters worse, Umma believed Molder had learned Korean instantaneously. "She's bilingual," my mother claimed. How humiliating, for me—to be one-upped by a dog.

My father also noticed Molder's ascending status in our family hierarchy. When Umma came home from work, the dog would gallop to the garage, wrap her tan paws around my mother's thigh, and vigorously hump away. My mother laughed and laughed. It was discomfiting to see Umma objectively getting dommed, and that she appeared capable of openly welcoming acts of arousal.

Umma routinely recoiled from my father's slightest touch, so witnessing these intimacies must have agitated him. On one night, he called me over to the garage Smelly Fridge, which contained kimchi, other stinky foods, and his silo of beer. He cracked open a Tecate and poured a pool into his cupped palm for Molder to slurp. My father chuckled, enrapt by the vulgarity, as if we were staring at a toddler who'd learned to curse. He signaled me the "shhh" sign, his face beet red not from embarrassment but rather the Asian Flush, the bigger tell—he'd been drinking for some time. Though I was not her lackey anymore, I informed my mother promptly.

The next scene I watched from the distance I'd come to inhabit in that house: Umma darting to the garage, shoving my father once, twice. The shift in her stature, how she embraced Molder, escorting her to the yard. The acoustics of that space, my mother's disdain magnified in the reverberations. The awkward aftermath of a failed prank, the way my father wiped palms to sweatpants and sucked his teeth then chugged the rest of his beer. His red face blank except his eyes, which seemed to affirm a twinge of awareness rarely left exposed, suddenly bare, remote, and in the next breath gone.

Soon after, I left for New York. My parents' marriage went kaput. Here's what mattered, what stayed the same: walks with Molder on quiet nights, Umma yanked along, flailing but refreshed of purpose. When my father returned home less and less, or during the intervention, or after he moved out, Molder was there on the other side of the glass, waiting patiently for Umma to open the door.

Until an afternoon windstorm. Rain pelted my mother's windows at work. The trees outside bent unnaturally, and she imagined the ones on her block snapping, like takeout chopsticks. She drove home, fretting how she'd find Molder, soaked, startled, or worse . . .

There was the Jindo, shivering but wagging her sickle-shaped tail. Umma wiped the dog's paws with a towel and let her into the house. They fell asleep together on the guest bed. Each stormy night they repeated the routine until Molder stayed inside for good. Finally, it was undeniable. Molder could do what I couldn't: sit there and listen for hours, absorbing every sound like a wall—the real Korean daughter Umma had always wanted.

* * *

JINDOS, SO IT IS SAID, retain no "dog odor" and groom themselves like cats. This made Molder an impeccable indoor companion, one of "us Choi girls" as Umma put it. By Canyon Lake, I'd come around to her role in the surrounding disorder. Laurie and I needed her there as much as Umma did, for the stability. Molder moseyed around the house as if she'd lived there her entire life, which likely had nothing to do with an innate sense of geography. Maybe she felt at home because of the person, not the place, to whom she now belonged.

But for a human? I couldn't personally see anything appealing about Canyon Lake. The nearest attraction was an outlet mall, where retailers included L'eggs hosiery, SAS orthopedic footwear, and a Wetzel's Pretzels. I was counting down the days until I could get back to the city because, at twenty, I felt on an atomic level defined by my life in Manhattan.

This was the early Aughts, pre-smartphones, in the heyday of Gawker and Nerve.com; you didn't have to belong to New York media to voraciously lap up the catty minutiae. The way you told a story trumped what actually happened, although the particulars could be just as tantalizing: pithy musings on socialites, party queens, or canonical scammers like the Hipster Grifter—a tatted Korean American woman wanted across state lines for writing bad checks, notorious for seducing bearded Brooklyn men. We read blogs (frequently updated and overly confessional) where voicey scenesters chronicled their sexploits. Some landed those white whale blog-to-book publishing deals. And the slice of New York attuned to this gossip eagerly refreshed the same choice sites every morning while noshing on their hangover bodega egg-and-cheese. Snark and cynicism earned a palpable social cachet, and though adhering to such an outlook did not equate to a personality, you could certainly feel as if you belonged to a substratum of New Yorkers by parroting along to this unspoken manifesto.

Maybe cynicism had been a matter of survival, as if rebuffing earnestness could somehow soften reality's blow. We had come of age between burst bubbles: the dot-com boom gone bust, economic damage post-9/11, and just when it seemed possible again, the subprime mortgage crisis exploded any prospect of linear, adult milestone attainment. Canyon Lake marked my mother's ninth purchased home. Meanwhile I, newly saddled with student loan debt, could not entertain the thought of buying anything permanent for myself one day, down to the chintzy bed frame I'd procured on Craigslist. I did not know what I wanted to be, which was at odds with how I could make money—not scrambling from gig-to-gig type cash but life-changing loot. So if you were like me, treading in that trite but tortured limbo, you might have chosen to not pay close attention. Recession, recession, recession. So omnipresent that the point of the word, the stakes, altogether eroded for me. Shit looked bad, but for adults. The fact I was becoming one, thus inheriting not even the now-mess but the metastasized future-mess of all that economic fracas was too daunting to fathom. I didn't want "real life." I preferred getting wasted at Happy Endings instead, waking up in last night's clothes then surreptitiously barfing in a bodega bag on the F train while heading to bottomless brunch.

Which is to say I, like my mother, was undergoing a frenzied, personal reclamation. I could not comprehend the parallel nature of our conditions. So I scoffed at the outlet mall, and the lava lamp night light, and every item in the thrift store she drove us to one afternoon outside Canyon Lake's city limits.

A tiny brass bell clanged a mournful tune as we entered the disarray. Shelves of musty shoes and watchful dolls greeted us. The racks were overstuffed with Members Only jackets, Hypercolor tees, acid-washed denim, and other fads time forgot—the kinds of clothes people had begun to reclaim again, for irony's sake, in New York.

As far as I was concerned, my mother and I were nothing alike, down to our tastes. In reality, I was a walking Mad Libs variation of Umma's identity crisis, though my blanks were filled with contrasting details. Rather than a too-youthful wardrobe, I wore vintage dresses, mostly floral frocks, empire, A-line, or high-waisted, and one unforgivable teal dress with gold snaps whose previous owner could have only been a 1980s New Wave flight attendant. I still dyed the front sweep of my hair a throbbing shade of red, too, which required multiple steps: bleaching (to strip the dark color to the tone of dead grass), followed by the overlay of semi-permanent scarlet goo, a soppy-headed waiting period so the color could take, and then monthly reapplications. It wasn't as if I disliked being Asian. I didn't alter my eyes or skin, though I had been offered these opportunities as gifts from family members on several occasions. I was hoping to create distractions, to preventatively indicate I was a "different" kind of Asian.

I did not want to talk with strangers about what it was like to be

Korean, speak Korean, cook Korean—matters they felt comfortable, if entitled, to inquire about with indefatigable intrigue for the sake of their own satiation. Engaging on that level would require admitting I didn't know anything about my family's homeland and, in turn, some essential part of my own self. I was perpetually disarmed, unequipped with clever retorts. Later, I'd replay the scenes, letting my bumbling fester until spewing out in regrettable fashion choices.

You can put a top hat on a toad, but that won't alter physiognomy; all you'll see is one funny-looking toad. My red hair and black smoky under-eyeliner and granny dresses only seemed to fuel curiosities. I didn't care as long as I could look in the mirror and see what I wanted to see: someone who didn't resemble her mother.

In the T-shirt section, I scored a black-and-white number screen-printed with the phrase "Shalom y'all!" As I joined Laurie and Umma near the faux fur coats, a mustachioed man approached us, grinning a Swiss cheese smile. His eyes bulged, bumfuzzled at the sight of us, as if he'd never encountered an Asian before, let alone a trio.

"Y'all three generations?!" he exclaimed.

I pointed to my sister. "You think *she* gave birth to *me?*"

My mother laughed her stunning, witchy cackle, which left her keeled over, breathless. I could always break her this way.

The man shrugged, the bell clanged again and like Pavlov's dog, he scurried away.

Back at the Canyon Lake house, Molder awaited, splayed in a patch of sun by the patio door. She wore a necklace emblazoned with DIVA in bubble letters, and the distinct expression of learned tolerance. At some point, Umma orchestrated a listening party, playing on loop the bossa nova CD she'd purchased in South America, along with a petite cherry-red leather jacket. She sat on the couch in the outfit, swaying and humming with her eyes closed, lost in a rapture I had seen last in church, when she sang on Praise Team. My sister and I exchanged glances that weren't even the "knowing" kind. What was there to know? We had watched these types of major personality shifts on episodes of *Law & Order: SVU,* but to see a fluctuation of this nature in real life left us speechless. Until we absconded to the liquor store, blasting Joy Division along the streets that could easily double as Yankee Candle fragrances—Cinnamon Teal, Cool Meadow, White Sail—screaming: What the fuck happened to our mother?

It was easier reacting to these changes antagonistically. I did not possess the clarity to do the harder, kinder introspection, to allow room for the possibility my mother's vacillations might lead to something promising and permanent. Doing so would require a level of vulnerability I could not risk. If I loved Umma now, would this version of her stay?

After Laurie and I chugged bone-dry martinis and everyone retired for bed, I raided my mother's pantry—a mini pharmacy stocked with prescription drugs—for anything remotely recreational. In those days I was beginning to chase the distinct notion of "elsewhere." This is easy to do in a place like New York. At Sin-é on Attorney Street, I went to shows where everyone pretended not to notice Sean Lennon while an indie band mumble-moaned through its set list. I guzzled whiskey gingers at Mama's Bar, wondering why that former '90s heartthrob was taking so long in the bathroom. I wasn't the Misshapes type, preferring instead Smiths Night at Sway, where I noodled around to Morrissey beside Chloë Sevigny and Ben Cho in the mindless camaraderie of party anonymity.

I had come to California skeptical of my mother and her life because the one I was living I believed, absurdly enough, was somehow more anchored in reality. She kept erupting into sonorous crying jags, repeating: "If I ever did anything right, it was raising my two girls. If I ever did anything right . . ." We thanked her, praised her, rebutted her, consoled her—she was a tireless provider, a good mother, a great mother—but she continued, "If I ever did anything right . . ." The words began to diffuse into syllables, sounds, then howls between hiccupped breaths, with the same refrain reprised the next evening and the next, until the thanking, and praising, and rebutting, and consoling particalized into meaningless white noise, revealing the futility of our exertions.

When I was a child, my mother rarely allowed her inner anguish to bubble forth like this. But I do recall several nighttime car rides together, when Patsy Cline's "Crazy" played on the radio. She'd crank the volume and sing along, bawling in a similar cadence of refracted abandon: "I'm crazy for feeling so lonely . . . crazy for feeling so blue . . ." I wanted to ask what was wrong. But her gaze remained fixed on some unknown distance, and I knew not to disturb her. Once the song ended, she'd zip up her misery, and we'd drive on.

Patsy's song is about heartbreak. Not once had I witnessed my parents exchange affections. I'd wondered if this marital dynamic was a Korean thing. Or if the matter she mourned had less to do with lost love but rather the absence of love in her life in the first place.

Rather than stay by her side in Canyon Lake, as I would have done as a child, I turned away. Another act of cruelty, perhaps, but I couldn't parse which Umma she might summon next: the starved and drunk one, electric with grief, or the callous one I seemed to ever-disappoint in my youth. So I flew back to New York, leaving my mother behind the walls of her desert mirage.

A sound returned to me thereafter, while waiting tables or at Max Fish knocking back muscle relaxers I'd stolen from my mother's pantry. Not Patsy nor the bossa nova melting in and out of earshot between Umma's crying. It was the resonant wail I'd overheard in Canyon Lake, reverberating from outside, into the house.

We had come home, still giggling about the man at the thrift store. An hour had passed when Umma decided to prune the tree in her front yard. I followed the sound and found her there, wearing a sequined T-shirt, the phrase *Cutie Pie* shimmering in the sun. Her elegant hands, the ones she inherited from Halmoni and passed on to me, gripped the clippers until her knuckles blanched to bone white. Yet there was softness, not as expected. Skin like wet tissue. The tree's branches tumbled down, slicing Umma up like razor blade confetti. Tufts of dust clouded around her feet. Molder barked from the driveway. Halmoni marched over, urging Umma to stop, calling her by her birth name, meaning Beautiful Sound. But we both knew. There was no stopping her. So Halmoni stepped aside and we stood together, listening and squinting from the sizzling hot pavement; a trio of the same eyes, the same skin, the same hands; one woman who bore the other who bore me—three generations.

. . .

My mother often reminds me I am "one hundred percent Korean." I am unsure what it is she's implicitly suggesting. Her tone is boastful, like how some people describe acquiring high-quality luxuries like Egyptian cotton sheets or the finest beads of Osetra Imperial Gold caviar. It is a privilege to obtain a thing distilled to its essence. I imagine what my mother is saying has something to do with fortitude; what she, and those who came before her, withstood so I might exist. A lineage like this considers physicality but nothing of the mind. It does not acknowledge what is inherently lost the farther we move away from a place of origin either, across oceans and time, generation to generation, the natural degradation, the slightly altered outcomes, something like attrition.

Lineage is simpler to speak about in dog terms. Entire organizations are dedicated to the study and preservation of the Jindo breed. Park Jong-hwa, at the Mosan Jindo Dog Research Centre, south of Seoul, has devoted much of his work to breeding out certain undesirable characteristics so as to make the Jindo more appealing to prospective owners worldwide. These attempts would alter something intrinsic about this quintessentially Korean dog and, while common practice by competitive international dog breeding standards, are diametrically at odds with Jindo preservation efforts.

The state-run Jindo Dog Research and Test Centre, however, located on Jindo Island, founded in 1999, spends approximately $1.7 million annually on "systematic and scientific" Jindo conservation. DNA and paternity tests are administered, and dogs who are up to scruff receive official certification. Those who do not meet standards are required to leave the island.

We did not conduct DNA tests on Molder to confirm her purity. I will probably never submit my spit to confirm Umma's "one hundred percent Korean" avowal either. But I do wonder what else I have inherited, seeable and unseeable, desirable and undesirable, from those who came before me—and what parts no amount of effort can conserve.

· · ·

IN THE SUMMER OF 2007, my mother left California. She'd spotted a job ad in a trade journal for registered nurses. The words resounded like a siren call until she answered: *Get away from it all in beautiful Ketchikan, Alaska.*

She hinted at her imminent journey north over the phone. If she'd been dropping bigger clues, I wouldn't have noticed. Too busy slamming cheap bourbon at Home Sweet Home on Chrystie Street, dancing my ass off to Soul Clap or yammering with strangers beside the taxidermied art. That sweet black curtain of Forget, sweeping open and closed, night after night. Somehow I always managed to crawl back into bed unscathed, where the thoughts I'd kept at bay burbled over. I imagined where my father was living. After his supposed trailer stint, I heard through the grapevine he'd moved into a no-frills boarding house, meals provided, still in Rowland Heights. When he drove by our old street, did he ever think of me?

Meanwhile, as a dry heat wave scorched through Canyon Lake, Umma began packing her long underwear into a suitcase. She'd sold what she could of her belongings at a garage sale. Sentimental objects—family vacation albums, knickknacks, furniture passed down from my grandparents—she distributed between two new friends from a Korean church in Riverside, Grace Jung and Grace Huang. My mother stopped into the local AAA, an agent gave her maps, and they plotted her path. At 2 A.M. Umma locked up the Canyon Lake house. Departing this early, she'd arrive in Sacramento by dinnertime. Molder sat in the front seat of her truck as they ventured past the city's security gates, onto the empty road.

She saw no sign declaring with certitude, YOU ARE NOW LEAVING CALIFORNIA. Instead OREGON WELCOMES YOU and OREGON THANKS YOU / COME BACK SOON blurred by her window. Then, WELCOME TO THE EVERGREEN STATE, then water and wind, to the land of wild forget-me-nots and four-spot skimmer dragonflies, once a prospector's paradise replete with hidden gold.

"I left, just like I was going to work," Umma said. "And I did not look back."

BOB'S CABIN
3BR, 1BA

Located conveniently seven miles from downtown
Ketchikan, AK. Remodeled kitchen; cast iron wood stove in
living room; sun room; large deck with unobstructed ocean
views; and a hot tub.

Partially furnished if desired.

August 27, 2007 12:34 PM

Email Subject: 2 city slickers and a white pony . . .

I was going for a morning walk with Molder last week and I saw a white pony coming toward us.

Molder started to run after him immediately. In panic I ran after Molder so two of us were running. In the meantime 3 of my neighbors with a camera on each running after the pony. The pony took a look at Molder and disappeared into a nearby bush.

To my ignorance it was a rare sight of a mountain goat! Even to my neighbors. We are not very popular around here since we chased a mountain goat away, kidding . . .

Things are good. I joined all women's hiking group and planning to go next week. There are so many trails to explore. The city of Ketchikan invests a lot of recreational stuff.

One of Orthopedic doctor invited me to his dinner party this Wednesday. All of us are new in town so it will be good to talk to each other.

Talk to you later,
Chris and Molder

The Great Alaskan Umma

FOUR TRAINS, TWO PLANES, three states, and twenty-eight hours of travel had led to a caesura. Our plane had been circling the same gray patch for thirty minutes. Do we turn back or wait for a break in the storm? The captain had not reached a decision, so we hovered above land, though no land could be seen from the windows. What presumably existed below: the panhandle, Misty Fjords National Monument, the world's largest collection of standing totem poles, and Ketchikan—the forty-ninth state's first city; rain capital of Alaska, Salmon Capital of the World. Home to five square miles of rainforest, peaks, channels, and creeks; home of the nation's highest postal code; and now home to my Korean mother.

Soon the dense rainfall dispersed into a soft spray, and we made our precarious descent toward the churning black water of Tongass Narrows. The airstrip materialized just as our wheels touched down. Passengers clapped as we skidded to a halt.

At Ketchikan International Airport, I entered what could have easily doubled as a bank lobby. Departures listed domestic routes only, to neighboring Sitka, Juneau, Anchorage. The same woman who greeted me at the gate also helmed Baggage Claim and Security and ambled from post to post. Interestingly, I was not yet in Ketchikan but a seven-minute ferry ride away on neighboring Gravina Island. I followed the signs for the dock.

It was September 2007. Since heading north, Umma had been dispatching updates to my sister, me, and the Graces. Her most recent email revealed a level of interiority previously unknown to us. But could we trust it? She'd lived in Ketchikan for less than two months.

At the Arrivals waiting room, before the exit to the ferry, I saw her. She was wearing yellow rain boots dotted with pink sunflowers and a windbreaker with *Ketchikan, AK* stitched onto the lapel. Both hands waving, she said, "Welcome to Alaska!"

I hopped in her truck for the tour. "This is the downtown!" my mother chirped. And we drove by the city center outfitted with curio and jewelry shops—selling kitschy ulu knives, gold quartz, and carved ivory—shut for the off-season lull. "This is the docks!" And we passed the wide-planked esplanade and cruise port, now blank without its massive ships. "For the excursions!" And we spied the most popular attractions in town: the Great Alaskan Lumberjack Show grounds and Dolly's House, a museum dedicated to Ketchikan's most famous madame and bordello. "For the sal-monz!" she said. And we noted the salmon cannery perched on its skinny stilts above George Inlet. On the last wooded stretch home, as light flickered through the trees, strobing the windshield, she said, "Does it get any better than this?"

The weather would soon turn, but she was ready.

Umma had packed my old ski bib. I'd worn those puffy-looking overalls when I was eleven, back in the mid-'90s when we schlepped across the West Coast on bank holiday sorties or budget weekend getaways starred in Umma's AAA handbook. She'd seemed miserable on our trips, her mouth crimped into a downhill slope, yet it was she who insisted we venture outside Arcadia ("for the cultures," as she put it). My father had stayed behind to man his shop—a completely reasonable decision that struck me as a convenient obligation. Perhaps this would prepare us; the void he left in time no longer a variable but reified, the clarity a kind of solace.

So each winter, Umma, Laurie, and I road-tripped to Mammoth Mountain. After the five-hour ride north and west, we checked into Alpenhof Lodge, a German-inspired alpine motel-cum-chalet. Umma made us gear up before boarding the shuttle bus to the ski resort. I'm talking goggles, headbands, ski boots, neoprene masks, down coats and bibs. Naturally people stared. Who wouldn't at the sight of not one but three Asian Michelin Man impersonators?

On the commute Laurie assumed the role of navigator and selected our trails for the day. We started with green circle runs (easy) and blue squares (intermediate).

I rode the chairlifts with my mother—an entire production. When the bench seat swung around to scoop us, Umma squatted nervously, anticipating contact. Yet she never seemed prepared upon liftoff, limbs splaying, hands frantically clinging to the rails. When the ride shook to a stop midway, as it occasionally did, our bodies bobbing high above the snow floor, she kept very still, eyes transfixed on the exit ramp.

At the slopes, Laurie and I darted down, carving S curves into fresh powder on Sleepy Hollow, Hully Gully, Clover Leaf, and Gremlin's Gulch. We waited for our mother at the bottom. Same as it ever was.

Except for one year, when Umma carried on a bizarre ritual. She launched after us in jittery, wide strokes, careening toward the orange-netted barricades blocking the sides of the trail. Then, like a push puppet, she collapsed and slid face-first down the mountain, her skis dragging the whole way down. The third time around, she busted her lip.

"What are you doing?!" we asked.

She hobbled upright and clumped a mound of snow against her mouth. A coil of blood seeped through the bright white. "I fell . . ." she said sheepishly.

On she went, going knock-kneed, skittering downhill flat as a pan-cake, grappling at her poles to rise again, and shuffling back into the lift line. No breaks. She embodied both Sisyphus and his boulder, in a trap of her own design. And yet I could sense with each fall, she was getting closer and closer to some internal place of achievement, where pain met pleasure. It must have been gratifying, thwacking through one known sensation to glimpse the other, only to rest, for a moment, in the unaccountable between.

At the Alpenhof that night, my sister and I sat on the pea-green pullout waiting for our Swiss Miss to cool. I was looking at the tiny marshmallows inside my mug when Umma pulled her pants down in the hallway. A dark blue bruise, the loose diameter of an acorn squash, bloomed on her upper thigh.

"It's a hematoma," she said proudly. "If it gets worse, I might have to drain it."

My sister and I sipped our cocoa. I was thinking, "Was this what she wanted?" as new snow cascaded outside our window, and our mother winced her way to bed.

*   *   *

GERMAN FOLKLORE HAS IT that once a beautiful maiden named Lorelei sat atop an enormous rock, awaiting her lover's return. While she remained faithful, her lover did not, and upon realizing he'd never come home, forlorn Lorelei jumped headfirst off the cliff and into the Rhine River's choppy current below. Thereafter, Lorelei's spirit lingered on the rock, where she combed her hair and sang a dulcet melody. Many sailors, entranced by her song, shipwrecked against the treacherous shoreline and perished. Some say every now and then you can still hear Lorelei's voice, echoing softly against the rock, vanishing into the hills of the Rhine Valley.

Loreley, the German biergarten where I worked, was located on the Lower East Side of Manhattan, between the Bowery's wholesale restaurant supply depots and Chrystie Street's grassless, drearily maintained Sara Delano Roosevelt Park. Lorelei seemed to me a macabre patron saint for a hospitality business, though she did effectively lure revelers to the bar who then crash landed out of sight, beyond Stanton Street. The bar's owner, a fiftysomething part-time iPod DJ, hailed from, rather fittingly, the city of Cologne. He'd gussied up the bar with "dad's basement" type flair. German flags and football scarves, ceramic steins with pewter lids, and a life-sized stuffed goat nested beside two flat-screen TVs.

The logic escapes me now, but at the time I believed working in an establishment I would never choose to visit recreationally equated to a sound separation of church and state. My commute was a six-minute walk from Allen and Broome, and for a while the fast cash seemed appropriate compensation for pouring hundreds of frothy beers into their comically oversized glassware. Bartending was supposed to be a stepping-stone job, until I figured out a plan.

In college, I'd worked with a close-knit editorial team for a handful of successful independent films (*Lost in Translation* turned out to be a biggie), cut in boutique post-production houses where facility staff zipped around on Razor scooters; the kinds of places where you might bump into a Coen brother at the fully stocked fridge or small talk with Michel Gondry in the communal kitchen on Cinco de Mayo over free chips and guac.

When that work dried up, I'd pulled together a couple part-time jobs. One was a somewhat coveted position at Kim's Video on St. Mark's— known by filmmakers and cinephiles alike as a mecca for out-of-print movies, rare international DVD releases, and customer service of an Olympic-level antagonism. Some third-floor clerks (in the infamous Rentals) straight up roasted you on the spot if they deemed your movie choices repugnant. First floor, in music, my colleagues were shier, amiable and, like everyone else employed by Mr. Kim, retained encyclopedic yet obscure expertise. I was, by these standards, underqualified. I worked on the second floor, the middle child: DVD sales and vinyl. The opportunity came my way via an on-again-off-again paramour—the first of my many entanglements with emotionally impoverished men (one genre in which I would come to possess near virtuosic knowledge). He knew the manager, so I cut the line. It was a job many people pined for. Film nerds constantly dropped off their resumes, which we collectively used as scratch paper. I'd crewed on some of the movies we kept in stock. Some days, as I shuffled through stacks of used pornos in the customer buyback line, I couldn't help but feel I had peaked early in my career. But also: what career?

The city can cast a strange spell on a person. One night you're bar hopping with Supergrass and the next morning, you're hauling your hungover ass to man the check-in desk at a basic bitch yoga studio on North Seventh for eight dollars an hour. You could graze the perimeter of the good life, make a whole meal out of the scraps, presuming you belonged to a big, radical moment, which made you special. There must be something almost chemical that happens when you're in your twenties in New York City (see: Dimes Square). Hyperlocal goings-on can feel major, as if your experiences are a part of a consequential, cultural awakening. Maybe this is true of any era, like the New York Beat generation, except we had no Ginsbergs, even if plenty pictured themselves just as revolutionary.

I did not consider myself a "writer" back then. Something a fiction professor in college once said boomeranged back to me whenever I entertained the thought: "You are not a writer unless you've published a book." Couldn't tell you a single thing the guy wrote, but when a person can zero in on a nascent desire and then quash it in the same breath, as if nothing had been mentioned at all, well, I suppose you never forget it.

I preferred taking creative nonfiction with a gentler, remarkably patient professor. She introduced me to Didion and Baldwin (you never forget that either). These classes happened to coincide with my family's implosion, so I dumped every raw emotion and budding resentment onto the page. My writing was like any beginner's: overly expository, oscillating between mawkish confession, amateur stand-up comic bits, and unfiltered pain, always meandering around the deeper reflections. I wasn't any good yet, but the mode itself intrigued me—taking lived experiences and elevating them, through language, into art. I didn't know a genre of literature like that existed. The discovery blasted an idle part of me open, to the ambiguous promise of potential, while simultaneously leaving any semblance of a clear direction forward scattershot. After graduation, my ambitions diffused into obtuse, floating conundrums: How will I make money? Can I make money while pursuing something "meaningful"? What "work" feels "meaningful"? What is "meaning"? What is "life"?

I focused on the immediate issue: coinage. A friend who bartended at flashy Bowlmor Lanes in Union Square told me how cash tips flowed there like Monopoly money. So I switched from café work to cocktail waitressing and eventually faked my way into the biergarten. I got hired because the server who took my CV was impressed by one credit I'd listed: the time I helped edit Criterion Collection DVD extras for an early Soderbergh movie. I threw that on to pad out my job history. It had already become clear I didn't have the knack for post-production long-term. I didn't care for the caste system or serf-like wages, and while working on films tickled my interest in show business, editing just wasn't my bag.

At Loreley, cash did not flow like Monopoly money, but it was enough to survive in the way I wanted in 2007. I made enough scratch to comfortably lollygag around downtown and Williamsburg, doing bumps in the bathroom with "new friends," seeing wherever the night took us. During that time, it seemed plausible to one day be plucked from the Gawker comments section for one's extemporaneous witticisms and anointed a writer-of-note overnight. Writing was the latest vessel into which I could channel my aimless creativity, and somehow the efforts, I'd decided, would manifest eventually into a "profession." I was working on a screenplay, then a novella, then a novel, then a memoir. Between the daydreams and errant editorial gigs and side-hustling, every first of the month I managed to scuttle together rent before repeating the rigamarole again.

To be in Alaska, where my mother now lived, seemed to follow the absurdist logic of my world. Which isn't to say I accepted her monumental relocation with ease. On my trip in September, I distracted myself from any concerns by nosing around town. I took a zipline tour through the rainforest. I stopped by Creek Street, the old red-light district, and Dolly's House—the "den of iniquity" wallpapered with cabbage roses. The sun set around 9 P.M. In the extended daylight, I spent afternoons keeping my eyes peeled for the motherless baby bear known to scavenge in the neighbor's garbage. And at night, beyond the tourist strip, I wandered over to Hole in the Wall, a locals' hangout where a woman named not Debbie but Webby tended bar.

Ketchikan was filled with unusual folks who had settled, or stalled, on their way elsewhere. Umma had taken a job at the local hospital on a whim. My zipline instructor, a towheaded Idahoan, was about to leave for a missionary trip to Uganda. He took me out on a dinghy docked at Hole in the Wall. The oars streamed phosphorescent ribbons in the dark water while the sky above cloaked us in stars. After a night of clothes-on writhing on his twin bed, I returned to my mother's short-term rental. She glanced up from her knitting and asked, with veiled curiosity: "What are you doing with that white boy?" She let the question dissolve, perhaps to avoid my inevitable rebuttal: "What are you doing in Alaska?"

Technically I didn't need an answer. Alaska has maintained a beguiling mystique in the American imagination. It is a place where adventurers seeking "primitive recreation" disappear into nature at the risk of life and limb. The geography itself can confound the uninitiated. The state is so huge it could comfortably fit California, Montana, and Texas within its borders. The ecologically diverse landscape contains volcanic mountains, boreal forests, the arctic tundra, robust coastal ecosystems and waterways. The state—ensconced by the Bering Sea, British Columbia, and Canadian Yukon Territory—lies a blink away from Russia, and as close to Tokyo as it is to New York City. The culmination of these idiosyncrasies also thrust a folksy political jester like Sarah Palin into national conversation, discombobulating any notions outsiders might have initially held when contemplating the Last Frontier.

But why *is* Alaska the Last Frontier?

The terrain itself exudes untapped potential. In the late nineteenth century's Klondike gold rush, many a prospector migrated through the Canadian Yukon and southeastern Alaska, in search of untold riches. The flourishing copper mining, fishing, and canning industries sustained steady interest in the region during the early twentieth century. In the 1970s, the verification of an oil field in Prudhoe Bay further enticed job seekers, leading to rapid population growth well into the 2000s.

While some have ventured to Alaska in search of transformative wealth, others come to abandon the constraints of capitalist society altogether by entering the wild. Of the state's 222 million acres of federally protected land, some 57.8 million acres are considered "designated wilderness," meaning Congress has placed protections on the area to keep it naturally intact, where human presence is to remain unobtrusive. Millions more have been "proposed" as wilderness, which may perpetuate the idea that parts of the state have yet to be explored by mankind. This draws a particular kind of individual, seeking remote, pristine conditions, as well as those of a more philosophical breed, looking for radical isolation.

People have been escaping to Alaska for decades, pursuing the answers to the unanswerable, as if life's greatest riddles might be deciphered through forced exposure to the extremes. Those who have voluntarily abandoned civilization and its creature comforts to live off-grid have published dozens of memoirs: *Wild Men, Wild Alaska: Finding What Lies Beyond the Limits; To Hell with Togetherness: The Story of an Alaskan Family Living Together on a Remote Homestead West of Anchorage, 1957–1962; Impossible Beyond This Point: True Adventure Creating a Self-Sufficient Life in the Wilderness; Alaska Wolff Pack: The true story of an Alaskan family, whose dreams came true in spite of fires, floods, shootings, and an airplane crash; Alaska Bound: One man's dream . . . One woman's nightmare!*

These tales chronicle harrowing, swashbuckling escapades, as if to test one's limits through primeval, back-to-basics experiments. I'm sure it's no coincidence the solo narratives are written mostly by men (women authors typically relocated with a partner or family). And aside from the occasional Indigenous figure's biography, these stories frequently revolve around white people who have voluntarily subjected themselves to peril.

Perhaps the most known is Jon Krakauer's *Into the Wild*, which recounts the two years before twenty-four-year-old Christopher McCandless wandered into the Alaskan bush and died, starved and alone. Before moose hunters discovered his decomposed remains in a junked bus off the Stampede Trail on the outskirts of Denali National Park and Preserve, before donating his life savings to charity, McCandless was a freshly matriculated young man from a wealthy East Coast family, poised to follow the successful, linear path white men of similar stock are often afforded. One of his favorite authors, Leo Tolstoy, had sought to denude himself from inherited wealth by roaming among the destitute. Similarly McCandless aspired to, as Krakauer puts it, voluntarily take up residence on "the ragged margin of our society . . . in search of raw transcendent experience." Or as McCandless himself confessed in a journal entry, he wished to pursue the "great triumphant joy of living to the fullest extent in which real meaning is found. God it's great to be alive!"

To some this story may be one of astonishing privilege—a white man writing about a white man suffering indulgently, by choice, for the sake of ontological clarity. But it is also a compelling account of hubris and the fragile, human desire to quench our deepest longings—as if we might at last know ourselves when left with nothing but snow-packed, deafening silence.

"Alaska has long been a magnet for dreamers and misfits," Krakauer writes, "people who think the unsullied enormity of the Last Frontier will patch all the holes in their lives." But as the author posits, McCandless was not one of these run-of-the-mill, foolhardy types. Before disappearing into the tundra, surrounded by the frozen boggy sprawl of muskeg and alder groves, McCandless had already lived on the fringes, train hopping and hitching across the American Southwest, at one point even managing to canoe to Mexico. Alaska, to McCandless, was indeed the Last Frontier—the world at its crudest, truest form. And he'd planned to make it out alive.

Narrowly escaping death, like magic, is an act of stunt performance. The suspense is titillating, toggling an audience between terror and thrill so they might feel the exhilaration of survival.

To be clear, my mother was not interested in "roughing it" in bush country. Like the one million tourists that plodded through Alaska's port towns each year, she initially encountered the state's splendors from the comfort of a cruise ship with my grandparents on a trip the year prior to her move. The first stop was Ketchikan.

Still, rarely do adventure narratives, in Alaska or anywhere else, revolve around lone Asian women. The closest modern-day account might be that of Su Min, the fifty-six-year-old housewife who ditched her chores and husband to road trip across mainland China in 2020. Su became an internet phenomenon—the Chinese auntie-turned-feminist-icon single-handedly table-flipping centuries-old subservient gender roles. All she took with her was a rice cooker, mini fridge, and the tent she could erect atop her hatchback. "I've been a wife, a mother and a grandmother," Su told the *New York Times*. "I came out this time to find myself."

Houdini-ing your way out of the old life, leaving bystanders with only a cloud of smoke, can be an attractive exit strategy, exhilarating to behold, and empowering for those who have mastered the illusion of disappearance. It means you are leaving no definitive outcome for onlookers to judge the successes or failures or whatever else lies on the other side, once the smoke clears. We don't typically hear about the postscript, after the trip ends, when the adventurer must inevitably return to whatever they left behind, in all its stultifying stillness.

* * *

December 9, 2007 12:05 PM

Email Subject: Not enough snow to build an igloo?

How did you all do for the post Thanksgiving black holiday sales?

I gave everybody a day off except the traveler. She doesn't get paid if she doesn't work. I went for few hours, reviewed 7 policies and call it a day.

New house is very airy and bright when sun comes out. I spend a lot of time looking out from my living room and just enjoy the scenery. I'm reading about the Queen Elizabeth I and her golden years. And some knitting to pass time.

Last night it started to snow on my way to attend hospital Christmas party. It was OK, nothing special. I went there for the political reason, you know.

After the party I couldn't drive up to my driveway so I parked my truck way down the road and I hiked

up to my house. Imagine me with my heels and fancy black pants and all. This morning city cleared
the snow on the road and I can see my truck from
my kitchen window. It brings me back those fond
memories of our family ski trips when my girls
were little.

I guess I have to shovel the deck so Molder can stand
outside and inspect the scenery. Of course snow
shovel came with the house. It is way of life here.

In 10 days Jennifer will be here. And Laurie on
Christmas Eve. I am very excited! I am still working on Jennifer's mitten. Hope to finish for Santa's
travel time.

Love,
Lady Christina and Princess Molder

• • •

THE CHRISTMAS PRIOR, in 2006, we'd spent in Canyon Lake. By then
Umma had visited three continents and seven countries on her globetrot-
ting kick. The prints she brought back from her travels hung on the walls
(tango dancers splashed in amber and scarlet sensual strokes and a pocket-
sized snapshot of Santorini). Otherwise, maximalist holiday décor gilded
every remaining inch, as it had in her three previous houses. The plastic
tree had been immaculately resurrected. No family trimming traditions.
She needed the gold and green baubles distributed evenly beside the glit-
tery strawberries and tiny wreaths, with the popsicle sled I constructed in
'89 front and center. And a family of bronze ducks in red crushed-velvet
capes, mid waddle in the hallway: Umma, Laurie, Jennipah, and the father
one she displayed with the group, for show. And a wooden train set. And
the pint-sized animatronic Santa and Mrs. Claus bears who popped and
locked like the old Chuck E. Cheese band. And the seventeen-inch LED-lit
candlestick decoration (that, unbeknownst to Umma, resembled an erect
penis) glowing from my bedroom window like some X-rated bat signal.

The gifts, however, had taken a noticeable turn. They were hand-made, female wares procured from the local flea market: quilted paisley tampon cases and matching quilted passport holders; for my sister, a sparkly business card case, for me a beglittered pill box; and a trio of pastel-tinted Swarovski crystal bracelets adorned with personalized charms (a pair of flip-flops for Laurie—"Zapatos!" Umma pointed out in Spanish—a teddy bear for me, and for herself, a pendant engraved with the word "Faith").

A year later in Alaska, no Santa and Mrs. Claus bears, no train set, no candledick. My mother had moved into a cabin she rented from a former New Yorker named Bob, who attached spiky cleats to his trainers to run in the snow. He checked in on Umma from time to time ("just a nice friend," she preemptively mentioned).

The two-bedroom was cozy, rustic, and comfortably fit Umma, Laurie, me, and Molder. The sun set around 3:30 P.M. Each night we warmed ourselves by the wood-burning stove in the living room. Molder slept by our doorways, stirring in the middle of the night to rotate stations and keep watch. Each morning we took breakfast in the sunroom, admiring its panoramic view of the ocean, whose stippled current wended into the horizon. I ate as I had when I was little, devouring bowls of glutinous rice mixed with yolky fried eggs, sesame oil, and soy sauce, pinching up morsels with salty seaweed laver between my chopsticks.

Umma did not prune trees in Alaska, though she did chop, without injury, her own kindling. She had become resourceful in other ways. The best, nearest Korean markets were back in the lower forty-eight—at shortest by ferry or car, a twenty-seven-hour commute. She improvised a new kimchi, with ingredients from the Super Walmart on Don King Road. Red radishes replaced the moo, Mexican chili powder for gochugaru, broccoli tossed in, for crunch. She left the jar to ferment on the countertop and prepped enough for our stay. "How's that for imagination!" she told us.

What does one take with them in the flurry of escape? On her desk in the sunroom, beside Bob's boombox set to Ketchikan Public Radio, Umma displayed select tokens from her adventures: a toucan-shaped bookmark from Costa Rica; photos of Laurie and me on a cobblestone street in Madrid; Molder as a puppy behind the Arcadia house's back screen door; and one of Umma solo, her teased-up orange bouffant wind-socking off Copa Cabana beach.

"You didn't bring anything else?" I asked.

She shook her head and, after a moment, added: "Anyway, they just a worldly pojession."

This made sense when we walked the circumference of nearby Ward Lake. Stands of Sitka spruce and western hemlock undulated around us, framing handsome, snow-splotched mountains. Molder sauntered along, pausing occasionally to scan the terrain.

A Jindo in Ketchikan. As far-fetched a premise as the best of any Jindo lore. One website I stumbled upon claimed Jindos appeared on a list of ancient canines in *Chilhyeongeulnori*, a wall painting from the Silla dynasty (668 to 935). This account also notes Jindo-gae translates, rather spuriously, to a "shrimp-eating dog," making no mention of the island for which the breed is named. Then there are the legendary tall tales like how the dog is the progeny of wolves; or how three Jindos once hunted and killed a Siberian tiger; or how, according to my grandfather, Jindos are so tough, "they can even eat rock."

When we got back to Bob's cabin, I noticed the cyst on Molder's spine, which resembled the cyst situated on Umma's back. I wasn't sure if she'd become like Umma or if Umma had become like Molder. What was uncannier: my mom and her dog in Alaska or that they'd found each other in the first place?

On Christmas Eve, we did not eat kimchi and rice but a homemade chili, and my mother went back for seconds. Her gifts this time seemed geared toward Asian bonding. Umma wrapped my mittens inside a cloth purse she'd purchased at Easter Seals Thrift Store, made from kabuki-inspired fabric. The women printed on the purse had slanted eyes. The checkbook cover and coin purse, made of chinoiserie-style faux silk, imparted a slanted-eyes quality, too.

It wasn't as if Canyon Lake Umma had vanished entirely. For a good hour, she repeated her old mantra: "If I ever did anything right, it was my two girls. If I ever did anything right . . ." We had learned to let our mother go to these places. Laurie and I silently sipped mulled wine until, appeased by the purge, Umma teetered half-asleep, half-drunk to bed.

The next day, we had a White Christmas. I hadn't seen snow like this before: a steady float of feathers flecking the stark black sky. We topped off our mugs with more mulled wine and took a night stroll. We walked with no route in mind, onto some vacant, unlit path behind the cabin. Umma had knitted something for each of us, so on our tipsy stroll, my sister and I wore our new accessories while Molder trotted beside us in her hot-pink sweater. Our mother led us with the gifts we had given her, clearing the way with her new hiking boots and headlamp. It was quiet, save for the squeak of fresh snowfall puckering underfoot. Beneath the wobbling lamplight, I could see Umma, her eyes locked on the path yet her mind noticeably elsewhere, as if she'd panned out to savor the moment and inscribe the full picture of us. That's how she forged ahead, pausing every so often to look back as we followed her into the night.

. . .

December 30, 2007 1:08 PM

Email Subject: Achy breaky heart = umma's heart . . .

Nothing seem different yet, everything is.

Of course I have always loved my girls and I always will until the day I die.

For some strange reason, this time is different.

I keep looking for them in this tiny house thinking they are still here. Like a senile woman I go to my spare bedroom checking the bed if Laurie is sleeping peacefully, or touching on my left side of my bed looking for Jennifer. I stay awake most of last night trying to deposit these fond memories to my memory bank. I don't want to forget these precious few days ever.

There is an old Korean saying that 80 year old mother still worries about her 60 year old son/daughter crossing the street safely every day. Can you hear me?

As neurotic as I am, I worry about you sometimes more than other times. I don't think I will ever not worry. It's just mother thing, you know.

* I worry if you made it home safely every night.
* If you are eating well, is there enough food?
* Is Jennifer drinking too much?
* Are they sick?
* Is there enough money to live?
* Are you dating someone nice and honest? Is he treating you respectively?

But most of all, are they happy? Are they not depressed?

You are the best thing ever happened to me.

You are so beautiful and so smart. So perrtty!

For some reason I am so emotional this morning. Maybe because I am listening to Bosa noba surrounded by the incredible natural beauty outside.

I am still aching from the hike up the Silvis lake yesterday. It was so icy and slippery. But it was so nice. I will run with Molder again later this morning.

It would be nice to hear from you once in awhile, just to say you are OK.

Love,
umma

*   *   *

BEFORE I LEFT ALASKA for the last time, I necked a mini bottle of Jäger-meister and left it bottoms up in the snow in front of Umma's house. It symbolized some loose vow, I had drunkenly decided, to leave the bier-garten days and the red hair and this sloppy phase behind me.

My mother was right to worry. Before she moved to Ketchikan, there were a couple weeks in which a cosmos of bruises bloomed across my upper arms. Blue-black clusters at first, their most satisfying stage, pain-ful but impermanent (even with self-harm, I could be noncommittal). I had taken to punching myself, right balled fist pounding the left side, left pounding the right. Only shoulder to triceps, so as to be easily con-cealed by a short-sleeve tee. I wanted the hidden shapeless thing throb-bing inside me made visible, the abstruse sharpened to its finest point.

Maybe that's why we don't usually get to see what happens inside a cocoon. A life gets messy and rots before it emerges in its evolved form. The human mind is really something. You can watch a person unravel and assume the same could not possibly happen to you.

I was wrong about molder. Yes, the word connotes decay in the sense of disintegration, a crumbling—as one definition contextualizes, a turn to dust: *a house that had been left to molder.* As a noun, a "mold" can be a person or thing that shapes another, filling a cavity, a need, a void. It references prototype too: a fixed pattern distinctive in nature or char-acter; the frame around which an object is constructed. In other words, the place from where we came. Maybe this means no matter how far you go, the circumstances that have shaped you can never be fully escaped.

Getting your shit together isn't as easy as changing the scenery. A new city or town cannot fundamentally alter who you are. But, removed from our usual contexts, maybe an unfamiliar terrain can jostle us into a place of reckoning. You don't need the Last Frontier to get there. It's an appealing narrative to entertain, though—that Umma could have changed so quickly, graced overnight with a settled spirit. Maybe then we could be settled with each other again too. I wanted to believe in the tall tale–ness of such a return.

Wilder things have come to pass. Take the 1993 story of Baek-gu (meaning white dog). In the town of Donji-ri on Jindo Island, a halmoni's white Jindo bore twelve puppies. The woman, well into her eighties, was too old and too tired to deal with the nuisance and decided to sell the dog to a trader. Off Baek-gu went to a family on the mainland, in the city of Daejeon. Seven months later, the halmoni heard a commotion outside. The dog had traveled 186 miles, including a narrow, 484-meter suspension bridge, under which the Uldolmok Strait—the fastest sea water current in Asia—churns ferociously below. Baek-gu waited until the woman opened the door. And from that night forward, the Jindo never left her side.

. . .

Umma lived in Alaska for ten months. This is not to say the woman couldn't hack it. She wouldn't see the lush boreal forests to the north, nor any of the state's interior, like Denali's merciless, unalloyed terrain. Hers was never meant to be a backcountry survivalist story. Alaska marked the beginning of a different undertaking: Every year or so for the next decade, Umma would move to a new city, from the Oregon Coast to the Sunshine State.

She never read *Into the Wild*. The book is filled with McCandless's musings, in journal entries or postcards and letters he'd sent throughout his wanderings. Yet it was as if she'd heeded his call for itinerance, like what McCandless sent to an elderly man he'd met in the California desert, quaking from personal loss. In the letter, he wrote that it will appear foolish at first, hurling yourself toward the "endlessly changing horizon, for each day to have a new and different sun." It will feel unnatural, inhabiting such a different way of life. But do not be afraid, he assured. You have lived many years, and you will live many more, so why not seize what's still possible from this strange and beautiful life? Do not settle down. Keep going. "Just get out and do it. Just get out and do it. You will be very, very glad that you did."

. . .

Nearly a decade after Alaska, I unearthed a collection of my mother's photos. We'd lost countless albums and heirlooms throughout Umma's relocations, so it's possible I'd gained the pictures for safekeeping. They were stored in their original drugstore envelopes. And they happen to document a mysterious period of my mother's life: the year, post-separation, when she started sending postcards from around the world.

At twenty-eight I no longer lived on the smelliest street in Manhattan. I'd found another cheap apartment, this time above a Brooklyn bodega, in a building with a fake front door. My street had a high English name and a smattering of regal pin oaks, which decorated the comelier, northern stretch of the block where I did not reside. On more occasions than I care to admit, I passed strangers urinating in broad daylight steps from my mailbox. If the building were to ever burn down, no one would be surprised. I was still bartending, now in a speakeasy whose jazz Manouche soundtracks snapped my life's anachronisms into focus—the rift with my father, the stagnant writing career I'd claimed to pursue for years, both frozen in time.

Peeking into someone else's private memories is an intimate act. Dozens of unflattering, low-angle shots my mother had taken of herself (in a pre–front camera lens era) filled the rolls, with landmarks or her face accidentally cropped out of the frame. The stumpy, grounded half of the leaning tower of Pisa, for example. Umma's body swallowed inside a giant Dutch clog. Her chin aboard a London double-decker bus. In most of the pictures, she's showing teeth; it doesn't look like she knows how to smile.

Then there was Costa Rica. Another slew of images: brown fuzz (a monkey?) tightroping a phone line, a hazy zigzag (boa constrictor?) nestled in a pile of leaves. But also a set of clear, candid self-portraits. Her perm is out, springy and tousled. Wide jungle fronds splay at her shoulders. Finally, nearing the end of her trip, inside her bungalow where the peach-painted walls warm her skin and the room, the corners of her mouth upturn softly.

I have nearly identical photos from Costa Rica. Monkeys (hairy splotches) carousing in sky-high vines, an eyelash viper (a cloudy coil) camouflaged on a tree trunk. I flew to Costa Rica on my twenty-ninth birthday. The week prior, a patron at work drunkenly spilled a craft beer on my butt. I caught myself glaring at her, looking positively homicidal. At home I came unhinged, pausing between gasps for sips of wine. The uncertainty that once thrummed with possibility had all but drained, leaving only a question to knell in the void: What now?

On a whim, I escaped the States for as long as I could afford (four days). I remember arriving on Costa Rica's Caribbean coastline at midnight, driving through velvet darkness to my beachside bunga-low. I fell asleep to the hum of a million little living things secreted by shadows. I hoped I'd awake an improved person, granted instant clarity overnight.

I don't have pictures of the dismal moments, like when my jungle guide's feral dog chased me and I fell face-first onto his gravel driveway. Or when the cocoa farmer's apprentice insulted me in Spanish while toasting my beans. I did relish lying in a hammock outside my room, where I took my own unsuccessful self-portraits. I returned to New York sun-kissed but, to my dismay, otherwise unaltered.

Real change is not instant but a long process, a kind of honest work. Then one day you reach a point when you can look, maybe only briefly, with clear eyes, and simply let go. My mother knows this. She has yelled my name in many far-flung places, from the top of mountains or while riding Greek donkeys.

The first time I heard her was in Ketchikan. Summer had lingered in long, temperate days. My mother, Molder, and I walked until the blacktop of South Tongass Highway ended and we entered the footpath toward Beaver Falls. Molder sprinted ahead, flicking sticks and peb-bles with her back paws. We caught up to her at a trail rest area, where she sniffed a candy wrapper on the ground. "Hey," Umma playfully scolded, "you a kongju. Princess don't eat trash."

As Molder took off again, we climbed higher and higher through the dense forestry until the trees thinned and the air sharpened and a clearing appeared. We stopped there, at Upper Silvis Lake, to consider its pristine acreage. The sky, a saturated, steel blue, matched the surface of the lake.

"Sometimes I yell your names to the water," Umma said.

"What do you mean?"

"Laurie-yah! Jennipah!" she bellowed, her voice ringing around us. "Like that," she said. "To the lake."

"Why?" I asked.

She was looking out beyond me, the water, the trees, even the snow-caps in the distance. "Just to say it," she said. "Just to say something."

It would take another ten years for me to yell her name too. First while standing upon a summit in the Icelandic highlands and then again while perched on the white cliffs near Cochiti Pueblo in New Mexico. It soothed me to see how the mesas pleated into an opulent skyline, or how miles of slick deltas wove through black sand, vanishing into a new horizon. I sang and called her name over and over.

Can you imagine? Each time I shouted, she echoed back.

PART TWO

THE CARSON MCCULLERS CENTER
FOR WRITERS AND MUSICIANS
2,148 sq. ft.: 4BR, 3BA

From www.exploregeorgia.com

"Visit the home where internationally acclaimed author Carson McCullers grew up in beautiful Midtown Columbus. McCullers was born and raised in Columbus, and her experiences shaped her writing of classic novels like *The Heart is a Lonely Hunter, Reflections in a Golden Eye, The Member of the Wedding,* and *The Ballad of the Sad Cafe.* A tour of her childhood home grants you insight into not only McCullers' life and work but also provides you with an idea of Columbus in the first half of the twentieth century.

Located on a quiet residential street in the Wildwood Circle/ Hillcrest historic district in Columbus, the Smith-McCullers House Museum is open to the public by appointment. Please try to give at least 24 hours advance notice when scheduling a tour. There is a suggested donation of $5 per person.

The Carson McCullers Center for Writers and Musicians is dedicated to preserving the legacy of Carson McCullers; to nurturing American writers and musicians; to educating young people; and to fostering the literary and musical life of Columbus, the State of Georgia, and the American South."

Signs and Wonders

I.

FOR ALL THE LIES I dispensed across the Southeast in 2017, here is one truth: A few months prior to my arrival, before I packed up my life in Brooklyn, bought someone's grandma's Camry, and drove, I had no clue my destination, the city of Columbus, existed in Georgia. If I were the big believing type, I might have attributed the turn of events that followed to whimsical notions such as chance or fate. It began with a very of-this-world, human error though: a bungled deadline. I'd missed by a few hours the application cutoff for a writing fellowship—a nine-month gig that, due to its literary clout, balanced out the fact I'd be taking residence in Arkansas. As some consolation for all the mad-dash, Southern-centric proposal summaries and personal statements I'd already composed, I searched the internet (likely "writing fellow-ship South") for a contingency plan, thus unearthing the not-in-Ohio Columbus. There are, evidently, at least fifteen American towns and cities called Columbus, five in the South alone. This one offered writers a three-month stay in a house/museum—the former childhood residence of novelist Carson McCullers—located a two-hour drive from Atlanta. I submitted my materials with a week to spare.

At this point in my career, I had unmistakably busied myself into a corner. Sure, I'd cobbled together a smattering of respectable bylines since graduating from an MFA program. But none of that labor equated to a livable wage (a lesson they most certainly do not teach you in said graduate program). Dollar-per-calorie, bartending had proven the most lucrative part-time job that did not sap my creative energies. I'd anticipated this line of work to be only temporary, and yet thirteen years had somehow evaporated in the blink of an eye.

Working in hospitality will teach you myriad lessons in humility, such as the amount of self-respect you are willing to relinquish for a buck. But the most potent reckoning foisted upon me during that time was of the existential sort: how the vitality I so profligately frittered away in my twenties with cute-but-poor-arch-support footwear and 4 A.M. close-outs and shots-shots-shots might one day add up. As I stirred, swizzled, and whip-shaked past thirty, it had become clear my nights behind the stick were increasingly untenable on the body. Or worse— what if I could never afford to stop bartending?

Meanwhile, I had spent the better part of a decade revising a book that draft after draft seemed more like a figment of my imagination. Friends had ascended various professional tracks, accruing 401Ks, exceeding six-figure salaries, amassing traditional adult milestones (marriage, children, dream home and car), and when I allowed myself to pause and snap-to, I was startled to the point of bewilderment: The rest of the world had carried on with life, yet I had only managed to grow older.

During a night off, the weight of my predicament fell upon me with the precision of an anvil. I was watching an episode of a competition cooking show featuring a challenge at the legendary Rao's, a red sauce Italian joint in East Harlem. Famous patrons included Joe Pesci and Lorraine Bracco, the latter of whom served as a guest judge in the episode. For a prelude to the meal, requisite introductions had been made: owner, chef, but notably a Mickey Rooney–esque older gentleman donning a vest sequined in rainbow paillettes. "Name is Nicky Vest," he croaked, "and I'm the bartender in Rao's for the last thirty-six years."

Nicky Vest appeared for less than ten seconds, yet I can recall little else of the show. His glinting image throttled me forward twenty years, to an all but inevitable future: me, in the denim pinafore I'd been known to sport at work, my French-twist brindled gray, the new heft in my hips and trunk leaning into the dusty backbar. "Name's Jenny Overalls," I squawked, "and I been the bartender in Rucola for the last thirty years." Regulars could recite my bygone literary laurels like folklore: "Did you know I was once published in the *Atlantic* online?!"

So it had been the harbinger Nicky Vest who initially spurred my mopey ass to assemble an escape plan. Never mind how in the applications I'd cobbled together semi-bogus circumstances worthy of a months-long tenure. Though I did not have proof, the idea seemed pretty legit. Two-pronged, it went something like this: Religion is fundamental to Southern identity but discussed solely within a white–Black binary; there are Korean fringe churches along the Bible Belt who might share the same extreme beliefs that sent my paternal uncle to the clink.

I had recently published a piece about a 1996 murder in which this uncle in question had played an instrumental role in a deadly exorcism. The case belonged to a concurrence of similar exorcisms across the country and abroad, involving Korean Pentecostal–adjacent zealots who'd strived to free evil spirits from their mothers, aunts, or wives (the victims always women).

As my mother often reminded me: "Koreans are everywhere. Any place you go, you'll find us." She had proof in this theory; of the five states and eight cities she'd wandered through coast-to-coast since splitting with my father in 2005, she always found a Korean church to join nearby. Per this logic, and a map search of area Pentecostal (or Full Gospel) Korean churches, a profusion dappled the Southeast, off desolate highways and parking lots and country dirt roads. I posited these places indeed existed and somehow, in three months, I'd visit them all.

Attempt a project like this and someone is bound to mention The Church of Jesus with Signs Following, particularly the book *Salvation on Sand Mountain: Snake-Handling and Redemption in Southern Appalachia*. In it, author Dennis Covington investigates an Alabama congregation whose rite of serpent handling appears methodologically kindred to my uncle's former habits (practices such as the laying on of hands and various forms of miracle-making). One involved venomous animals, the other a Korean folk belief system—Shamanism—and its power for mystic healing.

Unlike Covington, I was not a journalist with pedigreed reportage experience. I positioned myself instead as a loose, self-appointed authority on Koreanness, in both cultural and religious capacities (insofar as my parents were born in Korea, and I grew up attending an all-Korean church). There were glaring holes to my proposal (how could I infiltrate the congregations without speaking Korean?). These specifics I set aside; surely the committee wouldn't choose me. Then, as if willed by divine intervention, they did.

The whole scenario reminded me of a similarly shoddy plan I'd concocted in the seventh grade. My teacher Mrs. Bartczak awarded extra credit for a variety of vague, humanities-related projects. Hellbent on sliding my B+ to an A-, I asked to present my family's New Year blessing bow at lunch. She agreed, and I fancied myself quite clever, capitalizing on my sparse knowledge of Korean traditions for the sake of what I now see as a truly negligible GPA. When it came time for the bow, Mrs. Bartczak decided I ought to give my presentation in front of the entire class. She also opened the retractable wall separating our room from Mr. Malloy's next door, expanding my audience to a total of forty students. Already dressed in my petal-pink hanbok, I couldn't back out of the deal.

The classroom's linoleum floor looked filthy, but I knelt to the ground anyway and blessed Mrs. Bartczak in my phonetically memorized Hangukmal. When I got up, she handed me a dollar, which was part of the act. Then she asked me to expound further on the history of the tradition. ("Why do you receive cash? Can you translate the blessings?") Having expected nothing beyond the bow, I stood speechless. Mrs. Bartczak thanked me and limp applause peppered the room. What I recall most vividly happened on my way out to change. I'd locked eyes with a classmate, a girl who, unlike me, had been raised to speak and write Korean. She stared with this incredulous smirk as if she saw what I saw, and God saw: the truth.

What did I know about being Korean?

Nothing at all.

* * *

THE MCCULLERS HOUSE exuded the rustic charm one expects to find below the Mason–Dixon: a creaking porch and gabled roof, canopied by ancient magnolias. I'd missed the trees' window of beauty. Barren of their pendulous flowers, they now shed seed pods that crunched like tiny skeletons beneath my car tires. It was August in Georgia which is, as some might say, hotter'n blue blazes; hotter'n a blister bug in a pepper patch; hot as the hinges on the gates of Hades (even Satan's sweatin').

But on this house no gate could be found, nor any outward-facing hinges, just a brass door knocker hanging from the jowls of a lion whose mane was in need of polishing. That first day, that first week even, I chose not to consider the signs around me, like how the front lawn looked fried, hoofed bare in patches. Or how past residents had experienced encounters: sheets allegedly ripped off one writer's body in an otherwise empty bedroom; another writer beseeching the specter of a man to leave her be.

Before departing for Georgia, I'd jokingly told friends about how I planned to install myself in one dim corner of the house, silently rocking in a rocking chair, offering museum guests an "immersive experience." I did not consider how the rocking chair bit implied I might, in the course of a few months, become a haunted fixture myself.

On Day One though, I stood in the pebbled driveway with a dumbstruck glow, for the possibility and luck, and the eight rooms (all mine!) in which to roost throughout my Herculean productivity. I came to disappear from MTA subway delays, and lazy paramours, and social network distractions, and Jenny Overalls, to reappear in New York at year's end slimmer, accomplished, transformed.

Off a main drag in town, I'd passed a roadside marquee whose block letters portended HE THAT IS DISCONTENT IN ONE PLACE WILL SELDOM BE HAPPY IN ANOTHER. I thought, *What does Aesop know anyhow?* then swung open the door and stepped inside, drunk on the delusion of newness.

•   •   •

ANOTHER TRUTH: It is quite possible I had not read, to completion, a single Carson McCullers book before moving into the author's childhood home. Her personal history I found more enthralling, like how she moved to New York City at seventeen to study piano at Juilliard but lost her tuition money on the subway. Or that she published her first novel at twenty-three. Or how sickness plagued much of her life through recurring strokes and alcoholism. At twenty-nine, she became paralyzed on the left side of her body and at fifty, by then the author of nine books, she passed away from a brain hemorrhage in Nyack, New York, a thousand miles northeast of the Southern Gothic birthplace from which much of her literary identity had been formed.

I also moved to New York City at seventeen, but that's where our commonalities end. I had no prodigious talents to speak of (in fact, I'd tried and failed at piano as a child, along with four other musical instruments). At twenty-three, my writing did not launch me into literary fame. I could instead be found sneaking shots from the Jägerator with my Mexican barbacks, who were sisters (*"Hermanas!"* we slurred together, glasses clinking). I amused them with anecdotes about my father's slangy Spanish, how he spoke like a true LA vato. I never talked about my mother even though, back then, I could hardly shake her from my thoughts. She was living alone in Alaska, but my mind kept slipping back to a moment when I was a kid: watching her naked figure stippled behind the shower glass; the forceful way she scrubbed the tiles with disinfectant, how she choked from the toxic mist—a private exercise in pain, as if to test how much she could take and tolerate, how much she believed she deserved.

To evade this story, I drank enough to wipe the mind clean, closing out bars with coworkers, babbling about the art I wanted to create, before passing out in the perpetual darkness of my crypt-like apartment. I was unbound by time in a different way then, because time appeared limitless; I could figure out what to do with my life tomorrow, or tomorrow, or tomorrow.

Ten years later, in Columbus, I had completed nothing resembling a book. So I began my fellowship with the hope I might channel Carson's industrious spirit and leave Georgia, manuscript in hand.

Living in a house is one thing, but living in a museum is another. My new residence bore the palpable air of a mausoleum. The main display room contained tall glass cases, spotlighting a modest collection of Carson's belongings: her silver-handled cane, cigarette lighter, spectacles, even her voice locked into the grooves of an LP (a recitation of her third novel). Framed photos depicted her in decline, her gaunt face tucked above a crisp white bed sheet, her mouth—as if caught mid-scream—gaping, strained.

There was also a garment the program director pointed out during my introduction tour, which he identified as Carson's kimono. Before leaving the room, he unceremoniously placed a plastic garbage bag over the garment. I returned after he left, removed the trash bag, and stared. No obi, no eri, no panels upon panels of fine, starched fabric. This was not a kimono but more likely a dragon robe—an A-line cut of silk with long belled sleeves and a rounded neckline, once the everyday dress of Chinese emperors from the Qing dynasty. Dragon robes were worn by Korean royalty too, during the Joseon era centuries ago. I'd glimpsed these costumes in the period piece VHS K dramas my mother and grandmother rented by the dozen from a local Korean video store. Tape after tape, always the same: noblemen and women stuck in some rice paper–walled room, a shocking confession, the zoom to a man and his glued, wispy goatee, shared gasps, and those dragon robes, dusting palatial grounds upon brusque character entrances or exits.

According to Christie's auction house, genuine surviving dragon robes are exceedingly rare. I wondered where Carson procured hers and if she also incorrectly called it a kimono. Would anyone in her world notice or care?

Asians account for 2.6 percent of Columbus's population. I imagine for those 5,400 people, visiting a somewhat obscure fiction writer's former home does not rank as a top life priority, as it certainly would not have for my immigrant parents. I wouldn't have been raised in this historic neighborhood either—Wynnton, an antebellum streetcar suburb boasting Colonial Revival architecture, replete with flowering dogwood and honey locust trees, riots of pink azaleas bursting from every block come spring. Local historian and journalist William W. Winn once described Wynnton as a kind of Arcadia, tranquil save for the odd cat burglary. Until a late-1970s serial killing spree, in which a man nicknamed the Stocking Strangler raped and murdered elderly lone women, terrorizing the neighborhood for two years. That chapter is now considered something akin to lore, lacquered over by time's passing and new generations of Wynnton's enduring white and middle-class families. The people who looked like me lived scattered at the edges of the city. I saw myself reflected in small-town capitulations: the chinky font of Chinese take-out signage, the one pan-Asian grocery store called Oriental Food and Gift.

A Georgia.org video, however, implies Koreans are not only visible but positively thriving throughout the Peach State. In "Korean investment in Georgia," women backbend to pound samgomu drums and Ssireum wrestlers spar in a cloud of sand. We see Koreans laughing over Korean barbecue, Koreans shopping in Korean supermarkets, plus picturesque mountains, beaches, and the verdant undulations of a golf course (because Koreans love golf). The three-minute reel, narrated in Korean, concludes with an invitation: "*Let us show you the harmony and success you will find here in Georgia, USA.*"

By Georgia, they really mean Gwinnett County, located thirty miles north and east of Atlanta. At the time of a 2014 survey by the U.S. Census Bureau, 41.9 percent of the 52,431 Koreans living in Georgia resided in Gwinnett. The county even earned a distinct moniker from the local tourism board in 2016: the "Seoul of the South." When I was growing up, I knew nothing about Gwinnett, but families like mine have been discreetly populating the area for decades.

As early as 1980, an increase of construction jobs diversified a predominantly white, outer suburban Atlanta, and Mexican and Central American migrant workers soon set roots alongside Asian immigrants. In 1985, when the state of Georgia opened an office in Seoul, the Korean community had only just begun to develop off Buford Highway, which connects metropolitan Atlanta to Gwinnett's westerly edge. Interstate 85 helped foster the swift spread. Those looking to flee Tri-State and D.C. Korean neighborhoods could travel a straight shot south along I-85 to opt for an up-and-coming hamlet with warmer weather and cheaper rent.

From 1990 to 2000, Georgia's Korean community grew faster than anywhere else in the United States, by a staggering 88.2 percent. Compared to other Koreatowns though, the concrete numbers can seem underwhelming (Los Angeles's Korean population hovers around 326,000 people; Queens, New York, 220,000; Gwinnett's, a mere 30,000). But in the land of Bojangles and Piggly Wiggly, the Korean presence is striking. Entire pylon signs are written in Hangul, plaza after plaza. Nowhere else in the Southeast can one find such a density of contiguous Korean businesses, which flourish in the hub city of Duluth and have trickled into neighboring Suwanee, Norcross, Lawrenceville, Sugar Hill, Doraville, and Peachtree Corners.

The community is so interdependent that in 2007, Duluth mayor Nancy Harris initiated a special task force, citing the need to "assimilate and live together" while mitigating a unique problem: Koreans often reported crimes to elders rather than local authorities. When the police did respond to calls, they could not decipher the business signs, posted exclusively in Korean. This type of insularity lies in direct contrast to certain regional ideals: Southern hospitality and a public, down-home, flag-wielding American patriotism. Yet it seems Koreans have quietly settled in the gulf between Black and white Southern spheres, by choice, for some time.

Now there are Gwinnett-based Korean newspapers, Korean banks, Korean beauty salons, Korean after-school programs, and even a local Korean TV station. A halmoni could carry on for weeks without ever speaking English to a single person, filling her prescriptions with a bilingual pharmacist, booking a trip with a Korean travel agent, buying fresh-baked bread from a Korean bakery. But where did she worship?

The internet can't help you the way a Korean grocery store can. No matter where you are, no matter how small the town, chances are you'll find a makeshift trading post near your Korean market's door. This is where local classifieds are advertised, posted beside an abundance of free religious multimedia.

My second week in Georgia, I drove to the gold standard of Korean markets, Super H Mart, in Duluth. A shelving unit near the entrance contained sermon recordings from more than thirty local churches: New People Church, Stay Community Church, Atlanta Jesus Way Church, Gideon 300 Mission Church, Atlanta Truly Beautiful Church, Jesus Hope Church, the Christ Centered People Oriented Korean Church of Atlanta. There were hundreds of computer-burned CDs, each packaged with custom-printed labels and paper sleeves.

I stashed as many as I could in my bag, along with a few brochures. One was from as far west as Ontario, California; it proposed a tract that could prove a "most precious gift" for those in search of answers to life's greatest quandaries. On the front panel, a tempest of cumulonimbus clouds surged beneath the words "God's plan of Salvation," typed in jittery script, as if etched into stone tablets. "But it is confusing because there are so many different religions," the leaflet professed, among a sundry of impassioned arguments:

"The ancestor of mankind is not the monkey, but Adam, who was made in the image of God!"

"Video sermons will change your life."

"You are in great peril!"

II.
Atlanta Beloved. Duluth, Georgia. Sunday Service

AN ADDRESS ON ONE of the CDs leads me to an industrial property site located two miles from H Mart. I obey the sun-faded signs for Atlanta Beloved Church toward the back of the lot, passing a succession of warehouses with high-dock loading platforms and rentable office and storage spaces before reaching a dead end. I'm looking for cars packed bumper-to-bumper, or any indication of the 150-plus all-Korean congregation I'd watched in the Beloved Vimeo sermon linked on their free CD.

The video captures, via an impressive multi-camera operation, a cavernous sanctuary with vaulted ceilings, Broadway-caliber lighting, and a state-of-the-art sound system best suited for a theme park or amphitheater. Together the aesthetics look awesome, in the old-fashioned sense—awe-inspiring, as in, "Our God is an awesome God, He reigns from heaven above." These are lyrics from an immensely popular contemporary worship song called "Awesome God." Across denominations it is a song everyone seems to know, even though its creator, Rich Mullins, stated in *The Lighthouse* (an online Christian college magazine) in April 1996: "You know, the thing I like about 'Awesome God' is that it's one of the worst-written songs that I ever wrote; it's just poorly crafted."

I do not see anything awesome when I finally spot the building number for Atlanta Beloved, which is posted on a heavily tinted glass door.

An ajumma lets me in, and I follow her perm into a windowless backroom, where a slim man in a green striped polo with hyphens for eyebrows greets me in broken English. When he smiles, the hyphens pitch heavenward, adjusting his expression into one of gentle curiosity. We bow. "Praise at ten thirty," he says. Above us, fluorescent light panels checkerboard the ceiling, casting the room with the bleak anonymity of a DMV.

"I saw a video online," I say. "Where is the big church?"

"Ah, in Seoul. This is . . ." He searches for the word. "Branch-y." His hyphens upturn again, this time imparting humility. For fear I might not return, he motions toward a gigantic Tupperware filled with English translation headsets.

I return an hour later, sit in the back row of chairs that face a whitewashed cinder-block wall, and place one of the provided fleece blankets on my lap. We watch a projected recording of the home church's service, where a shoeless twenty-person praise team croons on a stage 7,000 miles away. The camera pans to a cellist and two electric guitarists shredding wicked Van Halen–esque riffs. In a separate soundproof room, a drummer jams on a twelve-piece kit. Meanwhile, at Atlanta Beloved, a trio of stand-up speakers (the kind that might blast Jock Jams at a pep rally) stand idle beside a roll-down gate. The incongruence is unsettling. Around me a dozen Korean congregants, mostly of the AARP age bracket, have convened in what could easily pass for a post-apocalyptic bomb shelter, while bobbing along to what could easily pass for a hologram.

These modest surroundings remind me of my family's home church, a cobwebbed pile of linoleum and brick located between a Wiener-schnitzel hot dog stand and a freeway off-ramp in El Monte, California. The nicest room was Big Sanctuary, where the adults attended Korean language service. The interior design theme was of the broadly purplish sort, with grape-colored pew cushions and matching stained glass. On the burgundy carpeted pulpit steps, I'd performed countless holiday musical numbers with the Sunday School kids. For our closing tunes, our teacher would typically kneel at our feet with cue cards, displaying English phoneticized lyrics of a Korean hymn. Some more than others (me) fumbled their way through the verses discordantly, our tongues straining to mimic the beat of our parents' language. At the end, we'd stand straight and at the count of three, bow.

Twenty years later, little has changed; I fumble through the Korean praise lyrics. Even with the translation headsets, my mind wanders during the sermon. I can smell the briny scent of seaweed soup wafting over from the kitchen. No doubt the women of Beloved prepared the post-service meal, just as my mother and the other wives dutifully had at our church each weekend.

At Atlanta Beloved, the video benediction concludes and the woman beside me introduces herself. Helen is in her forties, with a dove-like disposition. She has brought her own foot rest, back rest, and tissue box. She asks if I am a student, and I say yes, because sometimes it is easier to lie. Then she invites me to lunch.

We collect in the mess hall, slurp on miyukk soup, and share Styrofoam plates of kimchi. I ask about the more eccentric moments in the sermon: the pastor's various rants (heresy accusations) and raves (miraculous healing in the congregation; how a deaf man could hear again, and a blind man could see). I can sense my line of inquiry lacks subtlety. Thankfully she doesn't fully understand me. Helen apologizes for her English. I apologize for my Korean. She asks if I can speak in tongues. I shake my head. Helen smiles and shares how the gift came to her at this church, with these people. I wonder what it must be like, to place trust

so freely with strangers. After offering me seconds, she invites me back
for healing prayer.

*   *   *

I HAVE ALWAYS BEEN the easily spooked type. I grew up a latchkey kid
in the 1990s, parents gone by the time I woke up, still gone by the time
I fell asleep. As a precautionary measure (a ruse in the style of Kevin
McCallister), I hoped to present to the outside world the illusion of a
bustling home life by cranking the television volume high, switching
on every light, then shutting everything off before bed so my mother
couldn't nag me about the wasted electricity.

Unhappy as she was then, Umma managed to love me in her own
measured way. When our schedules overlapped, usually on weekends, we
watched her favorite programs: *Murder, She Wrote, Unsolved Mysteries*,
and *America's Most Wanted*. During commercial breaks, she interrupted
our shared silence with warnings: *Do not open the door to strangers! Do
not go in cars with strangers! Do not get kidnapped by strangers!*

She never elaborated on what might happen should these instances
transpire. Still, the endless imagined possibilities and the unknowable
nature of what the world had in store terrorized my thoughts. I can
pinpoint exactly when those fears sent me hurtling over the edge. I was
home alone, watching the show *Quantum Leap*. The episode was called
"The Curse of Ptah-Hotep." On the eve of a sandstorm, Dr. Sam Beck-
ett (played by Scott Bakula) time-travels to 1957 and into the body of an
archaeologist studying the tomb of an ancient Egyptian pharaoh. Accidents befall the research camp and its inhabitants, who attribute their
misfortunes to a curse. Sam scoffs at this theory, suspecting a dodgy
local doctor to be the source of calamity. And dodgy he is. The doctor
tries to steal a jewel from inside the pharaoh's tomb, which triggers a
failsafe. In the last seconds before the tomb shuts, Sam rolls out, leaving the doctor/thief trapped with a reanimated (and greatly displeased)
Ptah-Hotep. The screams, muffled behind stone, reverberated in my

head for months. It was the vastness, of all I could not see, belying one's infinite capacity for suffering, that haunted me most.

Though to me danger lurked around every corner, historians marked the '90s as a relatively peaceful era in the world. Long-held notions shattered: the Soviet Union at last fell; the internet entered the common household; cable networks like CNN prevailed, standardizing the twenty-four-hour news cycle.

I wasn't fully aware, but the decade also marked an unfavorable period, optics-wise, for Koreans. Woody Allen and his pseudo-adopted daughter Soon Yi Previn publicly revealed their sexual relationship (a deep and public shame for "our people," is how my mother put it). North Korean dictator Kim Jong-il succeeded his father Kim Il-sung, and rumors fixated on the Dear Leader's eclectic tastes and mythic origins (his preference for Hennessy, his birth heralded by a double rainbow). And more shame, of a different sort—the lingering stigma unearthed by the Seoul 1988 Summer Olympics, when restaurants were ordered, by official presidential decree, to temporarily omit an item from their menus: dog meat. These incidents, so separate they seemed from my own personal experiences (I would never eat a dog), I observed with detached wonder, as if captured through a long-focus lens. The panorama, however compressed, felt too remote—my parents' country, my parents' shame, another world away.

Until July 1996. Most associate this month with the Centennial Olympic Park pipe bombing that killed one bystander and injured 111 others on July 27, in Atlanta, Georgia. But three weeks prior, a separate crime took place, closer to home.

It was Independence Day, and as for most American holidays, my mother had established a set of traditions that, due to her permanently sour expression, she seemed to perform solely for the enjoyment of others. In this case, a festive cookout.

We lived then in the Arcadia house. That afternoon, my mother was assembling her annual American flag pound cake dessert, slathering the top with Cool Whip, forming the stars and stripes with berries, when a *breaking news* mugshot flashed onto our TV. The man in the photo resembled my father. He looked lost.

As I recall, the anchorman mentioned a strange word—exorcism—and our family name. I shouted, "Look! That's Uncle, right?" Which is when my mother dropped her berries. She powered off the television and stepped outside, where meat charred on the backyard grill. I stared at her from the couch a good while after, waiting for an answer.

My father's mother, whom we called Figueroa Grandma (nicknamed after the Los Angeles street on which she resided), joined us an hour later. After releasing a brief, tearless cry, she assembled and consumed three double cheeseburgers and two slices of American flag cake. That night I asked my mother for details, but she talked about Figueroa Grandma instead. "She ate every crumb by crumb," my mother said, astonished. "But . . . I guess peoples got to eat."

When Umma eventually offered an explanation, it had been distilled to the point of absurdity: "Your uncle stepped on a woman and she died."

Another decade passed before I discovered the full story. Perhaps I'd avoided researching for so long because I wasn't ready to confront the depth of our family's depravity, or how that might reveal some kind of inescapable, immoral inheritance. Access to the truth was almost laughably simple. I Googled "Choi Korean exorcism LA," and the headlines instantly surfaced: "Exorcism on Trial: Korean Missionaries' Murder Case Pits Religion, Culture and Law" and "Exorcism: Case of Death by 'Deliverance' Poses Vexing Questions." The bizarre facts—a Korean Shamanistic healing ceremony, demon expulsion, a possibly cultish Korean Christian group—captured the life of a man I hardly knew.

Reporting in the *Los Angeles Times* relayed what my mother could not. That July Fourth morning, an LAPD patrol officer on the graveyard shift responded to a call from a Century City condominium. My uncle answered the front door, speaking in (as the patrolman put it) excited, incomprehensible "Oriental." A Korean American officer arrived shortly afterward to translate. A prayer session had gone awry. In addition to my uncle, two other middle-aged Korean men—Christian missionaries Reverend Choi Sung-soo (no relation) and Chung Jae-whoa—waited in the living room. In the bedroom, paramedics attempted to revive Chung's unconscious wife. Her chest was sunken, and her legs were covered from knee to hip with purple contusions—injuries, as Deputy Medical Examiner James Ribe would later testify, he'd witnessed in cases of vehicular trauma, like when a body is run over by a car.

Hours after the police arrived, Chung Kyung-jae, a fifty-three-year-old mother of two teenagers, was pronounced dead. The official cause: multiple blunt force trauma. Specifically, her heart had been crushed against her backbone; along with sixteen fractured ribs, her pancreas and the muscles of her abdominal wall were bruised. Less visible: early-stage gangrene developing on a badly damaged intestinal tract. The skin on her leg, which had ballooned from excess fluid, obscured swollen and mangled thigh muscles, symptomatic of imminent kidney failure. Which is to say the woman had suffered.

Out of all my uncles (two on my father's side, three on my mother's), this one had struck me as troubled, sure, but a murderer? Though he did bestow suspiciously firm, rib-squeezing hugs at Thanksgiving, my uncle was a deacon at a Glendale Presbyterian church—the same denomination as my family's home congregation in the San Gabriel Valley. We were "mainline," or so I thought. Real above-board type worship, with praise teams and choirs and English-speaking service for the first-gen kids. And we believed, like anyone else, in a Jesus born of immaculate conception who died for our sins then rose from the dead. I had never seen a person "speak in tongues." The phrase itself hadn't been mentioned in Sunday School or Bible study. The only exorcisms I'd witnessed had been under fictional, Catholic pretenses. There was Linda Blair, of course, with her cotton nightie and ghoulish, rotary head. Or the baffling 1994 storyline from *Days of Our Lives* (an age-inappropriate favorite of mine back then) in which a demon-possessed Dr. Marlena Evans levitated above her bed in silk pajamas.

One *Los Angeles Times* report described my uncle's crime as "a bare-knuckled, hands-on slaying." It marked the third Korean exorcism-related court case in the United States. In 1995, a twenty-five-year-old woman had been beaten to death in the Bay Area by members of a religious group known as Jesus Amen Ministries. Weeks after my uncle's arrest, a Chicago-area physician attempted to beat the demons out of his fifty-one-year-old wife. And in 2015, a forty-one-year-old South Korean mother was found dead in a Frankfurt hotel room following a two-hour healing prayer. The case in Germany echoed uncanny details. Of the five Koreans involved, the victim's own family members held the "possessed" woman down. They muffled her cries by stuffing her mouth with a balled-up rag and clothes hanger and beat her until she suffocated. By one account, the perpetrators practiced "a form of Christianity with influences from an ancient Asian Shamanist religion." Which form of Christianity no one could seem to determine.

My uncle's case remains the first of its kind to lead to a murder trial in the States. The circumstances of this envelope-pushing scandal puzzled Koreans and non-Koreans alike. "What we're trying to establish is that, based upon their cultural background, this was not such an unreasonable behavior that they were engaged in," defense attorney Christopher Lee claimed. The closest modern-day equivalent, religion experts asserted, had been an Appalachian snake-handler case in which a child perished from a poisonous serpent bite.

Neither Columbus nor Duluth belongs to Appalachia, but who knew what ensued behind closed doors. A 2014 Pew Research Center survey indicated two-thirds of Georgia adults considered themselves "highly religious." Couldn't it stand to reason that Koreans like my uncle had spread south and east, preaching a similar, dangerously persuasive salvation? Possibly. They'd have to trust me enough to show me.

*   *   *

IN THE SAME INDUSTRIAL LOT as Atlanta Beloved, one can find several other religious organizations including The Lord's Church (Korean), Jesus Life Church (Korean), and Ministerio Internacional El Gran Yo Soy. Though they occupy neighboring units to Beloved, it is nearly impossible to judge proximity. The complex is labyrinthine. On a weeknight, I drove around and around and could not differentiate one place of worship from the next; in daylight, none of them appear operational.

I choose to visit The Lord's Church because, like Atlanta Beloved, it is a satellite branch with a home base located in Incheon, South Korea. The Lord's Church, however, promises its ethnically diverse devotees a metaphysical portal to salvation. Also referred to as Holy Fire Ministries, the group was founded by Pastor Kim Yong-doo, an avuncular Korean man who espouses that, through marathons of late-night prayer, one can experience supernatural, spiritual encounters with Jesus, and dozens of other life-altering visions (say, one's own family burning perilously in hell).

It's unclear how the church is funded, though donations are accepted online, at church services, and at a series of international revivals, held everywhere from Belgium to Thailand; edited videos of such gatherings are posted on a regularly updated YouTube page. Despite its lo-fi, homemade quality, the clip I initially clicked on, entitled "Holy Spirit movement dance led by power," tallies more than 23,000 views. In it, a balding man sways to an instrumental version of the song "I Love You Lord"—another exceedingly popular contemporary worship tune (one I still know by heart), originally penned by Wisconsin native Laurie Klein in 1976.

The instrumental version in The Lord's Church video is more rigid than the ballad I belted out fervently as a child, featuring a steady synth snare, as if performed by a military band. The balding man is Pastor Kim Yong-doo, stout and in his sixties. He's wearing a dress shirt with subtle polka dots, a purple tie, a silver tie-clip, and pressed slacks. The look is put-together but unshowy, implying the value he places in his image—one of many considered curations.

When the camera pans out, we see the pastor is wearing socks and house slippers (does he travel with his own pair?), which clatter on the floor. There's also a full-sized microphone tucked clunkily between his shirt buttons. His eyes are scrunched, his mouth gathered into an O, his comportment somnambulant as he squats and steps, slowly swiping his hands up and down, in waves and figure eights. Eventually he heaves an imaginary cross onto his shoulder. The pastor staggers from the invisible weight. A voice off-screen translates Kim's Korean interjections into English while the snare drum taps its metronymic beat.

Suddenly, Kim collapses. Someone screams, "Oh, Jeejus!" The mic falls from Kim's shirt and a woman—dressed in a head-to-toe white, bejeweled ensemble—enters, sweeping the device away like a stagehand. A crowd of mostly non-Koreans are seated in metal folding chairs, mesmerized. A wide shot reveals they are all wearing house slippers too.

As Kim mimes crucifixion, his head lists, his fingers twitch, and the woman in white (Kim's wife) steps in with her phone to get a shot of the pastor wincing. Then she beckons three men to help lift Kim upright. He seems unconscious, except his brow is furrowed, which would make a skeptic surmise that Jesus had not inhabited this man's form for the last fifteen minutes; that perhaps Kim designed this scene with great calculation, because his congregants want to witness miracles unfold right before their eyes, and because miracles equate Kim to the Son of God. But if you are a believer, this scene is one reason why attending The Lord's Church can bring you closer to, if not into the very presence of, Jesus.

A congregant is so moved she drops to her knees. "I don't want you to make my suffering in vain," the interpreter translates. Kim's wife crouches with them, hissing into her own mic a slithering talk (tongues I think), which is delivered with theatrical pomp, warbly then breathy, Gollum-like. Her hand is outstretched, as if beaming invisible voltage through her fingertips. They go in turns, the pastor, the translator, the wife in white, Korean, English, tongues:

"For you I will come down to the earth . . ."

". . . You must change your mind, your heart, your soul, your attitude in order to survive!"

Another two women appear, also dressed in sparkly white—the uniform for Holy Dancers, who are gifted by God with the power of interpretive dance. Off-duty until praise hour, they film the pastor on their smartphones, their attention synchronous and rapt.

The voices circle as Kim gains strength with each pronouncement:

"Oh pitiful souls who end up in hell . . ."

"Only you who fit my expectation will enter my kingdom . . ."

"I will save them, I will change them, and they will come to me."

"Give your life. Hallelujah!"

"Hallelujah!" the congregation repeats.

The music peters and off-screen, the translator announces it is time to tithe. Right then, Kim opens his eyes and blinks pointedly, as if waking from a dream.

"Aigoo! Sehsangheh," he says, dazed, in the manner of a bone-weary village grandmother.

And the men help him rise.

III.

MY OFFICIAL WELCOME RECEPTION at the McCullers house was, to be generous, a sparsely attended affair consisting of a couple museum mailing list recipients unaware of the specific purpose of the occasion, the program director and his friend, and three students from the local university's creative nonfiction class. The guests were united by their shared interest in free food. Catering services had accommodated for greater fanfare: tessellations of cheddar and Colby Jack cubes stacked like lactose Mayan ruins; veggie sticks encircling a tub of ranch dip, shiny chafers of satay skewers, and bulk Josh wine. I nibbled on a grape as others engaged in the feeble endeavor of small talk—thesis projects, midterm exams, the weather. Then one bespectacled student, guarding a plate stacked with a silo of salami, piped up: "You know this house is haunted, right?" "Oh, definitely haunted," another student agreed. An awkward, tittering noise meant as laughter departed my body while I replenished my rosé. Then I handed the students Ziploc bags to hoard what they could of the spread. To my relief, they busied themselves quietly.

I did not contribute this tidbit to the conversation but within those first weeks, I'd sensed an illogical but incontrovertible ominousness emanating from the main museum display room, which contained Carson's "kimono." I had moved to the house not believing in ghosts, while also not *not* believing in ghosts. As in, I could entertain the existence of scientifically unexplainable encounters. Not exactly miracles but coincidences so extraordinary as to seem orchestrated by an entity beyond human capability—the invisible hand I once attributed to God. I hadn't witnessed anything unusual but had more or less concluded I was not, spiritually speaking, alone in the house—a fact I could not admit out loud to those students or even to myself, as that would surely shape a loose thing into a fixed matter, shoving the fear front-of-mind. Plus, I needed to continue visiting the churches from my H Mart CD haul—a task made no easier by the fact that I'd been reading up on Korean cults, thus heightening my metaphysical preoccupations.

In order to place my uncle's case into a larger cultural context, earlier in the year I'd corresponded with South Korean cult expert Dr. Tark Ji-il, a professor of religion at Busan Presbyterian University. While I didn't think my uncle had been involved in a cult per se, his behavior struck me as definitively compromised, if cult-adjacent.

I wanted to know where the line existed, if such a distinction could even be made, between what was practiced in that Century City condominium in 1996 and the extreme end of the Korean fringe religion spectrum. Perhaps the most known example of the latter is the Unification Church, a South Korean religious group originally founded in 1954 by leader, "true father," and second coming of Jesus, Moon Sun Myung. Reverend Moon's church had successfully evangelized in the United States by the 1970s and as far abroad as Russia and Czechoslovakia by the 1990s, claiming a worldwide membership of up to three million followers by 2012. Tell-all memoirs, international investigations, and even a *60 Minutes* feature exposed the inner workings of Moon's church. His devotees, whom the press nicknamed the "Moonies," had become synonymous with bright-eyed and brainwashed worshippers; they agreed to blind arranged marriages and mass weddings, sometimes moiling twenty-one hours a day, seven days a week, squandering their savings accounts for the cause. Ex-disciples confessed in widespread allegations that they often required intensive "deprogramming" in their harrowing reacclimation to life beyond the fold.

Organizations like Moon's are sometimes referred to as "new religious movements," a term sociologists popularized to veer away from derogatory connotations commonly associated with the word "cult." What falls under this designation is broad, applicable to groups whose intentions range from meditative and innocuous, such as Falun Gong, to manipulative and destructive, like David Koresh's Branch Davidians— more than eighty of whom died in an inferno during the 1993 siege of their compound in Waco, Texas. Dr. Tark prefers using the biblical term "heresy" when referring to Korean religious bodies that have diverged from mainline doctrines.

Terminology aside, the ubiquity is alarming. I came across so many Korean cult-related whispers involving celebrities, K-pop stars, and politicians, I began to think you could link almost anyone or anything, within six degrees of separation, to cultish activity. Notably, former South Korean president Park Geun-hye's entanglements with a cult leader and his daughter eventually led to Park's 2017 ouster and subsequent imprisonment. Even one of South Korea's most devastating tragedies in decades, the sinking of the MV *Sewol* ferry in 2014, could be traced back to a fringe religious figure. More than 300 passengers drowned, prompting a nationwide manhunt for Yoo Byung-eun, a billionaire described as the "de facto owner" of *Sewol*'s operating company. Yoo was the founder of the Evangelical Baptist Church of Korea, known alternatively as the Salvation Sect, which is categorized as a cult by Modern Religion Monthly—an institute and publication run by Dr. Tark. The Lord's Church and Beloved Church are listed on this same unofficial index of heresies.

Dr. Tark asserts it is nearly impossible to determine exactly how many Korean heresies are active today. He estimates the number is likely in the hundreds. An exact statistic is difficult to wrangle because many cults in South Korea consider themselves Christian entities. A 2015 census found that 27.6 percent of South Koreans identify as Christian and 15.5 percent as Buddhist, while 56.9 percent of the population aligns with no religious affiliation, other denominations, unregistered groups, or with the indigenous folk religion of Shamanism.

Korean heresies, Tark told me, typically ascribe to four principles:

1. God, or the second coming of Christ, or the Holy Spirit, is Korean.
2. The new revelation or doctrine is written in Korean.
3. The chosen people who will be saved are mostly Korean.
4. The new kingdom will be established in Korea.

Most of these religions gained traction during South Korea's three main periods of political unrest and cultural oppression: Japanese imperialist rule (1910 to 1945), the Korean War (1950 to 1953), and postwar dictatorship during massive industrialization (1960 to 1986). Tark believes this is no coincidence. "Military dictatorship [in Korea] needed blind supporters because they didn't have any democratic basis, and cults needed an umbrella under which they could hide from mainline churches or surrounding society's criticism," he said. New Korea-centric religions, which blend facets of Buddhism, Christianity, and Shamanism, appealed to those desperate for salvation in times of national and individual despair.

* * *

MAYBE IT WAS DESPAIR that led my mother to God. I think of the things she has had to conform to in America: a new language, a new profession, a new name. Whenever she moves, the Korean church consistently offers an open door to a version of herself that remains unchanged.

There is a difference, however, between the church itself and faith. The former, as an institution, has failed my mother in ways that would justify a loss of faith altogether. Something else drives her to these spaces, beyond conviction or creed. She may have left my father and that old El Monte sanctuary behind, but she has actively chosen to return to Korean churches in the years since. She may start over again and again, city after city, but her faith has never wavered. If anything, it has become the only remaining refuge of stasis in her life—immovable, permanent, and solely hers to know.

Many Korean immigrants like my mother have turned to God through times of uncertainty. During the 1990s swell of exorcisms, one *Chicago Tribune* writer concluded healing prayer rituals provided "quick-fix promises" to hardworking Korean immigrants "struggling for survival" in America.

For those raised in Korea, leaving behind one's home country is equivalent to "literally cutting off their roots and blood ties," says sociologist Ai Ra Kim, resulting in "a kind of social and spiritual death." In her 1996 book, *Women Struggling for a New Life: The Role of Religion in the Cultural Passage from Korea to America*, Kim focuses on Ilse women, raised in a collective Confucian culture. She posits Ilse women long tethered to oppressive, patrilineal traditions, raised in the shadow of stratified dynastic rule, have been historically drawn to the Christian church.

American missionaries first introduced Christianity to Korea in 1884, during the Joseon empire, when women lived in complete servitude to their male counterparts and families. For the powerless and poor, to whom the very idea of autonomy was unthinkable, the Christian church not only symbolized modernization and the Western world but a gateway to a new way of life. Missionaries developed pedagogical structures for women ordinarily excluded from educational opportunities; soon mothers and daughters could learn not only English but their own Korean alphabet, along with teachings in ethics and philosophy through the lens of the Bible.

Nearly half of the first 101 Koreans to arrive in America in 1903 belonged to missionary Reverend George Heber Jones's Incheon-based Methodist church. The 1882 Chinese Exclusion Act led to a workforce shortage of Chinese laborers, who had previously filled undesirable positions vacated by enslaved people. Thousands of Koreans relocated to toil in Hawaiian sugarcane plantations for fifty to sixty-five cents a day, a trend exacerbated by Japan's annexation of Korea in 1910. They were political exiles, born-agains, students, and those once castigated to the lower class, and they did what Koreans always do: They put their heads down and worked.

"Within a decade after the first wave of immigration," Kim writes, "Koreans had organized thirty-one churches and chapels in Hawaii and twelve churches in California." By 1990, approximately 70 percent of Koreans in the United States were affiliated with their ethnic churches—which functioned as community centers—and women made up approximately two-thirds of church membership. Some immigrant converts had no previous desire to attend. They were seeking kinship, thousands of miles away from home. And they discovered newfound empowerment by serving their congregations. Women could hold leadership roles as deacons and stewards. They became educators too, teaching Sunday School and Korean language programs for their first-generation children. The Korean church signified home, culture, and opportunity, functioning, as Kim puts it, as "more of a movement than an institution."

These spaces, however, were not entirely free of old societal conventions. Perhaps those early Korean immigrant women prepared Sunday lunch just as the matriarchs of Atlanta Beloved did, hustling to caretake while the men occupied themselves with higher spiritual callings. I imagine they tolerated far worse while seeking the false promise hidden within compromise. The truth is we may never really know.

* * *

SEVERAL *LOS ANGELES TIMES* ARTICLES published in 1996 and 1997 covering my uncle's case and subsequent trial referenced how cultural incongruities contributed to Chung Kyung-jae's death. In one article, published on April 6, 1997, experts claimed Shamanism "continues to strongly influence Korean thinking" because "a shaman, like a priest, is believed to possess special powers." The piece also described the exorcism as a combination of ancient Korean Shamanist principles mixed with Christian prayer. But in another article, Reverend Chun Soon-young, pastor of Valley First Presbyterian Church, disagrees. "This is an extreme case involving a fringe group of the Korean Christian community," Chun said. "I would say that what happened was almost cultist."

My uncle, who managed to negotiate a plea deal, testified that a demon haunting Ms. Chung's body had caused her to become " 'spiritually arrogant,' and 'at times she refused to obey' her husband." Though not a self-confessed shaman, Reverend Choi Sung-soo told the Chungs he was experienced in conducting exorcism rituals. The couple agreed to participate in ansukido, a combination of prayer and the laying on of hands, led by Reverend Choi, lasting for nearly two days.

I'm unsure why my uncle agreed to join or if he'd ever performed ansu prayer. But through this practice, the men violently expelled demons from Ms. Chung's body, stopping only for a church service in between the hours-long prayer sessions. The April 6 *Los Angeles Times* account notes all the defendants practiced Korean Pentecostal Christianity (a form of Charismatic Christianity), which emphasizes the possibility of modern-day miracles through the work of the Holy Spirit. Korean Charismatic Christians perform an aggressive variation of ansu prayer known as anchal prayer. Deputy District Attorney Hank Goldberg argued during the trial that Reverend Choi was an enterprising, if attention-seeking, exorcist and that he intended to perform a religious act so outrageous he'd be jailed and martyred in time for a Korean Pentecostal conference. However, in a profile of my uncle's congregation (which is Presbyterian, not Pentecostal), one member described the exorcism ceremony as "so out of the ordinary, it is beyond my understanding." In the same piece, the president of Southern California Korean Churches describes anchal prayer as a pleasant-sounding "religious body massage," unlike the April 6 story that says the technique can lead to "twisting or slapping" the possessed.

Accounts differ on the actual number of demons Ms. Chung was supposedly harboring, but my uncle claimed they successfully ousted several. Using their hands, feet, and even a wooden spoon, they prodded Ms. Chung's body until the object of their pursuit—a military spirit named Gundae—appeared near surrender, promising to relocate to a dog's body next door. The men took turns pressing on Ms. Chung, who pointed to the areas where the spirit lurked. Similarly in the Book of Mark, chapter five, Jesus expels the demon Legion from a man "and the impure spirits came out and went into the pigs" feeding upon a nearby hillside.

When Gundae promised to retreat, the men seized the demon's

weakness and ground their heels into Ms. Chung, as if stamping out brushfire. Reverend Choi then stood on top of Chung to force Gundae up through her mouth.

The men seemed unaware of their own brutality. "I was so close to it, getting rid of the thing," Reverend Choi stated at the crime scene. "Maybe I shouldn't have used the foot."

"There was not even one time that she complained or screamed out," my uncle told the police. "I guess that's what it takes to get the demons out."

IV.
Atlanta Beloved. Duluth, Georgia. Healing Prayer

MY GROUP CONSISTS OF all women: moon-faced thirtysomething Esther, Helen, and an older lady dressed outstandingly casual, in a baggy T-shirt, lounging shorts, socks, and slide sandals. She does not introduce herself. We call her Jipsanim (deacon). As we huddle around a folding chair, Helen introduces me to the group. I'm wearing glasses, no makeup, and a top I bought from Ross that covers my tattoos, to masquerade as the inconspicuous college student who can't speak in tongues and has come to walk with God again.

Jipsanim knows enough English to deliver a highly suspicious greeting, as if she's placed finger quotes around my name: "Welcome, 'Jenni-pur.'" She glares, her lips pursed, nostrils twitching, as if she's caught a whiff of something rotten. I bow and look away, scanning the room. The other three groups are carrying on peacefully; no signs of body crushing or demonic deliverance. Just closed eyes and hushed prayers, evoking a hope so hungry and plaintive it colors the already woeful space with another tinge of gloom.

I have returned to this office-space church because a weeknight extracurricular prayer session seems optimal territory for the loosening of personal boundaries. I want to witness for myself the confluence of faith, desire, and rapture.

For Beloved ansukido, one by one, we must sit in the metal folding chair to receive the mystical, synergistic power of prayer. The very thought of improvising a sincere healing request sends a hot flash through my body, and I begin to noticeably sweat. I can't take off my jacket because I've stowed my audio recorder in my pocket. I feel safer with the added layer, as if I can flee faster this way, should the need arise.

As the newbie I ask to skip my turn so I can observe, and Helen graciously agrees. We pray first for Esther's sciatica by each placing a hand on her upper body. The others take turns imploring God to cure Esther, voices cresting and falling, each a libretto.

When it comes time for Jipsanim's healing request, she describes with melodramatic flair the agony in her ankle, how she longs to be whole again, while clutching her socked foot, emphasizing every other syllable with a sort of guttural growl. Then she turns to me. "*I want Jennipur to pray for me,*" she says in Korean. "*Why won't you pray for me, Jennipur? Don't you want me to get better?*" There's something sneaky in her tone, almost virulent, as she smiles. I laugh nervously until Helen volunteers to speak first. My hand floats above Jipsanim's back, never making contact. The others pray while I think, *They know. You're a fraud. You're a fraud. You're a fraud.* I can feel Jipsanim's eyes on me even when she shuts them tight and moans "Ahhhmen, ahhhmen, ahhmen," as if in a trance, ecstatic to our prayers.

. . .

IF YOU'D ASKED ME what a shaman was in 2007, when I was still slinging steins at the biergarten, before I'd learned anything about my uncle, this is what I would have sketched for you: a fiftysomething white lady, barefoot and redolent of patchouli; maybe she's taken an online reiki course or read a book on energy work, and when you visit her "activated" space, it's all wind chimes, wall-hung tapestries, and YouTube Tibetan singing bowl tracks. This is a caricature of someone who might have adopted what is known as *neoshamanism*, a catchall term for a variety of practices that chase healing through altered states and communiqués with the spirit world. Much of this appears to be liberally borrowed from Indigenous cultures, particularly the use of entheogens or psychoactive substances, to impel transcendence or the sublime.

Whatever the case, Korean Shamanism—a prehistoric belief system native to Korea, also known as muism—belongs to an entirely different cultural stratosphere. "Gut" rituals, which involve dancing and music, are performed by shamans and remain common practice today, for events like business openings or groundbreaking ceremonies, to help clients establish peace and balance with surrounding energies. Sometimes they are used to exorcise evil spirits from spaces, places, objects, or even humans. And sometimes they serve as invitations, for the gods to bestow abundant harvests and good fortune. In the Korean baseball league, teams such as the LG Twins or Doosan Bears hold opening-day rites, splashing makgeolli across home plate or placing won notes into the maw of a decapitated pig's head posed by the dugout.

While Christian missionaries, Japanese rulers, and military governments all repressed shamans to varying degrees throughout Korea's history, they have returned to popular favor in the last two decades. Against the backdrop of South Korea's cutting-edge, technological landscape, the shaman is something of a shocking visual anachronism. They continue to wear Old World costumes. And they speak "in ecstasy," in the ancient Greek sense, meaning "to be or to stand outside oneself, a removal to elsewhere." To channel higher powers, they endure physical pain and a kind of psychosis in an act of ultimate self-loss. And they are almost always women, denied their very humanity; though they are chosen by the gods, even to their own bodies they do not belong.

I'd heard Korean women who immigrated from "lower-class" families were often susceptible to the mysticism of fringe, Shamanistic Christian doctrines. However classist and off-color, this is considered common knowledge. Seon Jeon, a linguistics professor at Columbus State University, whom I first encountered at my welcome reception, adamantly agreed. Seon and I met for coffee one afternoon, partly because I had begun to feel vampiric in my solitary habits. I wanted to speak to another human being who looked like me, without pretense, in daylight.

My project seemed to genuinely intrigue her. She had moved to Georgia from Gwangju, by way of D.C., in 2003 and attended a nearby Korean Presbyterian church housed, rather curiously, in a defunct movie theater.

Seon explained the Korean community in Columbus is directly tied to Fort Moore (formerly known as Fort Benning) military base. As at several other prominent U.S. military bases—such as Fort Jackson in South Carolina, Fort Liberty (formerly Fort Bragg) in North Carolina, or Fort Sill in Oklahoma—women who married American GIs in Korea relocated to the bases and their surrounding sleepy American towns knowing no one else besides their spouses. They, in turn, established Korean restaurants or small businesses and attended local Korean churches to retain vital cultural touchstones. After service, they could eat a Korean meal and converse comfortably in Hangukmal—practices that are, according to Seon, frequently discouraged in their mixed-race homes. Seon also reiterated the theory that GI wives are often regarded as uneducated and prone to mystical thinking.

The preconception that people of lower castes are inclined to mysticism goes as far back as the dragon-robe-era Joseon dynasty. The vocation of shaman was socially and culturally reserved for the "vulgar commoner" or cheonmin class. Known as mudangs, these mystics and healers acted as gifted intermediaries between the spirit world and the human plane. The royal court relied upon them for everyday matters, such as healing the sick or blessing harvests. They were universally deemed both skilled and trained religious professionals as well as abject social outcasts.

Ai Ra Kim describes the process of transforming into one type of shaman with chilling detail: "To become a kangsin-mu, one must pass through two rites of passage: sinbyeong, or spirit possessed sickness, as well as naerim gut, an initiating ritual, that involves suffering through a litany of symptoms: loss of appetite and weight, weakness, depression, hallucination, heartache . . . speaking in tongues, taking off clothes, constant washing of hands or bathing, singing, dancing, shouting, crying, mumbling, silence, and other 'strange' behaviors."

The shaman becomes a vessel, home to the spirit from whom one derives their mystical abilities. The process is, in essence, a voluntary death and resurrection. It occurred to me Chung Kyung-jae may have been a willing participant in her own violent ruin. Perhaps this was the fate she believed she deserved: unimaginable pain, but righteous pain—the affliction of being chosen to live outside herself, for a short while, in the final ecstasy of elsewhere.

* * *

FOR RINGING IN her sixty-fifth year, my mother had one request: to sweat profusely, Korean-style. Perspiring in the South may seem like a basic, cost-free experience, but my mother's birthday wish could only be granted by visiting a jimjilbang called Jeju Sauna, in Duluth. Named after Jeju-do, a volcanic Korean island, Jeju Sauna is a respite for Southerners hankering for a traditional Korean schvitz.

Jimjilbangs have expanded in popularity over the last fifteen years, beyond core Korean enthusiasts, as an egalitarian spa excursion. They're spotlessly maintained, affordable, and open twenty-four hours. Excluding the gendered locker rooms and wet saunas, the spaces are shared, decked out with cave-like detoxification chambers lined with salt bricks, mugwort, jade, and amethyst, for purported restorative effect (improved blood pressure, circulation, and cardiovascular health).

Jeju Sauna was the least impressive jimjilbang my mother had ever visited, but it did offer demiruh, or body scrub—a service where, for a nominal fee, an ajumma dressed in black underwear Brillos your naked body. As my mother prefaced before our visit, "Jeju will do the job just fine."

The "job," I'd supposed, meant that a trip to Duluth tempered a certain concern left unsaid. My mother had become something of a prodigal Korean, having drifted from the Asian-centric suburbs outside Los Angeles where I'd grown up, farther and farther away, across several state lines. Atypical for a Korean woman of her generation, raised in the rubble of civil war. But over the last decade, as she'd roamed from one city to the next, she could not ignore an almost primal call home, which surfaced in specific, arresting desires—the scent of fresh steamed rice or kimchi's electric tang or the sweltry interior of a salt-brick sauna—that followed her, no matter how far she wandered.

She lived now in central Florida, though I'd learned to accept her location was ever subject to change. The last time she snuck off for a job interview, I only found out through an email notification, which indicated a new sign-in for her account in Amarillo, Texas. "Did you move to Texas?" I asked over the phone. "Why?" she said, in the coy, avoidant tone I knew by then too well.

She did not move to Amarillo, but I have no doubt that if she had, she would've managed to find a Korean church within an hour's drive. Jimjilbangs were a different story, fewer and farther between. After her six-hour commute from Florida, we reunited at Jeju, both eager to lose a pound of water weight and the top layer of our skin for as little as sixty dollars.

I noticed a different service on this visit called chai-yok, or hip bath. For these vaginal steams, a woman rests atop a padded, seatless chair. Boiling beneath her nether regions is a cauldron of stewed mixed herbs such as wormwood, rosemary, and basil. The treatment supposedly offers a bounty of miraculous results such as vaginal tightening, uterus cleansing, weight loss, and menstrual cycle regulation. One *Fast Company* journalist described chai-yok as "sorcery for your vagina." In her trial, she endured a series of clench-worthy discomforts throughout the thirty-minute session, which she characterized as "an invading shower of scorching steam" upon the most delicate membranes of the female body. A reason she listed for withstanding the pain? "I want to feel as clean on the inside as I feel on the outside." Afterward, she reported feeling distinctly empty, but "in a calming way." Perhaps, like Chung Kyung-jae or the dozen women packed into Jeju's chai-yok room, she wanted to be freed of what invisibly besieged her.

No male-equivalent tradition exists in Korean culture. There is no scientific or medical proof supporting conclusive chai-yok results, either. But miracle-working and mystic healing are elemental to Korean folk history, and these beliefs have sustained for centuries.

I wondered about my mother, the open-heart-surgery nurse, the born-again Christian. She had never undergone a chai-yok. As a young girl, she accompanied my grandmother to many fortune-tellers and shamans. None of them mentioned how she would one day marry a black-toothed grifter in America, or how that man would bring her to God. It's the kind of story any prescient person ought to have portended:

Sacramento, 1977. Umma was twenty-four years old. She hadn't seen another Korean in a whole year. After riding a city bus downtown, she stumbled upon a Korean gift shop—Hangul characters coming into view, posted above the storefront, something like an oasis.

Umma walked inside and spoke effortlessly with the Korean shopkeeper, which reminded her of home. The shopkeeper handed over the telephone. The voice on the other end invited Umma to fellowship.

When my mother entered the church, the first one in America she'd step into, a large woman lumbered into the light, cooing salutations. As she showed Umma the sanctuary, the woman began to inquire beyond topics of divinity: *Are you single?* Yes. *Do you have a visa?* Yes. *Green card?* Yes. *Good . . . good.* The woman appeared worldly, spoke English, Cantonese, and Japanese fluently. She was a deacon, this was her church, and she had a son.

Despite the condition of his teeth when they met, he smiled wide and showily like the Cheshire cat. From the way he leaned his weight onto one popped hip, and by the look of his slacking shoulders, he did not appear exceptionally eligible or employable. But the deacon urged Umma to consider marriage. God had brought her here. Wouldn't it be better, to not be alone?

The deacon (my Figueroa Grandma) married them a month later in a motel room. Rush job. Because Grandma filed the paperwork, to this day Umma does not know the official date of her marriage. There is one photo from the church ceremony, which was held separately, weeks after the motel nuptials. An elder escorted my mother down the aisle. Head bowed to a supermarket bouquet of dandelions, she looked on the brink of tears, the velvet red pews empty behind her.

Promptly after the wedding, Figueroa Grandma relocated to Los Angeles with my father, where they squatted in foreclosed homes. My father hawked Italian gold chains at swap meets. Figueroa Grandma went door-to-door pocketing donations for a church that didn't exist. She kept a ledger of my father's expenses in a spiral notebook, which she mailed to my mother in Sacramento for reimbursement. Meanwhile, Umma emptied bed pans at a nursing home and waited. For what? For her life to begin. For a sign. Maybe she could leave, wake up somewhere else, start over. Then she got pregnant with my sister. She would have to wait longer. She would have to stay.

I've asked my mother on more than one occasion why she married a stranger. "Because I was lonely," she says. Nothing more, nothing less.

In Jeju's locker room, we examined our reflections in the mirror. The ajumma who scrubbed me had carried out the task with gruff haste, like a kitchen maid scaling a trout. We stood there naked, marveling at our scratches and new skin, her body and my body, side by side.

V.

THOUGH I HAD NOT fully realized it yet, an absence of spirituality had left a void in me so deep and penetrating, I could not seem to function without a stopgap faith. Upon the advice of a friend, I obtained crystals as a way of surrounding myself with positive energy—not something I had ascribed to in life before moving to Georgia, but as much as I believed the moon controlled the ocean's tide, it seemed plausible pretty rocks could furnish some type of elemental comfort. I suppose I could have opted for a more reliable source for this pursuit but instead nabbed, via Amazon, a generic gem variety starter kit plus an egg-sized labradorite stone sent from somewhere in mainland China. The reviews were mixed in terms of crystal "authenticity," but this concern was trumped by a need for expediency. The faster I could equalize the bad juju, the better. I needed the two-day shipping.

It didn't help that, six weeks in, I hadn't managed to squeeze out a single new sentence. I listened to my H Mart discs on a boom box while roasting sweet potatoes and baking Paleo banana bread, because I had decided it seemed possible to alter certain fundamental truths about myself, such as suddenly becoming the type of person who enjoyed sweet potatoes, bananas, or baked goods devoid of refined sugars and gluten. I suppose I'd never released the part of me who—with enough conviction or moxie—could transform into a superior, altered self. I could see the error in this too. Whenever I rifled through old photos, I was surprised by how much younger, thinner, or more beautiful I had looked only months or years earlier; and how at the time those pictures had been taken, I'd appraised myself resolutely a work in progress. It would have been sensible to value my current self beautiful, as is, rather than cycling through the same pattern of wistful flagellation. Though I did not commit my spiritual life to a fringe religion, or any religion at that, I noticed the parallel longing—an insatiable desire for categorical change. But the insight typically halted there. I lacked the will to self-correct.

So I roasted and baked food I didn't want to eat, and listened to sermons I couldn't understand, and fantasized about a future, better "me"—who, with incremental adjustments, might not be so inexorably destined for spinsterdom. I had been single for a while, a circumstance made ever bleaker by living in Columbus.

The internet deemed this my Jesus Year, the same age the Son of God had been when his life was, rather famously, curtailed via crucifixion. Blogs described this a time of ego-death; a chance, now fully jettisoned from adolescence, to abandon old ways and start anew. The crashing inertia of full-on adulthood could supposedly summon a sort of pre-midlife-crisis crisis. Meaning things got real ugly before one reached potential existential resurrection. Encumbered with a small island's GDP-worth of student loan debt and a microscopic savings account, I wondered how much uglier it could get. When I got especially down in the dumps, I took to pondering the label from the strainer I'd purchased at Super H Mart: "LIFE IS THE MOST VALUABLE INVESTMENT / MADE IN KOREA." I'd already banked on its philosophy, life itself my most valuable investment.

In the McCullers house, however, death accrued like a tax everywhere I turned. Some say when a ladybug lands on you, it's a sign of good luck. But what if you only found them dead? On the nightstand, along the windowsills, by the teapot, shells gone pale pink, every one of them belly-up. What stayed alive? Albino geckos the size of okra, skittering their see-through bodies across the beige carpet, as if the fibers themselves were mounting an escape. Umma called weekly and her unflappable nature permitted brief reprieve from the morose surroundings. Whenever I mentioned my unease in the house, she ignored me, noting instead nearby properties for sale, alluding to yet another inevitable uprooting.

Maybe a routine could help me feel better, one friend suggested. So in the mornings I stared at a blinking cursor, answered the kettle's scream. While my memory teas brewed, I stared at a bearded yogi pretzeled into a meditation pose on the side of the box. The teabag tags professed the assured piety of Bible verses.

Appreciate yourself and honor your soul.
Become part of the universe so the universe becomes part of you.
If you let yourself be successful, you shall be successful.

I collected the mail in the afternoon, mostly junk, often addressed to "Mr. Carston McCuller." Catalogs for bulk furniture, Valpak coupons, an entire compendium for commercial carpeting. At night I sipped on more tea while listening to the house awaken, cracking its knuckles and beams. Then I'd disrobe and plunge into the turquoise bathtub, with the nonchalance of someone who believed they were alone. With my back turned to the door, I did find myself wondering if someone somewhere was watching, whether hidden by the frosted window glass or through the mallards' eyes set adrift on the bathroom wallpaper.

This did not strike me as unreasonable behavior. I couldn't stop thinking about an article I'd read in September, reviving intrigue around the old Stocking Strangler murders. According to the local paper, new conflicting DNA evidence suggested, after thirty years, that the true killer may have never been caught. Maybe an innocent man could be exonerated. And maybe the real Stocking Strangler was still alive, an old man by now, walking around Wynnton, scot-free.

To make matters worse, I'd come home one day to an unlocked door. I messaged the director: "Hi there! Any chance you stopped by today?" He succinctly replied, "No." I proceeded to inspect every room, whipping around corners with the swaggering demeanor of a TV detective securing a crime scene. Most likely I'd forgotten to lock the door on my way out.

Once I'd searched every possible hiding place, when I believed I was truly as alone as I could be, I went to bed. From then on I kept pepper spray on my nightstand, beside my teacup of aphorisms and sun-charged crystals. Not once did I fall asleep without a light on.

*   *   *

WHAT DID I THINK might happen if I found myself in the presence of an intruder? I suppose whatever it was Umma had warned me against when I was a little girl: the unthinkable. I'd heard the word "rape" early, maybe too early, on one of my mother's programs. I couldn't make sense of these crimes as a child of God. The idea of such a violent violation stuck itself to the corner of my mind, lying dormant and obtuse—a looming horror so big and unbearable I could hardly comprehend it. I mean this both emotionally and physically. I wasn't one of those girls who explored her own body. Never took a mirror down there. Never got the talk about the birds and the bees. I learned about sex at night in our empty house, before my parents returned from Bible study. The man and woman I watched in a Showtime softcore porno writhed around naked. There were implications in their staged movements. How that corresponded to my own body remained an enigma, as did the male anatomy. I imagined their congress as a pillaging of the body. A ravenous desire. An act of devouring. It was a sin so deliciously depraved that the word itself (sex) I could not bear to say out loud.

Some children exhibit an uninhibited sexual awareness, but I was not that kind. What sort of kid was I? Two complete strangers on separate occasions had informed me I bore a striking resemblance to Tweety Bird. I had "big eyes for an Asian," as my mom would say, and pouty lips that could pass for a beak, and also an objectively large head for my body. Like Tweety, I exuded an androgynous disposition. In elementary school, I regularly wore boys' boxers as shorts. I liked girly things as well, such as Barbies, but often used them, much like my stuffed animals, to realize an active fantasy life, by weaving elaborate character backstories and narratives. The Barbies themselves I privately admired for their voluptuous figures and considered them the epitome of womanliness—an embodiment distant from my own reality. I did not imagine such a physique as part of my future.

I stayed cartoon-cute until puberty. I guess there's a reason you never see Tweety grown up. Puberty ravages some more than others, and I did not depart from childhood unscathed. Yes, the archetypal elements of a cripplingly awkward transition were there: thick ovate glasses; braces that forced my upper lip to curl into hiding; broomish, blunt bangs (courtesy of my mother's Korean beauty shop) concealing a forehead teeming with acne. While my classmates blossomed breasts and curves, I grew leaner. A promising competitive swimmer then, I did not become womanly so much as hydrodynamic. My shoulders and arms rippled with ropy muscles. I attained superhero strength. I could climb the P.E. rope in sixth grade without using my legs, or prop myself perpendicular to a pole like a flag by using only the grip of my hands. I considered these skills pretty neat until I discovered my peers were horrified by my physical prowess. How terribly naive; I had not realized I was supposed to become an object of desire.

It doesn't seem a coincidence now, how that time overlapped with a fervid period in my personal "faith journey." This spiritual awakening also served as my first, and perhaps only, experience of blind, unconditional love, and consequently the loss of that love—a heartbreak from which I might never truly recover. Blindness I believed was a necessary component to the equation, because if I could not see beauty in my own body, how could anyone else, of this earth, either? But God was an otherworldly force—supposedly the one who'd created this life and the next. I believed if He had created me too, then there must have been something in me worth valuing.

Though our family had attended church every weekend for as long as I could remember, I soon found new purpose in my convictions. I volunteered for roles in skits for church anniversaries, Thanksgivings, and Easter celebrations, and pursued each with the gusto of a seasoned dayplayer. I gifted faux frankincense as Wise Man #2, cradled a doll postpartum as the Virgin Mary, and stood gobsmacked at the mouth of an empty tomb, not as Magdalene or Joseph's wife but a woman literally referred to in scripture as "the other Mary."

Weekdays morphed into pre-Sunday preparation. I memorized verses to recite in Bible study and constantly rehearsed "body worship." The choreography borrowed from American Sign Language, and in the bathroom mirror I'd pump hand birds and cross motions with feverish pizzazz, because I believed. My mother didn't comment on this increased devoutness, nor did she mention anything about my performances. She was busy serving the congregation in self-effacing ways, quelling newborns in the nursery or heating cauldrons of kimchi stew in the basement for the post-service lunch rush. The pastor's wife, however, took notice and bequeathed unto me a title.

I was known then as Little Deacon. And I performed the role with grave sincerity. After lunch, when the other children headed home, I executed a variety of undesirable administrative duties, xeroxing and trifolding the paper programs for Second Worship, the college-age service. I handed out the pamphlets bearing the puffed-up pride of a mall cop. I wanted my faith to be recognizable, undeniable, awesome.

What ensued was not quite romance, even though pervading language in praise songs overtly suggested as much. "I want to fall in love with You; I could sing of Your love forever; how my soul longs for You; Your river runs with love for me, and I will open up my heart." God was all-encompassing: Father, Creator, Healer, Guide. I prayed to Him at home alone, and some nights I felt the unusual relief of being held in something greater than what I could understand. I believed if I could be good, and pure in my goodness, He could change me into someone worthy of love.

My outlook changed one weeknight during a Bible study led by the youth pastor—a wormish man with a hyena's cackle. He gave a short sermon addressing the general topic of sex, as much as one could while using the word as minimally as possible. I wanted to know what recourse a woman possessed in the case of rape. The discourse circled around the nobility in waiting, the devil's work of succumbing to temptation, the promise of chastity until marriage being a vow one makes to God first, and so on.

The session ended as it always did, with prayer. We'd been at it for a solid thirty minutes. A bit bored, I opened my eyes and watched as the youth pastor wept on his knees, allowing a rope of snot to land on a handkerchief he'd placed on the ground. By my estimation, the snot rope measured at least two feet long, unbroken from nose to floor. The sight alone was its own private punishment (I was supposed to be praying with my eyes closed like everyone else, so technically I had no business being disgusted by his unabashed release). But the methodical nature of the handkerchief arrangement disturbed me, as if he'd done this countless times before and had devised the solution after much trial and error. Meaning, he had the presence of mind to calculate that kind of logic. Yet he seemed to buckle at my questions during post–Bible study snacks. What about the R word (rape) and the A word (abortion)? Would the woman still be a virgin in God's eyes? Is she really supposed to keep the baby? I wondered about justice, resolution, revenge. He tucked his soggy hankie in his pocket and before he could answer, a party-sized Subway sandwich snaked across the buffet table stole his attention. He ate the way he prayed, with a kind of abandon. An iceberg lettuce shred dangled from his bottom lip for what felt like an eternity, and I realized: If this was the man God sent into my life for answers, I didn't want them.

If I were to choose one moment it was then—us virgins congregating on the metal folding chairs in the church basement, gorging on hunks of a super-sized sub. The answer suddenly seemed so obvious. I'd read as much in the Bible, seen as much at home: Women must suffer. From there it happened quickly. I prayed and prayed until one day I no longer believed anyone was listening, until all I could hear was my own voice, until all I could hear was silence.

VI.
The Lord's Church. Duluth, Georgia. Holy Fire Revival

Pastor Kim Yong-doo stands before his audience wearing a royal purple tailored suit and house slippers. The congregation is charmed by his stage presence, how he cracks jokes or how, for comedic effect, he twists his face up into clownish expressions. The delivery is slick, like that of a charlatan. Beside him, a Kinko's-style banner hangs on an easel, depicting Kim and his wife in a galaxy of stars and flames.

Some thirty attendees, who have traveled from as far away as Mississippi and Minnesota, sit in metal chairs, facing Kim's lectern. They are middle-aged white men, seven members of a Hmong family, Koreans, and several Black congregants including a woman dressed in an African wax-print kitenge.

Kim's interpreter is the same man featured in the crucifixion YouTube clip. He's tall, in his thirties with pointy Spock-like sideburns, standing stage left, at the ready.

It is hour two of Night One. Kim pauses after every line for his words to be echoed in English:

"Let me introduce my ministry.

The order of the service is to turn off all the lights and cry out to the Lord all together.

And you maybe also see the Lord and meet the Lord and experience his presence tonight.

Amen?

(Amen!)

Because the Lord will see how passionate you are, how much you're desiring to receive.

You will be able to *receive* the spiritual gifts and experience something miraculous things.

Hallelujah?

(Amen!)

Even if you're speak in tongues, there are times the Lord will open your spiritual eyes to *see* him.

Sincerely, with genuine heart, say, Lord, I want *you*!

[Shouting, with increasing forcefulness] Please, Lord, give us the tongue!

Of course the Lord is listening to your prayer very carefully.

But when you *show* your desperation in prayer,

that's when the Lord will see your tears and *touch* you with His physical hand.

When the Lord touches *you* with his hand,

you will experience an event.

All of sudden, you will feel like *vomit*, throw up, phlegm.

You're gagging.

Sometimes you are sneezing, coughing, you will feel the heat in your body continually without stopping, something from inside of your stomach will come out.

He will bring out what is *hidden* inside of you. Because you haven't been able to live spiritually.

The Lord will purify you tonight!

And also you will receive the *fire*.

Tangible heat and through the prayer you might fall on the floor!

Cleanse your mouth and change your language.

You might be able to experience hell because it's better for you to experience Hell Encounter.

[*Squeals* from the congregants; a breathy, *Yes!*]

When we talk about spiritual things like this, the evil spirits they're attacking me *physically*.

Evil spirits afflicting our lives with sickness, depart from us!

[Pops of high-pitched *amens* and *hallelujahs* scatter around the room]

Bless us Atlanta, Georgia!

Punch us with your mighty power!

[Booming now, thunderously] OPEN THE GATE OF HEAVEN GIVE US THE POWER TO SPEAK TO YOU DIRECTLY!

CAST OUT ALL THE EVIL SPIRITS CONTROLLING OUR LIFE FROM YOUR HOUSE!
DEPART FROM US EVIL SPIRITS OF SICKNESS!
[Both voices and languages overlapping] GIVE US YOUR FIRE! GIVE US YOU FIRE POWER!"

• • •

WHEN THE LIGHTS GO OUT, the remoteness of my situation crystalizes: I am sitting on the floor of a windowless office space tucked into the corner of a random lot in Duluth. From the main road, the lot appears vacant. There would be no way of knowing people have crammed into a back room in one of the rentable facilities from 7 P.M. to 2 A.M. for a four-night revival. Should something go wrong, I wonder how long it would take for anyone to find me.

A MIDI file composition blares from the PA system so loud the speakers crackle. The tune is a relentlessly peppy crescendo punched up with digital trumpets and cymbal clashes. It is better suited for a 1980s public access game show where, say, contestants maraud a grocery store for prizes. Or is it more like the intro to a TGIF sitcom, where the credits montage features a wacky neighbor and rascal siblings who pose arms crossed, back-to-back? I have time to mull this over; the tune will play on loop in the pitch black for an entire hour.

"*I want you to focus*," says Pastor Kim. "I want you to focus," says the interpreter. "Repeat after me: Lord I need you," they say.

"Lord I need you," we say.

Pastor Kim counts down in English: one, two, three.

Together we holler, "Holy fire! Holy fire! Holy fire!"

The squall atomizes in the darkness, giving way to splintered voices: weeping women, one sad soul's parched, lugubrious gasping. Beneath the peppy tune and wailing, a whir resonates—the hisses and snapped consonants of tongues-speaking.

Clear across the room, the only light glows—an EXIT sign, igneous red, above the doorway to the outside world we have temporarily revoked. Kim's voice explodes above the din, launching flares of glosso-lalia. He expels terse, then elongated interjections—a taekwondo type exertion (*huh!*) and a melodic *whoooooaa!*

Beside me, a woman has morphed into an archer. She is pivoting sharply left to right, aiming at invisible targets, releasing imagined arrow after arrow. It is unclear whether she is losing or winning her battle. Around the room, subtle curves emerge from the dark: slumped torsos, supplicant hands clapping and waving, arms cast heavenward like those of a toddler begging to be held. I feel the way I do sometimes in museums, when I can sense my own lack and search other peoples' reactions for whatever it is I'm missing—epiphany, revelation, awe.

I think of what Pastor Kim has promised us tonight, the supernatu-ral encounters in heaven and hell with Jesus. Previous experiences and visions Kim says we can expect:

- Evil spirits in the form of snakes slithering from your mouth
- A fire tunnel, reached only via prayer
- Sapphires and diamonds
- Jesus, in this universe, walking through walls
- Piggyback rides with Jesus
- Hide-and-seek with Jesus
- Animals (such as cows) rapping
- Flowers dancing in praise
- Your family in hell

I keel over and clasp my hands to mimic my neighbors' motions, in case anyone is watching me. The song loop and the cries and exultations thrash inside my head. I try to meditate, count my breaths. What comes to mind instead is the drive over.

I'd been late to the revival. For no good reason I'd left Columbus drag-ging ass, dreading the drive and the all-night worship sessions ahead. Nobody was forcing me to go. But as the final weeks of my fellowship dwindled, I realized I had very little concrete material to show for my time in Georgia: no manuscript, no greater grasp of my uncle's crime, only a giant question mark gaping above my fog-filled head. The morning of the revival arrived, then the afternoon. I did not want to see strangers pawing at hope—or rather, my own self reflected in our shared desperation. But this would be my one chance to witness Kim's ministry in-person. So I packed an overnight bag, aiming to make up for my dawdling on the road.

I rarely take notice of faces while driving on highways, associating my fellow commuters' habits with their vehicles instead (Maniac Miata, Slow-poke U-Haul, et cetera). But I distinctly remember the man in the champagne-colored sedan who lurched toward my passenger-side window. He did not expect to find me there. He was halfway through, cutting diagonally across three consecutive lanes when my car materialized in his blind spot, sandwiching him into a space he could only escape by colliding into me. I could see the whites of his eyes. Time suspended the moment like a held breath, stretching out long enough for me to watch his smug expression rearrange into a mask of panic.

I imagine I looked panicked, too, as my mind disconnected from my hands and tugged at the wheel, swerving me left, then right, then left again until the whole metal body I now belonged to began to rock, wheels alighting off the pavement, gravity coin-flipping whether I ought to tumble.

I'd once read what to do if I ever found myself in a vehicle submerged under water (POGO: Pop seat belt, Open window, Get Out). But I had not learned what to do to keep from flipping over on the highway. You are probably not supposed to slam the brakes, which is what I did next.

There was no noise when the car began to spin. I did not see my life flash before my eyes, just a gray-streaked windshield, pixelating like a kaleidoscope. The drivers around me parted, giving wide berth as my tires seared a black arc across the asphalt.

This is what it's like to sit stock-still and ass-backward on a highway: You feel a dumb kind of beauty. The senses sharpen. Eyes see a cloud-free blue sky, nose smells burnt rubber. Foot touches pedal, until hands speak to mind again, steering you forward, at first a crawl, 30, 40, then 50, 60 miles an hour, until you rejoin the current where cars plow past, as if the world hadn't stopped for an instant, as if whatever happened had never happened at all.

It dawned on me I'd narrowly escaped death once I pulled over at the nearest gas station. Though fully operational, the station looked run-down, its borders stitched in by leggy weeds. Beer-bellied men caroused beside the coin-operated vacuum. I inspected my car's exterior. Not a scratch on her. I wanted to curl into a ball and scream or sob but instead I hit the road. I didn't stop driving until after nightfall at the industrial lot, where I turned on my recorder and walked straight into the revival.

Here I was in the dark, where I could unload, unbidden. But I couldn't summon the tears. I closed my eyes and moaned the sound of sobbing, the way a sympathy-seeking child does after a minor tumble, hopeful the mimicry might spark actual waterworks.

An hour is an increment of time that can often feel fleeting. Once you've settled into a therapy session or deep-tissue massage, the minutes disintegrate and suddenly you're wrapping up, left wanting for more. This is not the case for Holy Fire prayer hour. There is no way to incon-spicuously track the passage of time. In the unlit dissonance, ten min-utes is ten hours and ten seconds at once. The game show tune repeats. My knees pop from kneeling. I can feel my mind sliding.

I hear Kim say the word "ansukido." His silhouette enters the crowd. He stands above each congregant, touches them on the head one by one. When he stands above me, I wonder if he can sense I don't believe. I wonder, too, if God had been on the road with me, if somehow I'd been spared. I'm thinking how this is impossible, as impossible as the fact that I spun out on the highway and I am alive. I'm saying, "I'm alive, I'm alive, I'm alive," when Pastor Kim palms my skull like a basketball, really grips it, gives it a firm shake, and then he's on to the next, and the next, until the game show tune fades and the fluorescent bulbs flicker on, blasting the room with bright white light.

· · ·

IT IS NIGHT TWO, 1 A.M., break time. Refreshments leave much to be desired: oblong cuts of room-temp cucumbers, a quivering onion dip tub, pale pink ham chunks, donettes in pelts of powdered sugar, bags

of Kenyan Safari tea. Instead of poking around the snack table, I ought
to mingle, for reporting purposes. But my head feels wadded and heavy,
as if filled with cotton batting. I hold a cup of hot water, so as to appear
occupied, and loiter in the corner of the lobby.

Someone has installed a makeshift greenroom there. Behind a curtain, I spot Pastor Kim and his team gathered around a small table, eating colorful bowls of bibimbap. The nutty scent of sesame oil wafts out
to where the rest of us spiritual peasants loam. My stomach growls loud
enough to be picked up by the recorder.

Eventually another upbeat MIDI file song filters into the lobby. We
take the cue and make our way back into the windowless sanctuary.

Repeat revival-goers know the drill: Pastor Kim, his wife/lead
holy dancer, the interpreter, and the Atlanta branch pastor (the spitting image of a Korean Alan Thicke) stand several feet apart across the
stage. Eyes closed, bodies swaying, they have already begun their own
divine reckonings.

Informal stations take shape. The scene resembles a convention,
where fans line up for their favorite celebrity meet-and-greets. In this
case, people queue to receive Holy Fire from spiritual elders. From what
I've gathered, fire baptism, known as Impartation, will allow believ-
ers to gain the gift of Holy Dance and, with hope, access to the metaphysical dimension they desire. Impartation is a rite of passage many
aspire to one day experience, as evidenced by the hundreds of pleas
posted on the church website's Prayer Request page. To some it is an all-
consuming pursuit: "Im desperate for this baptism of fire," writes one
forty-four-year-old from Sheffield, England. "I would like to visit The
Lord's Church for the summer conference . . . the devil is trying to stop
me . . . I'm so hungry for God. It's all I think about everyday."

The site is also where one can access Kim's self-published, six-volume
Baptize by Blazing Fire series as well as links to the church's revival
recap reels. Many members, like the man from Sheffield, might only
encounter Kim's ministry online, where (according to their profiles) converts of every color pray in the language only God and Kim understand,
from the Seychelles to Ghana, Borneo, and Brazil.

My presence here feels a little wasteful, like scoring tickets to the Super Bowl when you don't even know who's playing. What I do know is that those who follow The Lord's Church see Pastor Kim as both middleman and medium, currying God's favor and message while also endowed with unique powers unavailable to common man, such as the wielding of sacred fire.

By "fire," no one is speaking figuratively. I realize this when the interpreter undergoes what appears to be a personal cataclysm. As he prays in tongues, cupped hands raised, something threatens his concentration. He flicks his wrists, winces. What he is holding only he can see: a barely contained flame. Sparks scald his fingertips; he yowls from the burn until collapsing to the ground, lying there tucked and fetal, his whole figure engulfed in an invisible blaze.

The vignette belongs to a chaotic tableau. Beside the interpreter's squirming body, holy dancers glimmer in their bejeweled tunics and matching white spandex bell-bottoms, executing quasi-balletic movements, humming chipper la-di-da melodies in the busy, mirthful temperament of storybook fairy godmothers. Korean Alan Thicke flows through a series of tai chi–like positions. Pastor Kim rumbles in tongues, issuing personalized prophecies. After observing for a while, I finally get in line.

There are ten people ahead of me, including the woman standing before Pastor Kim, who is shrieking, *"Father! Father!"* in Korean honorific form. Everyone knows why. Earlier, she'd shared her testimony: During praying-in-darkness hour, she witnessed a chorus of angels descend upon her cancer-stricken husband, enveloping his frail form with a hopeful, miraculous tenor. Not because his prognosis had changed. Maybe it comforted her to know one certainty beyond his death: He was heaven-bound and when he got there, he would not be alone. At the time she'd seemed at peace with this, yet here she was, alternating between belly-deep wails and pleading Father God perhaps for comfort, quickness, relief.

She faints and Faith, the woman dressed in the kitenge, is ready to catch her. And with that the soon-to-be-widow's turn is over. The next

person in line steps over her shaking body. She stays on the floor, screaming again and again in Korean, *"Father! Father! Father!"* It occurs to me
how a revival is a sensible place to mourn; it is an occasion designed for
the display of open, conspicuous grief.

With Impartation now in full swing, waves of heartache and ela-
tion whirl wall to wall. One woman laughs and prances about while
another doubles over, yelling, "Owwwwwoo!" as if howling at the
moon. The interpreter has recovered and is standing again, ready to
dole fire. A woman I'd seen near the powdered donettes steps forward
and assumes the acceptance pose: chin tilted heavenward, mouth agape,
her body primed.

A teenager with a long curtain of black hair approaches me in line.
I'd noticed her, along with her younger sisters (twins, about twelve years
old), holy dancing at the start of service. The twins bear a discomfiting
air, not unlike the hallway-lurking duo from *The Shining*. These girls
say "come play with us" with their eyes, which are penetrating beads,
boba-black. The twins scurry about the room boundlessly energized,
disappear and reappear, giggling. I check my watch. It is two o'clock in
the morning.

"Jennifer, right?" the eldest sister asks.

"Right," I say, though I don't recall giving her my name.

The twins introduce themselves: Grace and Heather, they say, in
surround-sound.

"Have you gotten to Pastor Kim's books?" the eldest asks.

"I just started Book One," I say—partially true: a free excerpt, anyway.

"Oh," says the eldest, crestfallen.

I pull my sleeve cuffs over my wrists, to ensure my tattoos aren't
showing. "How did you end up here?" I ask.

"We were introduced by . . ." one twin starts.

"Friends," the other finishes. "Family friends."

"Do your parents come here, too?" I ask.

They point to their mom, and I recognize her immediately—the
screamer, Nora. In call-and-response Amens and Hallelujahs, her voice
rose above the others, vehement and tremulous. She'd even caught

Pastor Kim's attention, who'd mocked the treble of her exaltations. Nora and four of her six children (the twins, the eldest daughter, and a boy no older than eight) attended service weekly. "It is challenging," the eldest tells me. "But it is a blessing to have a place like this open twenty-four-seven. You don't find that anywhere else." I am thinking of the hundreds if not thousands of parallel organizations offering the same model but say nothing and nod.

It is possible Nora and I are the same age. She is slight, boyish, with unstyled, short-cropped hair and the expectant, woebegone gaze of a pound puppy. The thought of pushing out, then raising, six children is inconceivable to me. During instances such as this, I see myself from above, stunned by the course of my own life, by how different it could have been.

"She's . . . so young," I say.

"She's sometimes mistaken as our sister," one twin says, before dashing off.

The eldest tells me someone will be recording Nora's prophecy. I ask if she has ever received her own.

"I have. It was more of him telling me how I was currently," she says, which sounds to me like the opposite of a prophecy. "At first, the way I took it—well the obvious way." She pauses and grins bashfully, as if I ought to know why, then adds: "He did give me another prophecy that is in progress. I could tell that—"

A commotion erupts center stage. The holy dancers have congregated around Felicity, Faith's daughter. Felicity had been the subject of much talk throughout the revival, per her miracle-receiving potential. Pastor Kim had, on several occasions, encouraged her to rise from her wheelchair and walk, if the Holy Spirit inspired her. It is difficult to imagine. Felicity's legs, nestled atop a pillow, are without musculature, almost ornamental.

According to the Visakhapatnam, India, mission report video we screened earlier that evening, a woman had risen from her wheelchair due to Pastor Kim's ansukido. Footage cut to a sari-clad auntie side-sauntering down a parted sea of hands. Another miracle: Pastor Kim prayed over an elderly blind man whose milky irises, at the time of filming, glared blankly somewhere off-camera. We learned through a slow-pan across a printed letter update that, post-revival, the blind man's vision had been restored. This was the power of prayer.

Now it is Felicity's turn. She is encircled by her own chorus of angels. Holy dancers flutter their hands over her head, her wheelchair, her legs (which remain motionless). I wonder about Faith and Felicity outside the church, what they do, whether they feel the need to fulfill the mandate of their names. My middle name, Hope, I have come to consider an irony. It has been a very long time since anyone has described me as hopeful.

At this point I expect Nora's eldest to abide by natural social cues, peel away, and attend to other matters. Yet she continues: "Can you tell me your first impression of the revival so far?"

"It's really, um . . ." I search for neutral descriptors but settle on "overwhelming."

"Ah, I understand," she says with a sagely air. "How are you taking it in?" she asks. "Slowly or . . . ?"

"Yes," I dodge. Though I am not looking in her direction, I can feel her unbroken stare. The questions do not abate: What's your last name, Jennifer? Do you have siblings, Jennifer? Do you go to school? Jennifer, did you graduate? From where? What did you major in? Where are you from, Jennifer?

"Wow! So many questions!" I blurt, startled by my own obvious exasperation.

"You don't have to share," she says, unruffled. "I just want to get to know you."

We creep up the line, four to go.

As a means to distract from any suspicion, I begin my own informal interrogation. Her tone is eerily sedate as she answers. Her family grew up in a different church, the Christian and Missionary Alliance. ("CMA?" she says, as if I ought to know. "They're a denomination. Just like Presbyterian or Lutheran, but we're focused on missions.") She is nineteen, homeschooled, her family Hmong. So is the group from Minnesota I sat behind during service, the woman who brought seven of her thirteen adult children.

Nora's eldest is surprised I've heard of the Hmong. "How so?" she asks, head cocked. "When I hear people say they know, I want to know how they know. Because most of the time I have to explain."

"I mean I know *of* the Hmong," I say. As in, I'd Googled "Hmong in America" the previous night. As in, I understand they are an ethnic group that resides in remote villages throughout Southeast Asia and China—a sprawling diaspora, built upon a history of immigration; and without a land or country of their own, perhaps it is not a coincidence several Hmong Americans are drawn to The Lord's Church and the Atlanta revival, because of what a spiritual home can provide: a salve, wherever in the world they find themselves, when strangers they meet along the way have no concept of their people's very existence.

"Well," I add, "I guess I just know the basics." Flimsy assertions at best.

The MIDI track changes to another inappropriately chipper tune when I realize I have reached the front of the line. "You need a partner," Nora's eldest tells me.

A white dad in a Hawaiian shirt is also standing uncoupled. I introduce myself, seeing as how we're about to embark on this oddly intimate milestone together. "What's your name?"

"Daniel?" he says, warily.

Daniel and I watch as an avian woman with a tuft of white hair teeters before Pastor Kim. Her body is signaling an impending descent. Slowly, in an anticipatory way, she timbers backward, and Kim instructs in English: "Catch it catch it catch it!" Faith is there to receive her and lays the woman down tenderly, as if putting a baby to bed.

Daniel and I step forward, assuming the acceptance pose.

"*Put your hands a little closer together,*" Kim tells me in Korean. And I close my eyes, really close them, so no light can seep in, the way I once did as a child kneeling at my trundle bed, waiting for a sign. It is not unlike the way I'd learned to seek a different kind of rapture after shifts at the biergarten, blacking out in bars. Or how I'd find myself on someone else's mattress, writhing below the weight of a stranger, our staged movements, the pillaging of my body, the empty devouring. How my longing had left me still, always, bereft of answers.

Kim's voice is silken. Between slithering sounds, he looms in and out of English, chanting like a medicine man. My body is a bop bag; I teeter toes to heels. A tickle slinks down my cheek, because I have begun to cry. My knees buckle. "*You can fall*," I think he says in Korean. A thawing sensation flushes my body, as if I've just entered a warm room after shivering for hours outside in the cold. My hands drop. I stumble. Faith is there to catch me.

"Hallelujah?" Kim asks. I blink, wordless. Then, with finality, he says in Korean, "*Okay, we're done.*"

Outside, the crickets are chirping a tinny song. I spot a cat's eyes aglow; it disappears, reappears, skulking beneath a street lamp. When I lie in a friend's spare bedroom in an hour's time, I try to lasso my thoughts. There are sensible explanations for why I nearly fainted: the body's natural reactions to sensory deprivation, hunger, thirst; the Guantanamo-esque music torture of those too-chipper songs; resistance to the inevitable futile.

The next morning, I call my mother and tell her about the revival. A part of her will resolutely pray for the day I might return to God. Today is not that day.

I don't talk about the profound sense of emptiness I felt in the windowless church, or how being there only seemed to prove the irrevocable loss of my own faith. I ask her about fire. She shares a story I have never heard. In the '80s, she went to see a traveling preacher woman in Concord, California, who captivated the congregation with a tale of mythical proportions. "She was very highly educated," my mother notes. Maybe in another life, the woman could have been a doctor or a scholar.

When she gave birth to her first child, something was not quite right. A congenital limb condition, "no hands . . . something like that," my mother recalls—in Old World Korea, a sign of inescapable misfortune. Soon her second and third children were born like the first, and each entered the world—as the woman saw it—un-whole. "So that's when she said, 'This must be something bigger than my life.'" My mother may as well have been speaking about herself. I take this to mean the preacher believed there must be purpose to her pain.

After a rousing testimony, she led the congregation in prayer and said, "If Holy Spirit is coming, and if you feel something, don't resist. Take it."

Though the preacher had not called it fire, this is what my mother felt overcome her body: a lit match at her breastbone, no burning or fever but a soft warmth at her sternum, like an oil lamp chimney cupping a steady flame. The moment did not last long. The visiting heat left as it had come. "And just like that, it was gone."

VII.

WHEN THE WEATHER TURNED in Columbus, I kept the gas fireplace lit day and night in my bunker-like bedroom. In its flames I did not see God, but I did appreciate the suggestion of life in its improvised movements.

By then I had managed to attain some of my patron saint's prodigiousness, though not in the form of writing. I spent that last spell in the McCullers house swigging red wine while sob-singing to Fleetwood Mac's *Tusk* by the fire. Sometimes this led to a midnight binge of oven-baked curly fries and mint chip ice cream I promptly exorcized from my body by plunging the blunt end of a chopstick down my throat. If any ghosts lived there with me, I hoped they'd take pity. I was haunted enough already.

Posing as a spiritually lost person I believed to be parallel to my true identity had taken its toll. The work had rendered me a kind of specter, caught between whoever I actually was and my guileless simulacrum. It would have been easier being the latter, a believer, because when you lean on a higher power, there are always answers, absolutes. When I returned from the healing prayer circle and eight-hour revivals, I lay awake in bed, undone. What was I doing? Where was I going? When I got there, would I still be alone?

I needed to leave the house, partake in something uncomplicated and recalibrating. An acquaintance suggested I visit a Korean restaurant in Columbus called Golden Chopsticks. I'd received the recommendation already from several enthusiastic local Caucasians. In each instance I smiled politely while filing their referrals into the recycling bin of my mind. Nothing personal, but their expertise in the matter seemed questionable; anyway, would a Korean name their establishment something as debased as Golden Chopsticks?

Yes. They had. I found the no-frills restaurant in the southeastern part of town, beside a Dollar General whose ransacked shelves resembled a Soviet-era grocery store. To my surprise, Golden Chopsticks belonged to a handful of Korean small businesses in town. Though the population, at half a percent, may seem anemic compared to Duluth, evidence of a Korean presence in Columbus goes as far back as the 1950s. A short bulletin published in the *New York Times* on Sunday, June 7, 1953 (fifty days prior to the official "conclusion" of the Korean War), announced the approximately 150 South Korean Army officers training at Columbus-based Fort Benning would be required to return home.

By 1980, the Korean population in Columbus spiked as immigrants began to settle in pockets throughout the city. And where there are Koreans, there are churches. Five miles north of Golden Chopsticks, past a palm reader and Night Moves Lingerie, in a prefabricated metal office building plunked onto a faded plot of asphalt, a version of myself would enter a Korean Full Gospel church.

The first time I drove there, my foot pressed the gas pedal rather than the brake, and I found myself back on the highway. The dilapidated exterior reminded me of our family's old El Monte church, and I wasn't ready.

I'd passed through on the eve of a hurricane. "Irmageddon," as some called her, had already ravaged the Caribbean, her wind field cycloning and expanding to more than 220 miles in diameter, blitzing coastal and central Florida, bound for her final bow in Georgia. The basement studio may flood, the program director warned me. Not in the traditional sense, but a kind of groundswell, seeping up from beneath the carpets.

I thought of the Book of Revelation, when John the Apostle receives a series of prophecies signaling the end times, and thereafter a new beginning:

"From the throne came flashes of lightning, rumblings and peals of thunder."

"And the voice I had first heard speaking to me like a trumpet said, 'Come up here, and I will show you what must take place after this.'"

No job awaited me back in New York. I'd blown through my residency money. Insurance adjusters had recently inspected my Brooklyn apartment for inevitable sale. Plus, I'd gained ten pounds. *What must take place after this?*

Come December, I'd have to pack up my memory teas, cheap crystals, a Ziploc of yogi wisdoms, and the H Mart CDs with no device at home on which to play them. I would not know any more about my uncle than when I'd arrived. Nor would I leave Georgia with A Grand Unifying Theory on Korean Heresies in the American South.

But, in a roundabout way, I would wander back to what Dr. Tark had told me at the start of my project: "This will be a very meaningful search for you." I had entered each industrial lot and office-sanctuary expecting to uncover a phenomenon, only to confront an ordinary truth—the very essence of what my uncle, Nora, Chung Kyung-jae, or my mother had been seeking in these spaces. They wanted to relinquish themselves to a greater power, to vanish into something infinite and whole. The exhilaration of sharing an intensified emotional event, in sociological terms, is called collective effervescence. It's why villagers in San Pedro Manrique gather to watch firewalkers tread across molten coals every summer solstice in Spain or why Phish-heads caravan for months following their favorite band. But the communion of ritual is not exclusive to thrill or joy. Collective pain also elicits these moments of solidarity and inexplicable connection, which can soothe one of our most primordial needs: to belong.

The word "heresy," Dr. Tark says, derives from the Greek "hairesis," meaning "choice" or "thing chosen." Transcendence is a pursuit some spend their entire lives chasing—a yearning that makes us uniquely human. We want purpose, and meaning, and possibility. Perhaps then we are drawn together out of a desire to be a "thing chosen," so we might arrive, if only for a little while, to an anchored place, when we are not alone but wherever it is we belong. It must be a relief, for those who give their lives over to a higher power, to trust that a better future awaits them. To surrender and simply believe.

. . .

BEORE LEAVING GEORGIA, I surrender to a prayer.

At the Full Gospel church in Columbus, I sit in the parking lot and monitor an abandoned jungle gym; how a whorl of fallen orange leaves gather at the foot of a swing set, the empty seat propelling itself to and fro, its rusted chains chittering in the wind.

Then voices. A chorus. Sunday service. And as it was when I was a child: a room, a piano, a pulpit, blond wood pews, a polyester-robed choir, fingers flicking onionskin pages printed in the geometric script of my parents' language. An avuncular Korean pastor delivers his message with impassioned, melodic import as familiar interjections burst in his pauses ("Hallelujah! Ahhhhhhmen!"). A purple velvet offering basket stitched with a golden cross bobs through the aisles, which is when their eyes scan the room to behold me, and I behold them—a congregation of nearly all Korean women.

Something's not quite right. During announcements I give them my real, full name, immediately regretting it. Before I can sneak out to my car and jet past the palm reader and pawn shops and Waffle House and Goo Goo Car Wash, tires squealing back onto the interstate, back to the haunted museum, I am instead led by the elbows to lunch.

They seat me beside the pastor so I cannot leave. I bow politely and stare into my radish broth, and do not eat as they encourage but prod a spongey cube of tofu with a spoon until scurrying into the bathroom to jot notes behind a stall door.

When I exit, a woman with tattooed eyebrows, which renders her permanently startled, is waiting for me. She is their best English speaker and asks, "Can you stay little longer?"

Now I am ushered again by the elbows, out the side door, back into the main sanctuary, onto a pew. She purrs my American name with softened r's, the way my grandmother says it. The way all these women from the old country say it. I wonder if this is how it started with my uncle, with smiles, an invitation.

And suddenly I am triangulated: a gifted woman (a traveling preacher) to the right of me, the tattooed eyebrow lady to my left, the pastor standing before me, his sky-blue tie swaying by my nose. It is then I notice the gifted woman has only one finger on her left hand, a wide digit with a trim nail, which strokes my palm dexterously. She speaks in Korean, every other word lost, then partially recovered, in broken translation.

"*How many years do you have?*" the gifted woman asks.

"Thirty," I lie.

"*But your face,*" she says, disappointed, "*it's so young . . .*"

The tattooed lady has begun to cry.

"*What do you want, in life?*" the gifted woman asks.

"I don't know," I say. And after an earnest pause: "To be a teacher?"

Her agile digit is pressing the top of my hand now, pincering my fingers against her palm with surprising strength.

"*Did you ever play the piano?*" she asks.

"Yes," I say. Because I did, decades ago, when I was very young, and pure, swaddled in a rapturous, otherworldly content—the content of being saved. I was the kind of person then who wept in these spaces because of joy. I wonder if the gift this woman possesses might allow her to see that version of me from so long ago. Or can she sense the person I have yet to become?

The tattooed lady is rocking forward and back now. Her hands, cool and wrinkled, pin one side of me to the pew. She and the pastor are chanting, "Chooyoh, Heavenly Father," as the gifted woman shuts her eyes and releases a bolt of mystic vernacular. Her head is nodding, her brow is a crinkled line. A rictus stretches across her face: the transmission has been received.

It is time, to receive my prophecy.

Palmetto State Blues

Date: December 6, 2017, 3:39pm

Email Subject: 2+Bedrooms,+1+bathroom,
+living+room+with+fireplace,+large+kitchen

To: rvsmj-6350766100@hous.craigslist.org

Hello
Is this available? Chris

Date: December 6, 2017, 4:12pm

Subject: Re: 2+Bedrooms,+1+bathroom,
+living+room+with+fireplace,+large+kitchen

To: rvsmj-6350766100@hous.craigslist.org

Hello
Is this still available?
Plz let me know.

Date: December 8, 2017, 4:06pm

Subject: High+Speed+Internet+Access,
+Semi-Private+Entry,+Extra+Storage

To: vrmzc-6416444507@hous.craigslist.org

Hi
Is this 2 brm unit available?

Date: December 13, 2017, 12:21pm

Subject: ++Located+in+a+quiet+
neighborhood,+this+3+bedroom,+1.5+bathroom++

To: 4xg96-6409388307@hous.craigslist.org

Is this available
Chris

Date: December 13, 2017, 12:33pm

Subject: 1208+East+Muller+Avenue.

To: vrjcv-6392488080@hous.craigslist.org

Is this available?
Desperate Chris

COLUMBIA RENTAL
1,160 sq. ft.: 3BR, 1BA

From Coldwell-Banker:

Gorgeous remodeled stone bungalow in Forest
Acres . . . New landscaping, driveway, and front porch
lead into a large living room that opens into the dining
room. Gleaming hardwoods throughout the entire house.
Every inch of this home has been professionally painted
with designer colors. Kitchen features new solid surface
countertops, tiled backsplash, and updated cabinets. Three
large bedrooms with tons of closet space. Full bathroom
with reglazed bathtub. . . . This is a rare find!

My Sixty-Five-Year-Old Roommate

WHENEVER UMMA MOVED, she announced her latest change of address without much, if any, advance notice. Since Alaska, she'd gallivanted through seven different homes across four more states, with no foreseeable end to her newly adopted itinerance in sight. Once she settled into the new place, I was the first to visit. Though the structural particulars changed, to me it appeared as if her many relocations had been occasioned through the magic of transposition; each house contained the same select objects: the porcelain stash box from Shanghai, a tiny toucan painted atop a white feather from Costa Rica, license plates from the trail of states she'd left in her wake.

Then in December 2017, she accepted a job in Columbia, South Carolina, and asked me to help with the move.

I'd recently returned to Brooklyn after my fellowship in Georgia. I couldn't scrape together bar work and had drained my coffers chasing story leads. I'd been throwing permutations at the wall, hoping some iteration of my manuscript might stick. No job, no plan, no book. An answer to my problems had begun to brew, gathering low, gray, and ragged like a fractus cloud. I distracted myself by flying down to Florida, to help Umma and witness her latest exodus in real time. Together we'd caravan north for eight hours in one shot.

I did not expect her haphazard packing style: garbage bags filled with linens and sweaters, the rest of her clothes pulled straight from the closet—hangers and all—laid in stacks in her car's backseat. After loading up, I watched Umma's tiny frame fold into the U-Haul, her doll-like hand waving out to me from the driver's-side window. I locked the doors of her car, turned on the engine, and wept. There had been no magic. She'd unceremoniously uprooted herself so many times, packing and unpacking and repacking her life, as if the next place might hold an answer to whatever she seemed to be seeking.

That night we shared a bed at a Best Western Plus off Columbia's Two Notch Road. My mother had grown accustomed to falling asleep to true crime YouTube videos. She snored as the voiceover—a coroner's report detailing Jane Doe's freshly unearthed remains—blared from a miniature screen between our pillows. The next morning, we drove past a Lizard's Thicket ("Country Cookin Makes Ya Good Lookin"), Maurice's Piggie Park, and a Bojangles. The first house we toured, Umma signed a lease on the spot.

. . .

WHAT DID I OWN worth schlepping out of state? Returning to Brooklyn thrust whatever I'd left behind into the discerning flare of daylight. In my hedonistic twenties, I did not think twice splurging on twenty-dollar martinis at Bemelmans Bar in the Carlyle Hotel or tasting menus at buzzy restaurants with coveted reservations and soigné plate swipes or purchases of alpine cheeses and zingy cured meats from the larder off Flatbush Ave—only to come home to rickety Ikea furniture and jangly toilet handles and broken tub tile or moldy caulking and gunked-up cabinets covered in a film of kitchen grease and dust. I'd become blind to the deteriorating nature of my interior surroundings because of access to what lay just beyond my front door. I'd enjoyed bobbing in this chasm between luxury and filth, or, as the English-Irish painter Francis Bacon once put it, a life of gilded squalor.

Georgia had knocked me sideways and from that vantage I'd gained a new view. Surveying the detritus of my life was not unlike one writer's response in the *Los Angeles Times* upon viewing a retrospective of Bacon's paintings in 1989: To witness such an accretion was "to shudder with amazement and disgust." Perhaps even the spirited spark I'd arrived with at seventeen was now coated in an indelible grime, the kind that accumulates over years and years no deep cleaning could ever properly scale. In other words, I had become a cynic.

Living in New York can inure you. One minute you're on the subway when two complete strangers start singing the Chi-Lites 1971 hit "Have You Seen Her," amusing the whole car with an unexpected, if wholesome, interlude. The next minute you're avoiding eye contact with the unwell panhandler shuffling through traffic on Fulton Street, because he has been shuffling through traffic on Fulton Street for a decade straight and you wonder if ignoring someone's humanity has made you a bad person or if this is what is required of you, to live in such a place.

Are there also random acts of kindness and solidarity transpiring every day? Yes. But jouncing between these vicissitudes I worried had altered my grip on reality. Living in a certain Brooklyn microcosm required such internal negotiations regularly. I'm thinking about those of us who complained about neighborhoods changing, when moneyed fashion types then Gramercy bros started buying brownstones in Bed Stuy, or when acquaintances said, without irony, "I moved to Prospect Lefferts Gardens before all of *that*," as if we did not mutually enjoy the convenience of craft cocktails while listening to Biggie, or the nitro cold brew at the overpriced coffee shop, as if we hadn't outpriced Black and brown families with our versions of affordable rent, as if we weren't the reasons why the "changing" had initiated to begin with. It was the well-meaning gentrifiers' ouroboros. Was it worse when the person knew they were part of the problem or when they didn't?

Something else had begun to stir, storm-like, in my social circles. A noticeable shift happens when you enter your thirties. People you think will be in your life forever start families, leave the city, or simply fade into the periphery. It's a natural progression, neither good nor bad though quite startling still, to confront a fresh cycle of growing pains as a grown-ass adult. Departures had already commenced within my friend group. My own priorities had changed too. I wasn't fancy feasting or carousing around town as I had in my youth. I just wanted to work a job and finish my book.

In a 2015 interview, singer and author Patti Smith admitted New York was no longer the haven it once had been for artists and dreamers. "It doesn't welcome people that have very little, that just want to get a little job and have a little practice place to play with their band," she said. "But it's still a wonderful city, a great city, it's just, I guess, if you're scrappy you have to find a new way to get around in it."

To be scrappy in your twenties is one thing, but what about forty? Fifty? Sixty? Not everyone finds such gambles daunting; they'd happily sacrifice ease in favor of staying put in the city (New York or nowhere, as some say). They'd fight evictions tooth and nail, hustling and scrambling, never quite sure if next year or the next they'd financially be able to keep making art. I didn't have a partner with a high-paying job, nor did I come from generational wealth, so unless I stumbled upon a serious payday, it was only a matter of time.

I may have already reached my limit. I'd bartended a private party in the new year, which seemed like a straightforward cash deal: serve a multicourse dinner and drinks to well-heeled PR girlies in a Bushwick factory-turned-restaurant for a clean four-hour shift, then call it a night. But one of the drunkest guests took my coat home, leaving her thin sweeper sweater behind. Mistakes happen, sure. However, my house keys were stowed in the coat's pocket, and my roommate was out of town, and it was 3 A.M., below freezing. I curled up on a banquette, underneath the unlit Edison bulbs, watching my breath evanesce in the dark. The next afternoon, I'd wait at a friend's apartment for the culprit to return my coat. After half-hearted, hungover platitudes, she asked me if I'd squash things over drunk brunch. Scrappiness obliterated, I declined and headed home. I was already toast.

My mother had been the one to suggest I move in. No rent, no bills, free food—the choice was simple. Also, I had no other choices. And yet I found myself stalling.

"Did u call ur landlord," she texted.

"No. Scared to," I said. Shyster had been siphoning my electric, sky-rocketing the bill to a thousand bucks a month.

"Find out so u can move on. Come here," Umma wrote. "We r join by the hip so to speak."

"I'm not looking forward to driving long distance!" I said, avoidantly.

She sent the next notes in succession:

"That's only small part.

Lov u.

We r so much alike it is scary."

                            * * *

WITH THE PROSPECT of my own relocation looming, I did the least sen-sical thing one could do: I embarked on a research trip. I know, I know. But I'd been sitting on a small grant I'd received from a Korean arts foundation based in New York. I was supposed to use the award money to facilitate publishing a story about a contemporary Korean artist. The problem was . . . I knew nothing about Korean artists. I'd skirted that fact in my application; I hadn't proposed a specific project, either, just how I planned on writing about art from "a cultural standpoint." As the inaugural winner, I'd attended an awards ceremony the previous fall, been photographed in two Korean language newspapers (in articles I could not read), and met the benefactor of the grant in-person—the wid-ower of a Korean art critic. The elderly white man did not appear inter-ested in art himself. During our meeting, he looked distraught, as if he'd awoken in a different country. A glimmer of recognition sparkled every now and then, at the mention of his wife. Perhaps he didn't have to care about art if supporting what she loved brought the memory of her nearer.

Months passed. The foundation had been sending emails, checking in on my progress. A scene kept reappearing in my mind of the widower, alone at his dining table still set for two, the Korean newspaper clippings in his hand. "Bamboozled again," he mumbled, head shaking.

So in February 2018, I panic-booked back-to-back flights abroad to report on two promising shows. The first, "The Real DMZ: Artistic Encounters Through Korea's Demilitarized Zone," featured works of embroidery, installations, video, and photography. The project pried open an imagined dialogue between South Korean artists and an otherwise inaccessible place. The exhibition was, interestingly enough, located in Nottingham, England. The topic of Korean reunification had been dominating international headlines, more trenchant than ever with the 2018 Winter Olympics hosted in the South Korean city of Pyeongchang. North Korean leader Kim Jong-un had invited President Moon Jae-in to Pyongyang for a peace summit and later gifted Moon a pair of Pungsan (a North Korean dog resembling the Jindo). A unified Korea would even compete together in women's hockey. DMZ art coverage seemed like a decent hook to fulfill the writing grant parameters. But there were considerable hurdles.

I was, as one friend put it, a non-speaking Korean. Meaning when I was a kid, my parents had spoken to me in Korean, I'd understood some of it, and I'd responded in Konglish. This was fine for our rudimentary talk but was stripped of nuance. I have always identified as Korean, but being Korean American is nowhere near the same as being Korean-Korean. Was I supposed to write about a Korean-Korean's art? And what business did I have doing that?

I ought to have cleared this part up with the foundation. Instead I changed course midstream and tacked on a second trip, on the coattails of Nottingham. Via Helsinki, I'd head to Seoul, visit my grandparents, and catch a second show at Kukje—a contemporary art gallery in the historic neighborhood of Samcheong-dong. The Korean American artist Byron Kim was exhibiting several paintings there and would be in attendance.

It was odd to realize I'd never met a Korean American artist as an adult. In high school, I hadn't encountered Korean American literature, let alone Korean American art. I did know one guy ten years older than me; our families attended church together, and we'd occasionally cross paths during Sunday post-service lunch. He was an oil painter who lived in Long Beach, and while he had a playful sense of humor, there seemed to be an insuppressible sorrow lurking beneath the jokes. I eventually interviewed him for a class project, a day-in-the-life of an actual working artist. I didn't ask any practical questions, like how he made ends meet or what kept him in the game, because I was seventeen and just psyched to go to Long Beach. I accidentally filmed the interview in night-vision mode. All I recall of the footage now is how the army-green hues revealed something only implied in daylight, his vacant black pupils casting a refulgent, doleful glow.

In 2018, I couldn't find his work online. Was he still painting? I imagine Gen-Xers like him experienced innumerable challenges, coming of age during the Model Minority archetype's heyday. Typically, the goal for children of immigrants is to pursue a steady career path. Stability in service to your family, because they sacrificed their happiness for our ungrateful asses, et cetera. Safe money-making professions are preferable since failure isn't really an option. Creative undertakings require perpetual failures; they're compulsory to the process. Many dreams have shriveled while facing such uncertainties.

As far as first-gen kids go, I'm lucky. At no point did my mother actively deter me from pursuing a life in the arts (that would have required her to actually pay attention to what I was doing). Umma could be an ice-cold bitch but a Tiger Mom she was not. I think in another life she might have pursued an artistic path rather than the sensible, linear mobility of nursing. I asked her once what she would have done, if she'd had her druthers. Interior design or cartography, she told me. In another instance, I asked her if she had known any artists when she was growing up. "No," she replied. "I liked a few writers, but they all died young."

I suppose that was one way of stopping. But what made anyone else keep going?

There's a phrase Koreans chant during competitive games or when facing arduous tasks. 화이팅 is a phoneticized spelling of the English word "fighting," employed as an interjection: "hwai-ting!" or "pai-ting!" Sometimes instructors say it before an exam. People shout it during the World Cup. It's more patriotic than "C'mon!" or "Let's go!" and is meant to rally one's inner drive. Perhaps no better catch phrase encapsulates the Korean spirit. Hwaiting does not indicate probable victory; one is called into action merely to put up a worthy fight. I wondered about the artists who'd come before me, like Byron Kim, and whether they felt a call in their own work to "hwait."

In the span of a week, I went to Nottingham, then Kukje, met Kim, and returned to the States, eager to pursue a new inquiry based on Kim's paintings. But I could no longer avoid the shitstorm awaiting me in Brooklyn.

The city has a way of kicking you to the curb, and sometimes that exactness is so blunt, it might as well be lit up on a goddamn marquee. My roommate decided to move in with her boyfriend, so I had three weeks to either scramble for her replacement or scramble for a new apartment. I didn't want to scramble anymore. I could stay put, but for how long? Buyers had been showing up unannounced at my apartment, ejection imminent. I also got hit by a livery cab while riding my bike, right outside my front door. When my cat got diagnosed with a terminal heart disease, it was as if he'd personally sent me the indisputable message: *Lady, it's a wrap.*

My mother once told me, "Sometimes you gotta know when to hold 'em, when to fold 'em, and when to walk away." I didn't know she was essentially quoting Kenny Rogers, but both of them were right. I was thirty-three. The hustle had lost its luster. I'd spent half my life in the city. Now it was time to leave.

And so I sold most of my belongings, crammed whatever else fit into a minivan rental, and drove away from the only place I'd ever truly called home. It was raining. Just a sprinkle at first on the Verrazano. My sick cat sat statue-still as we crossed into Jersey, sheets of torrential downpour slapping the windshield, Manhattan blurring in the distance. After white-knuckling the wheel for thirteen hours straight, I pulled into an overgrown lawn. My sixty-five-year-old roommate greeted me. The diaphanous trim of her nightie fluttered like the gown of a ghost. Bullfrogs heaved from a nearby pond. "Welcome to South Carolina!" my mother chirped. "Hee-ha! You're home."

. . .

To LIVE WITH A PARENT, as an adult, is a strange gift. At a young age I'd surmised my mother's matter-of-fact, often affectionless demeanor had concealed her deepest aspirations—a mode she'd adopted in order to hunker down in a dreary marriage, to feed and care for her family. The late-in-life vagabond spirit she'd come to embrace confirmed my assumptions but made her newly inscrutable. Who was she now?

Over dinner, she didn't care for small talk, swallowed her kimchi and rice hastily, which summoned at meal completion a vociferous, lip-curling belch. She refused to shut the door while using the bathroom, so on my way to the kitchen I'd witness her zigzagged body enthroned, straining over various concerns. Which is to say in some ways, she hadn't changed much.

Neither of us had fully entertained the logistics of our cohabitation. My stay, I'd assumed, would be temporary. I'd get back on my feet in a month or two. It was only a matter of time until Umma uprooted herself again, and I had no intention of joining that circus. Job offers took my mother to random towns about an hour away from desirable cities of interest. Between her open-heart-surgery days in the '90s and my New York years in the aughts, she'd become a director for surgical services. Her skill set attracted offers from headhunters across the country. She managed people and operating rooms (I think). Whatever the case I could tell she wasn't scrubbing in as much, by looking at her hands. They felt like scouring pads when I was a kid, dried and scratchy from brushing down, elbows to fingertips, before surgery. The skin on her hands was now smooth. She had softened.

Of all places, I never imagined Umma would end up in South Carolina—"a tiny state that is half-dipped in the sea," poet Nikky Finney once wrote. Where were we living exactly? Online searches cull the pros (warm weather, relative proximity to the beach, Southern charm) and cons (hurricanes, income disparity, and bugs—lots of 'em). There are persistent questions about alligators: Are they a problem locally? (Sort of.) And what do you do if one chases you? (Run away in a straight line.) Perhaps it shares in common with Georgia the palpable sense of retrograde tensions. Beneath the quaint aesthetics, there is an abiding desire, for some, to bask in "the good ole days" despite what appetency for the past inherently suggests.

As recently as 2015, a Confederate flag flew at the South Carolina State House steps. That year, Dylann Roof murdered nine African American people during a Bible study at Emanuel African Methodist Episcopal Church in Charleston. Only then did legislators pursue the flag's official removal. The decision entailed thirteen hours of contentious debate. Roof was born and raised in Columbia. He chose to drive the 120 miles east to Emanuel AME because of its reputation as a long-standing institution within the Black community.

Charleston is located in the state's Lowcountry, a coastal region abutted by romantic marshlands, sandy beaches, and winding waterways. It is considered a gastronomic epicenter in the Southeast, where its younger populations enjoy their sustainably caught amberjack crudo or local oysters by the dozen with funky natural wine. Once the site of lucrative indigo and rice crop industries during the Antebellum period, about twenty-four of approximately 400 plantations remain today as historic landmarks and places throughout the county. Many have been thoughtfully preserved or restored for educational purposes. Several serve as wedding or gala venues for those who cannot grasp the macabre nature of reveling on historical sites of torment. South Carolina is abundant in such disparities.

Unlike Charleston, Columbia's identity is less distinct. It is the state's capital, located within a region unenticingly called the Midlands. There is a greenway, a riverwalk, a national park, a farmer's market, a zoo, and a Trader Joe's. While there are two HBCUs in town, Columbia's student community is often associated with the University of South Carolina— confusingly referred to as USC (with admirable impudence, as if the more renowned college on the West Coast with the same acronym simply does not exist). Other-USC is home to the Fighting Gamecocks, a middling Eastern Division football team with an enthusiastic fanbase. Due to the presence of Fort Jackson military base, there are Koreans in Columbia too—thus a modicum of serviceable Korean restaurants, markets, churches. And from time to time, gators have cropped up anywhere between the canal and the Congaree River.

Perhaps what characterizes Columbia best is its nickname; because it is often shortened to Cola, which is a kind of soda, it is known as Soda City. This arbitrary je ne sais quoi embodies a greater ambiance of ambiguity, as if Columbia might very well be a town pulled from a CAPTCHA *Are you a robot?* image test—crosswalks and traffic lights and buses from Anywhere, USA.

There is an allure to this imprecise, if malleable, status. In the 2022 Insider's Guide to Columbia, published by the tourism board, several cultural ambassadors describe their town as a "digestible city," where someone can "grow with it and in it." I was struck by the sincerity of one blurb, encapsulating the antithesis of cynicism: "When someone from here does something great, I'm full of pride. When my city does things that make us look awful . . . I feel regret. I'm critical of my town because I love it, and I dedicate my time to make it better." One could ostensibly contribute to shaping the character of a place still coming into its own, in turn providing a person with a sense of purpose and the desire to stick around to see through instrumental change. This was not why my mother moved to Columbia. But I did wonder what reason, if any, might convince her to stay.

. . .

MY MOTHER LIVED in Forest Acres—a park-dotted city within Columbia's metropolitan area, replete with well-groomed single-family homes. We lived on the outermost edge of the neighborhood, on a bedraggled street frequently used as the dumping grounds for abandoned furniture. Blocks away, in the rich part, one could find sprawling ranch homes or multistory Greek revivals impeccably maintained, down to the flawless white colonnades and the gas sconces that stayed lit night and day.

Our house was mortared with a mosaic of sturdy slate rock giving the facade a quirky Flintstones air. The landlord's son had been the one to leave a "Go cocks!" football sticker on the toilet—providing us with a little reminder of the world we'd entered any time we lifted the lid. A Korean Pentecostal church was located at the end of our street. It fit in because of its derelict quality (I would never see anyone come or go). Koreans didn't live in Forest Acres. According to my mother, who'd already found a Korean Presbyterian church to attend downtown, everyone else resided in the outskirts like Sandhills or across the Congaree in Lexington. They worked at Fort Jackson and owned small businesses like beauty supply shops and fusion restaurants. Or so she'd gathered. She didn't know many congregants on a personal level. Umma showed up for Sunday service, praised in the front rows, tithed, then bounced after benediction. Never once did she expect me to join her.

Umma had her life and I had mine. During the week, she woke up at 5 A.M. on the dot, drank coffee and munched on toast while the local news blasted. I didn't know what she did all day. I only saw how she looked walking out the door: like a million bucks, in chic Maxxinista head-to-toe ensembles, her glasses dependent on mood (vintage cat-eyes, transition lenses, or her designer red frames). Even though she immediately changed into scrubs at work, she made a point to project an image that garnered respect. She called out to me in singsong, "Have a super great day!" and sashayed away.

It's hard to say for certain what I got up to either in that first month home. A lot of wallowing, I suspect, which isn't so much a physical activity as it is an existential one. My cat died shortly after we'd arrived. I didn't expect to mourn Remy as much as I did. I had another, more likable cat (the Nermal to his Garfield) still alive. But oh, my pinheaded, big-bootied, feral boy. He hadn't been easy to love. Pet him too long and he'd bite you while shredding your arms with his back claws. Though neutered, overstimulation would provoke angry, hook-shaped erections and (spread-eagle) he'd sit up to bat them away, looking bug-eyed and abashed. You couldn't leave bread out, as he'd gnaw through the bag. And he often ate his own food too fast, upchucking the whole serving only to lap it back up again. But Remy, I'd realized, was the longest relationship I'd maintained as an adult. He'd terrorized many of my lovers over the last decade, all of whom eventually disappeared from our lives. Remy had lived across from Agnes on Allen and Broome, then above the deli in Brooklyn. But it was Columbia where he'd die.

In his final week, I found myself balled on the ground, professing desperate convictions I'd never before dared to utter aloud to anybody, let alone a cat. I wasn't ready for him to leave me. Or maybe it was the fact his departure marked the terminus of something bigger I could not yet face. I'd adopted Remy when I was twenty-one, irrepressibly hopeful about what lay ahead. Twelve years later, I was living with my peripatetic mother in a city I couldn't point out on a map. Not all endings are definitive. I'd left New York, yet part of me was still there, caught in limbo, haunting the trash-lined streets. But Remy had a heart condition Umma had come across in her O.R. days. We knew when it was time to say goodbye.

I held him in the sterile exam room. The vet, a perfectly nice woman, gave me the rundown about the injection. I wept and felt compelled to tell her how I'd adopted Remy from a shelter in Spanish Harlem but that he'd been born in the Bronx. Hand on doorknob, perhaps meant as consolation, she let out a mangled, "New Yowk Ci-tay?" It was like a cowboy from the Pace Picante Sauce commercials workshopping a Rosie Perez impression. And with that she left me to grieve in private.

I held Remy until he grew still. Then a man with a white ponytail took him away.

• • •

WHEN I RETURNED from the vet without Remy, my mother patted me on the back and said, "We all gotta go sometime. It's a facts of life."

She wasn't wrong. I knew by then I could turn to Umma for certain needs but not the tenderness I sometimes wanted. It was unfair to expect her to be a person she naturally wasn't or to then become incensed that she couldn't be the person I wished she could be. But I found myself incapable of resisting the pull of regression; it was easier slipping back to that younger self, confounded by her maternal shortcomings. Perhaps I confounded her as well, my prolonged dolorous state dampening the temperance of her home, my inability to swiftly move forward a matter of inefficiency.

It wasn't as if she lacked the capacity to grieve. Molder had passed two years earlier in Florida. When the Jindo was first diagnosed with lymphoma, Laurie and I flew down to say goodbye. The day after we left, Molder's health drastically declined, as if she'd held on, hobbling room to room while we slept, to watch us one last time.

Later, Umma sent a set of distressing photos she'd taken at the vet, including a selfie of her face contorted mid-wail, her free arm clutching Molder's splayed and lifeless body. At the time I didn't know what would drive a person to memorialize, then share, such a morbid scene. But doing so may have been her only way of showing us the extremity of her pain. It was like Umma: curt but effective. These days the loss of Molder resurfaces after too much wine, when my mother's mind wanders to the imagined place, where she allows herself to hold vigil a brief but candid moment of ache or desire. Her mind drifts and the world stops until she breaks her own trance to return to us undisturbed by the glut of sorrow.

Unlike Umma, I couldn't snap to my senses as dexterously. Was I crying over a cat? Not really. The event concretized a couple concerns I'd been holding abstract. Up until moving in with my mother, I'd fumbled from one opportunity to the next, presuming certain personal choices would remain continuously available to me and thus addressable in the future, when the variables (money, career, housing) stabilized. I could find a partner eventually, have a child eventually, or at least decide whether I wanted to pursue those conventions.

At a writing conference the year prior in 2017, women in my cohort were on the precipice of "breaking through" from emerging writer to writer-writer, as our fertile years had begun to dwindle. By the time we sold and published our books, we'd be well into our geriatric pregnancy years. Some discussed freezing their eggs, which can cost between $6,000 and $10,000 per extraction cycle (not including storage fees)—sums I could not conceive of acquiring any time soon. So I shoved the thought aside, with all my other "adult" deliberations.

It just so happens I'd already made those decisions, and without much cognizance or intention. Every possible break I actively chased had required a compromise until suddenly I was so far up a ladder, I couldn't make out the beginning or the end. Only one matter was clear: I was alone. People may mistake this as risk-taking or bravura. The truth is less thrilling; I'd been planning a few months ahead at a time, thus obscuring the ominousness of greater life choices—unaware that passivity itself is a choice. Evading important decisions does not in fact delay the passage of time. I wasn't old, but I was getting older. I could see the window of some other life sealing up and sailing off, with all my other chimerical notions. Or perhaps I deserved the outcome I'd found myself in: a version of the Maysles brothers' documentary *Grey Gardens* but Korean—Little Umma and Big Umma in the Deep South, lost in our respective illusions.

. . .

NOTHING WILL SLAP you back into reality like job searching in a mid-sized American town. Despite having earned undergraduate and graduate degrees, on paper it appeared I possessed no marketable skills. Remote positions were not common then, and while I had two essays greenlit for publication, it was evident freelance writing would not resurrect my finances. The previous ten years of work history, when examined in toto, appropriately summarized the helter-skelter nature of my pursuits. Film and television editing, writing (basically for free), artist fellowships, and bar work qualified me for nothing above the entry-level tier. Various employment websites filtered my available opportunities, each requiring additional skills: tree climber trainee for a shrub care company or on-call funeral home attendant. I was immediately prepared for two positions: bartender at an Episcopal retirement community or secret shopper.

Did I believe I deserved better? Not exactly. But I couldn't seem to reconcile the bottomlessness I found myself peering into. Did a decade and change twiddling away with writing really amount to nothing?

I did not express these frustrations to my mother. Umma had reshaped her daily habits around a lifestyle of solitude, and my mere existence in her home ruptured the equilibrium she'd created. Whenever I wanted to get my own groceries, she'd object from the couch, tipsy on her second prosecco: "There's plenty of food!" Yet the fridge looked bare, a tub of gochujang, a jar of kimchi, Walmart giardiniera, and a jug of neon Cuervo premade margarita mix blocking the bulb's light. Instead of conversation, she preferred rewatching the same episodes of her favorite woman-murderer show, *Snapped*, letting it blare in the background while decimating cartoon jelly beans on her phone. Between wine sips and nips of sliced pepperoni and pickled peppers, occasionally she paused to offer commentary ("Oh he's gonna di-eeeee!") or mockingly parrot along to local personal injury law or car dealership jingles. At dinner, she would not wait to eat together. If I timed my meal with hers and asked about her day, she'd grumble, "That's the last thing I wanna do when I get home. At work, all I do is talk."

To unmuddy my mind, I ran along the riverfront park. Before I headed out, Umma would stop me in my tracks to say, "Yeh, remember Chandra Levy." It was a warning, I guess. Levy was a young woman who disappeared while jogging in 2001; a year later her remains were discovered in Washington, D.C.'s Rock Creek Park.

I huffed along downtown Columbia's waterfront, below boas of Spanish moss draping the live oaks, past the old pump houses along the canal, perturbed by the sluggish walking patterns of local pedestrians. Everyone moved slower here, and I hadn't shed the impatient tempo of a city dweller, shuffling around desultory tourists. There were pockets of dense, forested areas off the trails but these were otherwise open, well-trod grounds, where every person paused to tip their hats or say hello. The confrontational pleasantries spooked me far more than any prospect of abduction.

Investigators had found Levy's last known location based on her final internet searches. I'd rather stay a cold case than have computer forensic experts rummage through my search history. What detectives could piece together from "bed bug symptoms"; "oil cleansing does it work"; and "thumb that looks like big toe" is anyone's guess. And aside from the job hunt, one recent revelation had inspired in me the impulse to walk into the woods and never return.

I had taken a career quiz. An article published in the *New York Times T* magazine—"Does Having a Day Job Mean Making Better Art?"—goaded my inquest.

"What is an artist supposed to be?" writer Katy Waldman asks. A fallacy one might entertain: the type "holed up in an airy turret with her materials, descending only to glissade through parties and openings," as Waldman puts it, "a product of our fetishization of genius." It's a rosy image that may have been possible in, say, the 1960s. I'd never entertained surviving solely off my musings. Nor had I equated myself to a "starving artist"—a cliché still lingering from the previous century. I wasn't opposed to employing a bit of strategy. A day job, aside from providing a steady salary, as Waldman elaborates, "might perform the same replenishing ministries as sleep or a long run" to the artistic process, like a sensible siesta spent grounded in the world of Normals, offering further inspiration once the artmaking resumes.

Seemed like a smart plan. But in New York I couldn't manage to kickstart a parallel profession. I'd toyed with copywriting, as I'd heard agencies often sought creative writers who'd capsized post-MFA. Those gigs required experience, which I couldn't manage to obtain without said experience. Composer Philip Glass was a plumber. He took house calls well into his recognizably successful years. Kafka's brotberuf, or bread job, entailed paper-pushing at an insurance company. Maybe I'd veered off with the whole writing thing and was better suited for an entirely separate vocation.

The career quiz provided sets of declarative statements. One's selections would then deduce strengths, weaknesses, and potential professions.

> I would rather be a clerical worker.
> I would rather be a carpenter.

> It's easy to laugh at one's little social errors or "faux pas."

It's hard to laugh at one's little social errors or "faux pas."

It is wise to make it known if someone is doing something that bothers you.

It is wise to remain silent if someone is doing something that bothers you.

I would read the instructions first when putting a new toy together for a child.

I would "jump in" and start putting a new toy together for a child.

I waited, gawking at the frozen progress bar. Had I broken the site out of incalculable purposelessness? After three attempts I got an answer: I was a BLUE person. BLUE people are drawn to creative occupations concerning theorization, design, reflection. Among the jobs I ought to consider: film editor, artist, writer.

• • •

BY MY SECOND MONTH job searching, I'd achieved minute but meaningful progress at dinnertime. Umma started to answer my questions, sometimes in full sentences. I even coaxed out an anecdote. She packed her lunch for work every day, but in one instance, she'd decided to dine at the cafeteria like the rest of her coworkers. Gristly chicken-fried steak. Brown green beans. Limp iceberg lettuce. She opted for rice, long-grain and loosened with butter. The server slopped a scoop onto her plate and asked if she wanted gravy. *Gravy . . . on rice*?! Outlandish. Before she could answer, a colleague behind her said: "She ain't *like* that." We cackled. She'd made an impression already.

The next night: silent treatment. Was she mad at me? No answer. Umma polished off her prosecco and tucked herself into bed before the sun went down, a voiceover detailing a corpse's dental record match mingling with the low sonorousness of her snoring.

Hours later, I realized I'd left my vibrator out on the ledge of the bathtub. It was an odd, oblong-shaped object one ex mistook as a Wi-Fi extender (when charging via USB, it radiated a router-like cerulean glow). Another ex had purchased the vibe for me. For reasons beyond even the salesperson's knowledge, the device worked up to twelve feet deep under water.

This was when I still imagined I could summon pleasure from my own mysterious depths. When I still entertained the idea of my own desire. I had likely pursued the activity out of boredom during an after-noon shower, in the same ambivalent way one responds to an invitation to an early meal out: *Sure, I could eat.*

I never left the vibrator out again. Frankly I had lost use for it in my demoralizing search for a new career. Nothing like a rejection from the Whole Foods cheese department to suck the libido right out of your gelded, useless body.

Between filling out boilerplate job applications, theoretically I could have been writing. Finally, I had the time to think about the grant project so I could place a timely piece for publication. But what I really wanted to stew on retained no timely allure at all.

Ever since Georgia, a very specific feeling had come to enshroud my spirits like a weeping veil. Despair is the best approximation I can think of to describe it. This is not torment or depression but a nimble sadness that tests and tugs at what you feel most purposeful in creating. I'd understood it as a kind of compulsion—one any artist experiences when honing, then sustaining, a craft. Despair if you don't get your ass in the chair and write. Despair when you do. Proust described it as "a long, sunken fatigue." Orwell equated the feeling to a painful affliction: "One would never undertake such a thing if one were not driven on by some demon whom one can neither resist nor understand." The despair never goes away, either, regardless of awards or accolades. One must find a way to manage it, perhaps for eternity, like learning to coexist peacefully with the anguished homunculus inextricably sprouting from one's back.

Not everyone finds the process harrowing. As prolific Japanese novelist Haruki Murakami once said, "To tell the truth, I have never found

writing painful. What's the point of writing, anyway, if you're not enjoying it?" Wow. Lucky bastard. He poses a worthwhile question though.
What *is* the point of pursuing such unpleasantness?

For the record, I do not believe in the "tortured artist" trope, which
sags with maudlin self-aggrandizing tedium. The process is not tortured
so much as torturous, pursuing a vision to ensure its actualization,
knowing only you stand in the way of its fruition, beyond the precipice
of "potential." It is a terrifying yet often invigorating impetus. Initially,
this drive produced in me no despair, only the promise of joy. I may
have even described writing as "fun," though what I felt when the words
clicked into place was more transcendent: incomparable exhilaration.
Embarking on a publishing career progressively squeezed the joy and
wonder right out of me. Near-constant rejection and infrequent compensation abraded my morale. Exhilaration returned in a pitter-patter.
I'd lost sight of the pleasure in the work entirely. I worried I might never
get it back. Surely then, what would be the point? Writing is a humbling
pursuit. It requires endurance. But for how long?

I managed to place an essay on the Nottingham show in an online
literary publication with far slimmer a readership than the foundation
had anticipated. To better fulfill the grant project, I burrowed toward a
new question: What could writers glean from visual arts practices that
could help us find a new way of seeing our own work? Specifically, I
wanted to know: How did the Korean American artists before me keep
going? When did they know it was time to move on and when it was
time to hwait?

* * *

I'VE NEVER SUCCEEDED much with traditional fine arts. I nearly failed
Intro to Art History in college. I could admire the prowess, the skill. But
wasn't I supposed to be feeling something? As others oohed and ahhed
before masterpieces, no grander "truth" appeared for me—except that
maybe I was a rube or a chump. I also tried my hand at oil painting, and
my reproduction of Goya's Manuel Osorio Manrique de Zúñiga por-

trait resembled an empty-eyed child clown. Aside from a general lack of innate talent, what I saw and what I could render did not align—a common obstacle any amateur confronts when venturing into a craft. There is a great divide between the art you admire and the art you make, and people spend entire lives devoted to narrowing the gap. This is the same in writing. Except the progress and work are physically intangible. With visual art, one could at least see and touch the thing they were in the process of creating, fortifying its realness.

As John Berger writes in his iconic book of art criticism, *Ways of Seeing*, there is an immediacy in comprehension innate to humans: "Seeing comes before words. The child looks and recognizes before it can speak." Seeing "establishes our place in the surrounding world; we explain that world with words, but words can never undo the fact that we are surrounded by it." Perhaps that's why completing a book felt so blindingly urgent; countless hours in a room alone could amount to something real, an object you could see and touch.

What I mean is that writing any story requires maintaining a level of fantasy. The work is constructed entirely in the mind, then rendered into marks on paper so readers can erect and render similar scaffolding individually, with their own imaginations. Without a reader, the creation is inert, or worse—complete nonsense. All to say, writers spend a lot of time in their heads, and that can take a toll. I periodically returned to a daymare that epitomized the absurdity of such a crisis. I'm frantically tapping away at my computer while the true product of my labor appears on the screen: endless pages filled margin-to-margin with Wingdings.

There's a good dose of delusion one must embrace when pursuing art-making long-term. The word "visionary" can describe one who possesses both foresight and imagination or it can allude to an illusory, deceptive, impossible-to-actualize ideal. Perhaps the treacherousness of breaching that void is what makes the endeavor echo with such profound melancholy. On the other side is an incomparable, soul-nourishing satisfaction, but it is you who either stands in the way or accomplishes the feat. Is this grandiose thinking? Probably. But what if you alone can see the sculpture hidden in the marble block? To prove the vision, one must chip away at the stone so the work can exist outside oneself as an object for others to behold. When I had yet to publish, writing retained a secret quality; it was a private act, devotional in its intimacy, radical in its openness to possibility. Then it became a space of expression, a communication to an unseeable audience. In my unemployable malaise, my thoughts returned to Byron Kim's Kukje exhibition—a series of works on the amateur's joy. What gets lost when the act is no longer private, for pleasure's sake?

I first stumbled upon Kim's work for obvious reasons: He is one of the most recognizable Korean American artists working today. Kim's oeuvre is said to exist somewhere between the abstract and the representational, meaning his paintings often take modernist forms (sweeping color fields) yet hold specific contextual relevance (unlike abstract expressionism's capacity for open-ended interpretation). This is best demonstrated in Kim's portrait series *Synecdoche*—the first work by any Korean American artist to be featured in the Whitney Biennial, in 1993. As far as the word "portrait" goes, these are not the standard sort; no three-quarter-turned face nor full-body pose. Kim spent an hour with each sitter to match their skin shade and painted the pigment onto a small monochrome canvas panel. Hung together in considered tilings, the panels have been excerpted in varying arrangements at the Museum of Modern Art, the Whitney, and the National Gallery; collectively they signify one of Kim's greatest fixations. As he once stated in an interview, "My work has mostly been concerned with the relationship of a part to a whole. How am I connected to others in the world, and how are we all connected to the greater whole?"

Twenty-five years after *Synecdoche* catapulted Kim to stardom, I wondered how he might be turning that question inward, with how he approached his own body of work. I was most interested in his *Sunday Paintings*. Every week since January 2001, no matter where he is in the world, Kim paints a segment of the sky on a fourteen-by-fourteen-inch canvas (small enough to fit in a carry-on suitcase). He jots contemporaneous notes onto the surface, to document the minutiae of the day: location, what he did, with whom he spoke. The project is reminiscent of On Kawara's *Today* series, or *Date Paintings*, initiated by the Japanese conceptual artist in 1966 and truncated by his death in 2014. One of these taken individually seems, at first glance, unremarkable: a month, a day, a year painted in white against a solid color, fashioned by hand with mechanical precision. If the piece could not be completed by day's end, Kawara destroyed it. He finished around 3,000 paintings in five decades. *Today*, like Kawara's other serial works, is an encounter with the marking of time, the mundanity of the everyday invigorated by how we see not one single date but the scope and entirety of one single life. A ritual and arts practice entwined.

Kim's *Sunday Paintings* differ in approach, making room for imprecision. He uses pencil or ballpoint pen for the diaristic scrawlings. Sometimes, admittedly, he completes the task on a Monday or a Thursday. The subject itself is trivial: clouds, fog, sky. Quick strokes, dapplings, a cottony swish suggesting rain. Bluest of blues some days, on others a square of overcast gray. These are odes in the spirit of the Sunday painter, an untrained hobbyist who dabbles in their spare time, for pleasure's sake, not yet bogged by despair and free of scrupulous self-critique. Cool concept, but if you're an artist at Byron Kim's level, what did it mean to paint like a novice? Was it even possible to return to such a mentality?

There is an almost imperceptible shift that occurs when one crosses the Rubicon from "amateur" to "professional." The amateur explores a craft out of curiosity. There is joy to be found, unhindered and low-stakes. There is lightness and gratification, too, in simply following each discovery as it unfolds, for what it can teach you. Maybe you present what you make to friends and loved ones or maybe you keep the progress to yourself. Maybe you get good at the thing and keep at it, finding more pleasure through the acceleration of your skills. And maybe that acceleration leads you to believe your abilities ought to be shared or acknowledged on a heightened, public level.

A "professional" pursuit of any art form, in this context, is somewhat general; not exactly achieving recognition but aspiring in that direction. It could mean wanting to publish poems, exhibit in a gallery, or enter a film into competition. Above all, it is the turning point at which one gears up, puts all of one's chips into the pot, and says, *I want to make a life from this*. It is a turning point because, to a degree, there is no going back.

Now there are stakes, rejections, and an enhanced rigor in the practice, requisite industriousness to evolve from the stakes and rejections. There are ways to engage with curiosity and play, but it is not, nor can it be, the same as "before." At least that's what a cynic would say. Maybe since starting his project in 2001, Kim had pioneered a way back to the amateur's radical openness, to ease. I'd decided to ask him in person.

At the time Kim and I lived a couple neighborhoods away from each other in Brooklyn, but I'd flown 6,863 miles to talk to him because sometimes you just say *fuck it* and follow your gut. In Kukje's austere showroom, he stood quietly as the interpreter beside him offered introductions to the flock of Korean journalists. It was a relief to see he was a non-speaking kind of Korean, like me. I don't know what an artist is meant to "look" like, but he was dressed in a sophisticated, casual manner: an untucked dress shirt, jeans, olive green blazer, sleek eyewear. Between the translation pauses, he had an air of timidity, glancing down at his feet, as if toeing an invisible pebble. With the *Sunday Paintings*, he told us he wanted to elevate the occupation of the "amateur," that the word derives from "amare"; "to love" something in a way only a novice can, to do something for fun, held a virtuousness worth memorializing. "Making art for me is not fun, generally," he added. "This project was something I could do without much pressure." His daily musings paired with a piece of the sky, these were not trivial choices. "It's this comparison between the insignificant life and . . . everything. Nothing and everything. Right next to each other."

I'd watched a video online in which Kim referenced his diptych from 2005, *Palms (Head Over Heart)*—extreme-close-up depictions of his hands. In turns the skin looks notched like concertina, tender like a cat's toe bean, or worn yellow-purple, like a healing bruise. He said he continued changing the paintings well after showing them because they no longer looked complete. Kim seemed bashful about this admission, aware of the subjectivity of doneness and the futility of that awareness, for it haunted him nonetheless. So in a Q&A lull, I asked Kim: Had the *Sunday Paintings* helped the way he treated his more "serious" work? Had he found ease?

He took a long pause before answering. "You know, that's a really interesting question that I never thought of," he said. "It's a question I'd have to think about." By then he'd already completed 707 *Sunday Paintings*.

The conversation carried on, but I was no longer listening. I was looking at one of the sky paintings, and another, and another—a turgid haze, a cloud cover slit open by pale blue parallelograms. They reminded me of what art historian Robert Rosenblum called the Abstract Sublime: work that places a viewer "on the threshold [of] shapeless infinities" until evoking a kind of transcendence. He was speaking of paintings by Mark Rothko or Barnett Newman. "These infinite glowing voids carry us beyond reason to the Sublime," wrote Rosenblum. "We can only submit to them in an act of faith and let ourselves be absorbed into their radiant depths." Such works conveyed an ineffability akin to nature's most quotidian, yet astounding, events: an expansive sunset or an eclipse—a raw, profound boundlessness. Everything and nothing.

Creating art requires acts of faith—secular faith—in the vision itself and in those who will encounter it. So I had a faith problem. In Columbia, while laser-focused on despair, I'd discounted the variable bubbling beneath all my concerns: uncertainty.

Why Am I a Bird?

A FTER NINE WEEKS IN Columbia, I decided to take a job at a strip mall restaurant, which served the anomalous fusion of Italian and Mexican cuisines. A supervisor, whom I privately referred to as Dipshit Doug was unimpressed by my thirteen years of New York bartending experience. This was a drop in the bucket compared to his tenure as managing partner at a nearby Ruth's Chris Steakhouse where, apparently, he'd honed a flair for paternalistic condescension and light misogyny. My bar manager, a twenty-five-year-old who proudly described himself as a mixologist, had devised a menu doomed to perform during peak service. I didn't want to bartend anymore, but the starting hourly rate with tips teased the promise of a livable wage. I worked ten-hour shifts hand-whittling blocks of ice, muddling ill-conceived cocktails à la minute as service tickets spat out from the printer in endless chains of bunting. We were always in the weeds. The all-male bar staff wore suspenders and sleeve garters and shouted creative variations of, "Behind!" and "Heard dat!" with such self-serious swagger there were nights that felt more like a community college production of immersive theater. Due to a Byzantine hierarchy, I'd been relegated mostly to barback duties, hauling five-gallon buckets of Kold-Draft or manually squeezing quarts of Key lime juice. My body throbbed from lugging beer crates and wine cases. I am not above such work. Physically, I could simply no longer swing it. If I was past my barkeeping prime, I wondered where else my abilities had expired.

I eventually quit the strip mall restaurant and decided I should become a bank teller. A regular day job, I thought, completely disparate from my innate interests, might provide those alleged restorative creative powers that continued to elude me. But a week before I began training, I was offered a different position at a local library branch. Essentially I'd carry out sales associate, desk clerk–type duties. Maybe being surrounded by books would help me finish writing one (ha!). The sedentary aspects of the role, along with decent benefits, clinched the deal.

Aside from the Fighting Gamecocks, boiled peanuts, and pimento cheese, Richland County—in which Columbia lies—is a place where people love the library. In 2013 residents voted to pass a $59 million bond referendum to update the public library system's facilities. A rebranding campaign came along with the overhaul. They dropped the "public" in their name and added a modern logo, perhaps to shift timeworn associations. No more *Shhh! Quiet!* Dewey Decimal, crusty keyboard–having, musty card catalog–keeping, microfiche-swooshing, unwashed gym socks–stinking stuffiness. These institutions would be different, not *public* libraries, but . . . drumroll please . . . *libraries.*

I hadn't stepped into a modern city library before moving to Columbia, and honestly, I was astounded. The main branch is a massive structure with an angular glass and concrete facade fit for an airport terminal or sports pavilion. Inside there are somewhat standard updates: ombré-painted bookshelves, curvilinear stacks, playful modular furniture, and electronic sensor self-checkouts. Among the thirteen total locations, there are also woodworking and fiber arts makerspaces, podcast and video recording studios, a teaching kitchen, a career development center, and a 3D printing machine. You can check out books, CDs, video games, and DVDs, of course, but also microscopes, Wacom tablets, a KitchenAid standup mixer, a sewing serger, live-streaming cameras, green screen backdrops, bubble machines, moving dollies, camping equipment, portable record players, pressure washers, metal detectors, and kits for bird watching, garden vegetable seed planting, and stop-motion animation.

The branch where I worked was named after the first published African American poet, Phillis Wheatley, and once served the city's Black readers during segregation. Integration began, albeit gradually and with considerable resistance, in 1963. Today remnants of that history are reflected at Wheatley's newer location, with its elderly white patrons residing in the winsome cottages of Old Shandon and the young Black families living on the other side of redlined Cherry Street's blighted divide. Wheatley reopened after a suite of renovations in the spring of 2018—an event hotly anticipated for all within a ten-mile radius. The space had been redesigned with serious snazz: ornate imported Italian tile at the entryway, reading nooks, barnwood plank paneling, a chalkboard wall, and spiffy electronics.

I would not be a librarian (you have to go to school for that). Here is what my job entailed: rotations among several stations, dictated by the weekly schedule kept in a protective sleeve and stored in a three-ring binder behind the front desk. For book drop collection, I pushed a wobbly library cart out to the curbside drop box and steered its contents on squeaky wheels back indoors, checked the items in, and sorted them onto either the internal reshelving cart or piles bound for the other branches. As a floor floater, I'd assist patrons with free services such as faxing documents and computer/internet use, or I just simply roamed through the aisles mindlessly edging book spines. If folks opted to check out their materials the old-fashioned way (with a human and not a machine), they headed to the front desk/circulation; this is also where one could inquire about fees, various titles, and recommendations. I preferred processing holds, which took place behind the wall partition, out of sight near the break room. You unloaded the materials from big plastic bins onto a library cart, then placed each item on the scanning pad, which automatically spat out a ticket with a patron's name (whoever placed the hold). You put the ticket in the item and then wheeled the cart back out to organize everything by patron name, ABC order, on the Holds shelves for pickup. Inevitably, once someone pulled their hold, the other items toppled like a house of cards. So while there were some advanced systems and approaches achieved over the years, no librarian had mastered the art of keeping the materials neatly stored. This would become perhaps the most mind-numbing part of the job: resetting a scene of perfection over and over again.

The holds were delivered twice daily in said plastic bins by a somewhat grumpy, perpetually perspiring fellow named Travis. After drop-off, Travis usually stuck around to graze on whatever cookies had been left out at the break room table, briefing us on the weekend banalities he and his wife and small children had recently pursued. I don't think he ever learned my name, and I didn't mind so long as I could silently dial into the doldrums of my new worker-bee life.

And I was new compared to my colleagues. All but two of us had been at the library for some time, collectively about thirty years. There was Sharon, a woman in her sixties who I seemed to startle whether I warned her of my general proximity or not. Her favorite dish from Lizard's Thicket was fried liver and onions. We often got our thermoses mixed up (she was a tea drinker like me).

Emmett was in his forties I think, a quiet, genial guy and a real gourmand, a fan of Juzo Itami's *Tampopo*. His mother, with whom he resided, regularly called for him on the library's landline. He positively lit up reading from picture books during Baby and Me story time. And he was endlessly patient, especially with the elderly patrons who shouted from the computer station, befuddled by the World Wide Web. He never showed his frustrations but for the way he emphasized certain words, by bugging out his eyes. After one difficult interaction with an ornery lady, I'd asked him if she was a problem person (every branch has a few). "She asked me if she could touch mah *beard* one day," he replied, eyes bulging.

My boss, Virginia, was the kind of woman you might imagine obtaining a library science degree: ebullient with a sort of bippity-boppity-boo energy. She sang in the church choir and in her free time, she and her husband were screening the AFI's top 100 movies, to watch-along with their favorite podcast.

Wesley, the children's librarian, was soft-spoken but secretly sassy, prone to the occasional knowing glance. He hid his sleeves of tattoos beneath plaid button-ups and enjoyed drinking craft beer or thrifting on weekends.

Wyatt occupied a mystifying dual role: security guard and desk clerk. This confused patrons, as he wore a library-mandated security uniform but also manned checkout. He provided security in that he was six foot seven and could potentially block the exit with his wall of a body. Loudest motherfucker to ever work in a library. Hailing from Appalachian Tennessee, he sported a musical accent native Carolinians could hardly understand. He sounded like a banjo twanging. When patrons approached him at the front desk, he boomed, "YOU FAHND WHATCHU WAS LEWKIN FOE-ERR?" He usually spent his shifts watching live broadcasts of Magic: The Gathering tournaments from the desktops at circulation. Once, when someone asked him for a book recommendation, he shouted, "I don't really read." It was amazing. If you could have formed a person least likely to work at a library out of clay, it would have been that man.

And then there was Miss Paula. Her smile practically glinted. She had short, platinum-blond hair and long fabulous nails that tapped pleasingly on the keys of her keyboard. People just showed up to talk to Paula, she was that likable. She was damn good at her job, too, understood the whole system like the back of her hand and was perhaps the only person I could speak to about the occasionally puzzling bureaucratic inner workings of the library. During her off-hours, she watched her grandbabies or attended big boisterous family reunions. When she wasn't at work, you felt her absence. She warmed up Wheatley, made it feel more than a place filled with machines and books—she gave the space life.

Those initial weeks on the job, I was powered by an anticipatory energy. I fulfilled my duties with the fervor of an inmate planning a jailbreak. Best behavior and such, because soon, blammo, I'd be out of there. I was a finalist for a sizeable writing grant, you see, and the prize money would be my golden ticket out of town. Where to? No clue. All I knew was I wouldn't stay. In the meanwhile, I volunteered to organize the children's stacks (most chaotic). I placed books written by peers prominently on the Fresh Picks tables. I volunteered to spearhead Special Projects I surely would not soon be around to follow through on, because I was busting out of the joint any day.

It wasn't a bad job, not by a long shot. But did it sting to see several films I'd worked on out on the shelves? After fifteen years, was I essentially a clerk at a video store again, checking the backs of DVDs for scratches? Yes, yes. It wasn't used porn, so I suppose I'd moved up in the world ever so slightly.

The thing about the library is you're dealing with the general population, and I'd been living in a New York bubble for nearly two decades. There were unfamiliar customs and behaviors to which I needed to acclimate. People moved without any sense of urgency in the South. Maybe it had something to do with the heat, so sticky and thick in the summer months even thinking made you sweat. And while folks gossiped mightily behind your back, to anyone's face you'd get good manners and a lot of sir-and-ma'aming. I am cursed with a highly expressive face, so I needed to learn quickly how to dull visible reactions with a blanket smile. Sometimes that meant checking out a laptop to a patron as if you didn't know he was a serial masturbator one offense away from permanent banning. Other times that meant sitting patiently with an elderly Black man in a head-to-toe red velvet suit, instructing him step-by-step how to RSVP and print a ticket he didn't need to attend a Trump rally. Once, I had to inform an absolutely hard-looking dude his account was locked due to a never returned copy of *Nanny McPhee*. Then there were the unspoken rules. A woman approached the front desk one day and hissed: "I won't let *her* check me out, seein' as how she's wearin' orange." This had something to do with football allegiances. Orange is the color favored by Clemson University, Other-USC's rival team. Wearing my favorite hat was akin to announcing I was a Crip in Blood streets. No matter. I'd be out of there soon enough.

Bad news started rolling in with the summer heat and its torrid, triple-digit temps. I got whooped in two consecutive wallops. My agent phoned to say the new pages I'd sent weren't working. She suggested the book ought to be about something else altogether, which meant I was back to square one. I didn't have the gas to throw permutations at the wall anymore, seeing which might stick. I'd taken her call during my lunch hour, in my 2001 Camry parked in the library lot. I tented a dollar-store sun shield around my head so I could weep in private.

I didn't get that grant either. The organization notified me by snail mail, and I recall standing in my mother's driveway, wailing. It was 99 degrees (Real Feel 103). Umma paused from pulling weeds in the lawn to assess the commotion. I showed her the letter, and after scanning its contents, she muttered, "Get over it."

I was still holding the envelope. Not five minutes had passed since I'd opened it. I was looking at the pile of junk someone had dumped across the street, and the derelict Korean church down the road, and the yellow pollen–covered mailbox, thinking about the library I'd have to return to on Monday, and every day forever maybe, because I had royally fucked up somewhere along the line, and the last chance I had to unfuck my way out of things had just withered into dust, and Umma was just standing there, all *so what*?

In fact, she doubled down: "I said, Get *over* it! Who cares." And she handed me the letter to return to her weed pulling.

Something broke inside me. I went apoplectic. Who cares? Who cares?? Obviously *me, I* care, the crying person, the one with feelings, standing right in front of her. "Don't you understand what this means?!" I was screaming so loud the neighbors' dogs began to bark. Before turning to go inside the house, I said the thing I shouldn't have said, pointing at her face, because I could be cruel too: "You're *not* good at this."

Ah, there she was. Same petulant girl with *The X-Files* poster hanging in her bedroom, who thought she was nothing like the woman who raised her. What a fool.

We didn't speak for days. I apologized, and because we had no choice (who else would we talk to?) we did what Umma had directed and moved on. I would save money. Reassess in six months, a year. So okay, I was in my thirties living with my mom. Things could be worse, right? Well, then my inner turmoil began to seep out of my pores. Dermatologists could not determine the cause, but my face erupted with painful cystic acne. And no, we aren't talking about a zit here or there but full-scale change of physical topography. These underground masses required steroid injections. Before each jab, the nurse would say, piteously, "Oh my. Well bless yer heart." Since I was already in a sorry state, I decided to fix my crossbite with teeth aligners too, which laced my speech with a lisp. Inadvertently, this allowed me to bond with one patron who needed help putting together a job resume. She had a lisp too, but from wearing gold grillz.

I wonder if she loved what she saw in the mirror. When I looked, I could hardly recognize my own reflection.

• • •

THE DAYS BEGIN TO OOZE together, one smudging into the next. I decide if I am going to become invisible, I want to control how I vanish.

So I wake up, hit the gym. Burn 630 calories. Pack lunch. No dairy, no grains, no sugar, no fruit. Show up to work late. Say to Virginia, "So sorry—won't happen again" (every morning). Off to book drop. Break. Front desk. Holds. Lunch in car. Meditate with app: Day 85 in current streak. Outside temp: Real Feel 100 degrees. Text from Umma: "Do u know circus is in town." Close library. Eat silent dinner with Umma. Log calories (max 1,250). Rinse, repeat.

Real Feel 101 degrees. 690 calories burned. Late. "So sorry—won't happen again." Spend two hours drawing library programming on white board with elaborate emojis and careful script: "Hello Baby! For ages 0–2 on Wednesdays; Hands on Art: Simple art and story fun for the very young. Dress for a mess!; Adult programming: 5–6 P.M. a presentation on will writing." Within minutes of its display, a toddler swipes the board clean. Take break in car. Fire up meditation app course pack: *Dealing with Regret*.

Real Feel 102. 710 calories burned. Front desk. "I'm looking for a book by my favorite author," says a little blond girl. "I love *The Jungle Book*. I love Richard Kipling."

"I think his name is Rudyard Kipling," I say.

"No," she says, a tinge snobbishly. "I think I know my own favorite author's name, Richard Kipling."

"It's Rudyard. Rudyard Kipling. Kind of a weird name, for sure, but—"

"It's *Richard*!" the girl screams, entering meltdown mode. "It's Richard it's Richard it's RICHARD!!!"

Real Feel 103. 616 calories burned. Holds, book drop, front desk, float. Avoid male patron following me in the aisles shouting Asian countries ("Thailand?! Japan?!") who hopes the right one will compel me to answer. Ask Paula what to do. "People will cross the line. You don't have to stand there and take it," she says. "And you don't have to let it hurt you either." Go back on the floor, spirits replenished. A different male patron, minutes later: "I'm looking for some kung-fu. You prolly speak Chinese, whatchu got?"

Real Feel 105. 720 calories burned. I'm working through hold requests, scanning a stack of DVDs when an actor–director ex's face pops up on one of the covers. It's like seeing a ghost. I wonder: What are the chances someone would request this movie in Columbia, South Carolina, and I'd be the one to process it? I report the item missing, walk to the children's library trash can, and throw the DVD away.

Real Feel 104. 635 calories burned. Week total 1,810. This month 2,461, last month 2,684. Meditation app: Day 120 in current streak. Dermatologist: three injections. "Bless yer heart," the nurse says. "What could it be?"

Real feel 106. New personal best: 1,025 calories burned in one session. New personal worst: I don't talk for a whole week. Very depressed, but I'm getting abs. "Are you okay?" Paula asks. "You doin' alright?" Emmett inquires, eyes bulging. I nod and nod. Stay quiet. Tidy the board books. Cry at the sight of one called *Subway*, an F train whizzing by on its cover. Relocate to cry in car during lunch break. Fetch book drop. Float. Even at home, I don't speak. Umma doesn't notice.

What could it be?

Therapist search, *Psychology Today* online database. Therapist option 1, profile description: "Would you like to live your best life? At the Southeastern Success Center, the focus is on seeking success by meeting therapy or coaching goals . . . out of the box thinking. Solution focused." Therapist option 2: "Hello and welcome to my webpage! Do you feel that you want to tell YOUR story and truly be heard and validated? If so, then we need to work together!" Therapist 3, bearing frog-like grimace: "Are you struggling to control or postpone sexual feelings and actions?"

I speak again when I go see Therapist 4. I'm staring at her faded foot tattoo when I ask, "Do you have experience working with artists?" We might be the same age. "I'm not sure what you mean," she says. "I work with everybody, at-risk youth, homosexuals, everyone." It's a weird answer, but I'm babbling now, about my messy Brooklyn exit, the cinders still hot to the touch, the ditch I'm in, how I can't claw my way out of it. Once I stop and take a breath, she says: "Wow, your life sounded pretty great in New York. Why would you leave?"

. . .

THE LIBRARY JOB, my mother reminded me, was a much-coveted position in Columbia. But what can I say, a genuine spell of depression can make a decent situation seem like personal purgatory. I couldn't see things clearly. Despair and the writing and the not-writing had turned my head topsy-turvy. One risk people don't mention much when pursuing nonfiction? Solipsism. I had become so unbearably self-serious, my mind a house of mirrors.

It took a children's book to set me straight. Hundreds of more alluring holds caught my eye over six months, ones with flashy colors or striking art. But this rudimentary science book, truly uninspired in design, stopped me dead in my tracks with its title: *Why Am I a Bird?*

The creature stares, its eye an orb of moonstone above a matte yellow beak. Under the title, there's the suggestion of a sunrise or perhaps the luminous perimeter of earth as seen from space, emitting an atmospheric glow. Then clouds, sky, and, peeking out from the bottom right corner, the animal in question perched on a bumpy rock. It is a plain bird with two stick-legs, a football-shaped body, a white belly, a round head, and a red spot, like a mole, protruding from its bill. Its slitted nostrils are flared, rendering an air of indignance.

As stated in the introduction, the animal kingdom consists of many species; some animals are small, some are big, some have feathers, some have scales (described as "plates that cover the skin"). Birds are one type of animal. Ostriches, sparrows, parrots, these are all birds. "But why?" the book asks. "What makes a bird a bird?"

The chosen specimen of this account is the herring gull. One photo shows the bird standing beside a scrub of tide, contemplative, as if pondering life's greatest questions (perhaps the one at the crux of this book). "A herring gull has a skeleton inside its body," the text reads. In order to be light enough to fly, their bones contain pockets of air. Additionally, "herring gulls have no teeth. Teeth are heavy." I'd never thought of it so definitively but yes, teeth *are* heavy. Nothing that flies has teeth. Did I ever really know a thing about birds?

I skimmed the pages on scavenging, nest building, egg laying and hatching. The peculiar red spot on the gull's beak, I learn, is a kind of panic button; when chicks are hungry, they peck at the red dot, and the parent bird opens its bill to provide food for the babies. As soon as the little gulls can fly, they leave home, continue the cycle. The tangential facts gripped me most. Flightless birds, for example, "also have bones with air spaces in them. This means that long ago, these birds must have been able to fly."

I cannot tell you why this book elicited such an extraordinary moment of epiphany. Maybe it was in the text's directness, its clarity. There was no room for abstraction. A bird is a bird for unequivocal reasons. If it has a backbone, lungs to breathe air, if it hatches from a hard-shelled egg, if it has a warm body and feathers and a beak (not teeth), it is a bird. Had I lost my mind? No. I was clawing my way out from the ditch, finally. Sitting in the stillness of something shapeless and immeasurable, the meaning of which I couldn't quite comprehend yet. Sometimes the truth of the matter is right there, plain and incontrovertible. And you might only take sight of it for a moment. But a bird is a bird, even if it can't fly.

. . .

HERE'S WHAT ELSE I learned at the library:

People read a shit ton of James Patterson; his seventieth publication of the year still accrued a 100-plus waiting list. Patrons adored page-turners and beach novels, like *Sullivan's Island* by Dorothea Benton Frank. They were also reading *Cheaper to Keep Her 3 (You Can't Afford to Cross Her . . .)*; *Around the Way Girls 8*; *Definition of a Bad Girl*; and most popular in the Urban Literature category, the *Thug Passion* series by Mz. Lady P. I spent an entire afternoon searching Mz. Lady P's Facebook page to scrounge for the *Thug Passion 4* release date because a woman had asked about it in passing. Similarly, a different patron wanted to know if we carried a children's book about a mouse who wore a striped shirt, or maybe it was polka dots, and the mouse goes on an adventure or maybe it lives in a garden, she couldn't remember, but could we find out? We would dedicate hours to these hunts, because we would do almost anything to encourage people to read.

I also learned about patrons from their hold requests. You could tell when someone was embarking on a new skill (ten books reserved on how to tie maritime knots) or if a student was preparing for a school project (eight books on the subcontinent of India). People were trying to get by on every level, with *The Dance of Anger: A Woman's Guide to Changing the Patterns of Intimate Relationships*; *The Five Languages of Apology*; or *Living Beyond Your Feelings: Controlling Emotions—So They Don't Control You*. There was *Alone Together: Making an Asperger Marriage Work*, which featured two arms reaching across a thick tree trunk, their hands adorned with handmade bracelets and wedding bands. And *Psychic Intelligence* by the Psychic Twins, who teach you how to "tune in and discover the power of your intuition." One patron blew through romance paperbacks *A Bull Rider to Depend On*, *A Ready-Made Amish Family*, *Her Cowboy Boss*, and *The Cowboy's Accidental Baby* in a month. Another lived for confectionary capers like *Charms and Chocolate Chips: A Magical Baking Mystery*; cozy, craft-centered *Knit to Kill*; and feline-inclined *Copycat Killing* ("No more pussyfooting around," the cover touted), by the author of *Sleight of Paw*.

You know what people weren't clamoring for? Contemporary literary writing. Least of all creative nonfiction. Which put things in perspective.

I also learned what the library means for a community. It is a destination for the elderly, who have otherwise been left in the ether of the internet's Big Bang. It's where they can check their email, look up doll collectors' stats and figures, or scan photos of the latest Oregon pumpkin regatta (an actual race where competitors sail across bodies of water in giant carved-out gourds). For many, it is a last bastion of independence—a place where one can drive a safe, short distance and speak, the old-timey way, to humans, face to face. I dedicated weeks to finding films for cinephile B. Sue, who wore stylish gray driving gloves and never entered Wheatley without a full face of makeup or her hair blown out and teased. "No Oriental movies, seen most of 'em," she instructed. "No British ones either. Can't understand a thang they're sayin'." At a certain point I had free rein with her queue and added to it as I pleased. She watched every one, like Abbas Kiarostami's *Close-Up* and Agnès Varda's *Cléo from 5 to 7*, caring for some more than others, and I looked forward to seeing her waltz through the double doors to deliberate on my selections in her no-nonsense way.

I even grew fond of crotchety Mr. Gentry, who had an adventurous musical taste, sampling CDs by Lorde, Major Lazer, and Enya.

"And how are you today, Mr. Gentry?" I'd ask.

"Well, I'm vertical," he'd grunt.

Or, "When you live by yourself, what else is there to do?"

Or, "S'matter of fact, brought back a DVD, didn't see the label saying it contained profanity. I don't need all that trash. Exactly what's wrong with this country. No class. Alexander Tytler, do you know who that is? Said, No republic, no democracy . . . we are on the brink of total collapse into chaos."

Then I'd watch his frail body tuck into a Cadillac and when he sputtered off, I thought about him at home, the frolicking melodies of Enya echoing throughout the empty rooms.

I regaled Umma with these stories during our newly established Friday night outing: sushi at the strip mall place off Decker Boulevard. Between dramatic pauses, one or the other of us panting from too much wasabi, she updated me on local headlines. "Did you hear about the

Hilton Head woman? Tried to save her dog and got ate up by alligator!" Or she shared her own stories from work. "Surgeons, ha. They such a divas," she'd muse, slurping her Nigori sake. "There's a Korean saying: Gotta give 'em another rice cake. So I smile. They have a no idea who they dealing with."

I could see a clearer picture of Umma coming into view after visiting her office at the hospital one day. A sign on her door greeted me: *Come on in!* written in that irreplicable scrawl of hers. There were teamworking strategies mapped out on easel pads, framed photos of me and Laurie, several of Umma from her solo international adventures, a Jesus fish with the word HOPE inscribed at its center, and a decorative frog sitting cross-legged holding a giant glass of wine.

Together we developed our own routine. On weekends we hit up Harbison for the Marshalls–Nordstrom Rack one-two punch or I accompanied Umma on trips to Matthews, North Carolina, for her perm and trim appointments at the Korean beauty salon. Every week we picked up bits and bobs at the Korean market. As it was in Georgia, various churches had left stacks of CDs near the front door, and from time to time I overheard a back-room Bible study group's hymns filtering over into the seaweed aisle. I wasn't writing, but I did jot contemporaneous notes, the minutiae of the day—location, what I ate, with whom I spoke—into a document with no specific intention or use in mind.

I noted how my mother called for Molder after too much wine. How sometimes Umma revisited the box with her dog's ashes stored beside the DIVA collar and hand-knit hot-pink sweater, both redolent still of Molder.

Seeing my mother that way always brought back a different scene, from Christmas 2014, in Key West, Florida. Newly dispatched from a rum bar's happy hour, Umma and I had lazed along a boardwalk, awaiting sunset. When we reached the pier, she parked herself on the pavement, leaned against the railing, and confessed: "My greatest wish is to live with someone I'm madly in love with."

A crowd began to form. Couples decked out in Santa hats wove through children playing chase. I stood speechless. While hotfooting it job to job, she'd mentioned no suitors, no date nights. As she repeatedly put it whenever I inquired about her romantic life: "I'm not into that kind of thing." It seemed at the pier, some buried part of her, summoned by daiquiris and our enchanting environs, had at last surfaced, insisting otherwise.

Shutters clicked as a pirate ship traversed a melting sky. Then my mother slumped over, smiling faintly, her thought carrying off into the breeze, already forgotten.

* * *

ON THE CUSP OF MY FIRST South Carolina fall, Umma and I returned to the ocean, road-ripping up the coast to Pawleys Island. At the beach I watched my mother in the water, standing with her black and white floppy hat, arms stretched to a T. She faced the shore, bracing for impact, which was of no use. The waves throttled her, one after the other, her wide brim waterlogged and droopy. There was that marionette body of hers again, head listing back and forth, this time hooting out of sheer exhilaration.

Umma's car navigation shuttled us back home through stretches of two-lane country roads and too-quiet expanses dotted with JESUS SAVES billboards and vinyl-sided homes plunked way back on unkempt lawns. NPR tapered out of range, as is habit in these parts, so I connected my phone to fill the silence.

"Should we play the song?" I said and cued it up, because I knew her answer.

The opening notes wended languid-like, with the twang of an electric lap steel guitar. We mmm-mmed as Shania Twain mmm-mmed. It wasn't the one where she's enthralled by womanhood nor the one where everything—including Brad Pitt—leaves her underwhelmed. The one we wanted was sadder. There's something pleading in her voice at this key, like the Saw Lady in the subway, who plays a carpenter's tool like a harp, its warped metal yielding an eerie ache. Maybe we'd transposed that ache because of Twain's backstory. She cowrote the song with mega music producer and then-husband "Mutt" Lange. They collaborated on most of Twain's breakout hits. Lange eventually cheated on Twain with a close friend, and for a stretch Twain wasn't sure she could write or sing without Lange. Then she got with the friend's ex-husband, who was not named "Mutt" and resembled a Prince Charming type, Colgate smile and everything, so the very bad event resulted in a happy ending. In some twist of fate, now the song is actually about how the unexpected thing, the thing that breaks you, can lead to something unforeseeable, something better. It's a ballad about being in love yet pangs with a kind of pre-heartbreak, dramatic irony weighting the chorus, which was presently upon us. And we really let loose, our voices cracking and fluttering. Umma was staring ahead, her mind having wandered to the imagined place again, until the final notes faded, the spacey synth echoing out like rings on a faraway planet. "One more time," Umma said. And we sang like this for a while, our sounds disappearing into the backwoods landscape, never taking our eyes off the road.

• • •

WHEN I SURPASSED my seven-month mark in Columbia, the weather cooled. Low-forties inspired the townspeople to sport their puffiest coats, as if entering a polar vortex. My skin was still a minefield. I'd paid off a credit card bill though, stashed some cash in the bank. Did I still want to leave? Hell yes. But, incredibly, I'd made a life there with Umma. Could I at last recognize what I saw in the mirror? Sort of. I'd shifted my way of looking, a trick I'd learned and nearly forgotten from 2014.

That summer I attended an artist residency. The heir to a gargantuan chemicals company hosted the private, invitation-only retreat. He was a painter with generous acreage on Maryland's eastern shore and invited people of varying disciplines to roost in old chicken coops and barns to make whatever it was they were making: intricate illustrations of avian creatures, realist still life, diffusions of inkblots dispersed on mylar. Lucky for me, a couple of us writers got to go. Everyone worked on their projects by day and convened in the main house, where we took turns cooking dinner at night. Before enjoying the meal, we sipped on gin and tonics while loitering around an unfinished puzzle, casually testing out viable combinations. The puzzle depicted a Hopper paint- ing, the one at the diner called *Nighthawks*. Some 40 percent of the image contained shades of black, rendering the correct placement of the poorly punched pieces difficult. Once we'd fiddled the thing together, a final cutout remained, and the leftover piece didn't fit. Somewhere along the way, the right piece had been jammed, imperceptibly, into the wrong place. No one else seemed to care we'd have to pull apart the whole pic- ture and start over.

At the dinner table, we talked about the peaks and pits of the day or rode the waves of generic party chatter. The conversation drifted inevita- bly to the topic of money—selling your work, staying financially afloat, and how rarely the two needs overlapped. Admittedly such associations may be American fixations, since one's industriousness and resultant creations are frequently attached to a value and, ultimately, a conflation of self-worth.

A realist painter named Lucas appeared untroubled. "I have no prob- lem selling my work," he said. It was true. He could capture sumptuous fur pelts, speckled robins' eggs, and aquamarine glass goblets staged atop knotty wooden tables with gilt-edged clarity—works that appealed to wealthy collectors greatly. I found his stance cavalier, seeing as how what he painted possessed obvious salability with no conceptual risk. The bearded twentysomething white guys, who had concocted well- intentioned but bland tofu banh mis the night before, had spent sev- eral afternoons melting beer cans for a sculpture; they did not rely on steady patronage.

I had visited Lucas in his studio earlier that week to get a better sense of his whole deal. A small bird lay dead on a table beside his easel. He had resuscitated a version of the creature, capturing its fragility for a work-in-progress. Occasionally Lucas faced away from the painting and held up a hand mirror. I found the repeated action perplexing. He didn't appear the vain type, based on his somewhat disheveled hair and unexceptional attire. Again and again, he placed the mirror beside his cheek, shifted his eyes back and forth, then swiveled around to continue painting. After some time, I asked: "What's up with the mirror?" It was the cheap plastic kind you could buy for a dollar.

"Oh," he said, suddenly aware of my company. "When I want to see the work with fresh eyes, I look at its reflection. A Da Vinci trick. Think he wrote about it in his journals."

Peering at the mirror's flopped image made subtle inexactitudes obvious, fixable. It was a method entailing no despair nor joy but a certain type of fight—urging only to continue looking at different angles to see the familiar or overlooked anew. Maybe then the missing piece could reveal itself, the entire picture made possible.

I was getting there, in my own time. Perhaps a library patron put it best one Sunday afternoon, upon seeing me at Trader Joe's, removed from my usual context, different clothes and hair, no makeup, no blanket smile. "Wow. Jennifer," she said, astonished. "Look at you! You're a real person."

. . .

REAL FEEL 44 DEGREES. 660 calories burned. At work on-time (miracle). White board duty: "Family Storytime, Fridays @ 10:30 A.M. Share stories, songs, & much more!; Baby, it's cold outside. Cozy up w/a snow craft; Excavation Exploration Box: Dig to solve a literary riddle! For school-age children; Adult programming: Holiday cupcake decorating!"

By month eight, I'd applied for a new job at a magazine in nearby Charleston. I prepped for the interview by reading copies delivered to Wheatley. The money was laughable, but I was ready for a change of scenery. Certain details about the library had started to grate on me. I'd struggled to negotiate a salary barely above minimum wage yet the children's play area was outfitted with bougie Design Within Reach felt baskets for storing building blocks, accompanied by sleek Finnish wooden stools that, according to my internet sleuthing, each racked up to $300. We even had $1,200-worth of backup fancy stools, stacked beneath a tattered Paddington Bear whose eye had popped out of its socket.

Due to scheduling snafus, I attended a new-hire orientation at the main branch a couple weeks before I'd give my notice. The group exercises reeked of corporate nonsense. At one point, I was instructed to choose a word card best summarizing my "personal brand." What did that have to do with working at a library? At the event's conclusion, we were provided stationery to pen a letter to our future selves we'd receive in one year's time. *Dear You Old So and So*, I wrote. *I sure as shit hope you're not working at the library anymore.*

So I wasn't a library lifer. That wasn't the point, was it?

"What is an artist supposed to be?" writer Katy Waldman asks. She is not a product of fetishized genius. Maybe she doesn't even always make art. Perhaps she spends months experiencing what the New Delhi artist trio Raqs Media Collective call "radical incompleteness." Their essay, "How to Be an Artist by Night," poses a different mode of embracing a life in artmaking. As students, we are taught a promise will be fulfilled at the end of our course of education; and once we reach a place of proficiency, we will ascend. But Raqs Media Collective contends "there can be no rigid separation between being someone and learning to become someone." There are no prescriptive steps; the process for a Sunday painter or a master of the form is ongoing, replenished by the drive of discovery and rediscovery. Practice becomes a daily devotional to what remains unexplored, following its expanding, unknowable horizons. How can one sustain such a practice? The answer, they write, is time: "time out, leisurely time, the kind of time that can be a vessel and receptacle for reflection," and with it a non-instrumental attitude, staying open to "unintended consequences," meaning no imperative toward productivity or industry. A paradox emerges. While cultivating the necessary conditions to create, "there is simultaneously a surfeit of obstacles (through constant demands to produce and perform) that hinder this search." In an ideal world, there is no hindrance in waiting, slowing down, languishing in each off-shoot life presents. We would be able to wander through every entropic portal, not certain where they might lead—to Alaska, to Georgia, to South Carolina, to Seoul. Like peering into a distorted mirror, whose reflection does not spawn a warped image of one whole self but rebounds pieces and parts worthy of individual consideration—new stimuli, new approaches, and in every refraction a new way of seeing.

This made me think of an article I'd read about the red-crowned crane—a revered image in Korea, symbolizing vitality and pictured on everything from my mother's opaline jewelry box to traditional watercolors and ancient scrolls. Unlike a herring gull, it is a graceful, folkloric-looking bird, bearing black and white feathers, a slender nape, and its namesake blood-red pate. The red-crowned crane is endangered; some 2,300 are in existence today. Much of its population on the Korean peninsula (1,600 as of 2022) survives in the unlikeliest ecological sanctuary: the Demilitarized Zone. Our perception of the thirty-ninth parallel is almost two-dimensional, a line drawn on a map. In actuality, the DMZ is a strip of land 160 miles long and two and a half miles wide that, for the last seventy years, has accidentally thrived due to the absence of human intervention. Such a place possesses a fourth dimensionality—a plane untouchable to man. And yet here was this odd, leggy creature, outliving its own mythological lore, moving freely across the halved country's borders, finding refuge on a slice of earth made unknown by time. The barrier of war sustains the birds' survival but, more importantly, its livelihood relies on our acceptance of mystery; to know this place would inevitably lead to its destruction.

Maybe faith requires us to lean into the not-knowing. And maybe in time those mysteries will reveal a purpose. Maybe not. Maybe they will reveal a greater truth or meaning. Maybe not.

It's like standing in the ocean, somewhere remote and rough. The water, a shifting field behind you, doesn't know or care that you're there. You cannot control the whole beastly thing but perhaps you can tame for one moment your place in it, to make one glimpse, one truth, however brief, known.

• • •

IN SOUTH CAROLINA, my book stayed unwritten. My damn cat died. I got no nookie. But I did not feel lonely. On jogs at the Riverwalk, I started tipping my hat back to passersby, saying hello. I would leave eventually. Until then I slowed down, took time, pondered the little things and the big things and questions with no answers. And sometimes, late at night, after Umma finished her routine and fell asleep, I shut off her true crime videos and lingered at her bedside, thinking about a story she'd once told me.

We shared a bed when I was a baby. No matter how quietly she got up in the morning, I'd wake with a start and inconsolably cry and cry. She often wore her work clothes to bed for a stealthier exit, but I couldn't be fooled. Every morning, the heat of her figure vanished, and I lay awake, panicked my mother might disappear from me forever. Then she returned and the universe realigned, my simple world made whole again.

I didn't know if she'd stay put in Columbia, if she'd pack up the next week or if I'd leave with her. But one night at home, tipsy on wine, before nodding off, my mother offered another confession:

"You left at seventeen. Exactly seventeen years later, you came back to me." She had that dreamy look, like the night in Key West, on the pier. "You are my me," she said. Then her thought, a wisp of a thing, floated off, already forgotten.

PART
THREE

Ways of Seeing

TULSA, OKLAHOMA
604 sq. ft.: Studio, 1BA

From visittulsa.com:

"Just across the tracks from downtown Tulsa's primary business districts, the **Tulsa Arts District** is a hub for creativity. Obviously boasting plenty of art galleries, the Tulsa Arts District also includes the Guthrie Green, music venues like Cain's Ballroom and Tulsa Theater, along with several James Beard nominated restaurants and bars including Sisserou's Caribbean Restaurant and Restaurant Basque.

Check out Living Arts of Tulsa for constantly rotating contemporary exhibits, or experience the legacy of one of America's most prolific folk artists at the new Bob Dylan Center . . . Explore fine craft at 108|Contemporary, or enjoy fine craft cocktails at Valkyrie. Dance the night away at Club Majestic, or try some of Welltown Brewing's incredible beers and seltzers from their rooftop patio."

Prism

IN 2020 I MOVED to Tulsa. I'd never pictured myself living in Okla-homa, but at this point I no longer questioned where the opportunities took me or why; it was a relief to know they took me anywhere at all.

After my stint at the library, I'd headed to Charleston, back-filling for a twenty-four-year-old at a local magazine. I was making less than when I was twenty-four, but working the "eat and drink" beat at any publication felt like a move forward rather than sideways or back. Part of my mandate included contributing a monthly food review that need not lean into negative critique. It's easy to be a snarky little fucker and far trickier to write about something you enjoy. Restrictions can feel, well, restrictive, but sometimes limitations force you to get strategic, which can lead to greater satisfaction, because the wins are harder won. These assignments crowbarred me out of a rut, wiggling free enough space for joy to reenter my writing practice. I dusted off my book project. Morale refreshed, I applied for an artist fellowship in a state I'd never visited; the two-year appointment included free housing, a studio space, a stipend—and I got it.

Before heading west, I left Charleston and decamped at Umma's house for a couple months. We both took well to the do-over. I packed her work lunch every weekday and at night cooked elaborate dinners she promptly amended with kimchi and rice. (Once, before even sampling the tagine I'd spent hours preparing, she deluged her plate with kimchi juice and inhaled the thing in five cartoonish bites.) There were bumps, naturally. Whenever the cable and internet were on the fritz, or the bidet temp felt three degrees cooler than usual—any instance in which something went slightly askew—I became suspect number one. "What did you do?" she'd accuse. "You're the only thing changed around here, so it must have been you." This was to be expected; she'd welcomed me back with no hesitation, but I had temporarily interrupted her life again. And she'd need to adjust again as soon as I departed.

Near the end of the month, a different interruption ensued: news of the novel Coronavirus trickled into Umma's morning routine until it was Covid, Covid, Covid every day, hour, minute. Incidentally, my mother's brusque matter-of-factness is quite useful during world crises. A woman of faith and science is not frightened by the prospect of death. She continued working at the hospital, unrattled. I continued packing her lunches and cooking us dinner, which she continued to amend with kimchi and rice. On weekends we cruised over to the rich part of the neighborhood. Passersby said hello and, under her breath in Korean, Umma mercilessly skewered them one by one. This was her way of making conversation (how far we'd come!). It reminded me of the time I'd explained to her the concept of a "basic bitch," to which she self-deliberated: "I'm not basic. But I am a bitch."

As we walked the winding streets, we passed split-level and Charleston-style homes. None of these properties were for sale and yet, for Umma, each house contained a possible choice to entertain or reject. "Aigoo no," she'd say. "I don't like a two-story . . . No, I don't like front door pointing to the east . . . Aigoo no, I need enclosed garage." They didn't appeal to me, either, more likely because owning a home seemed so radically unfeasible, I hadn't even considered what a dream one might or might not include.

For my mother, I'd assumed these assessments were mere thought experiments. She hadn't purchased a home in years. Columbia didn't strike me as a permanent situation anyway. Back in 2017, she'd bandied about the idea of buying a solar-powered van. Inside, she could fit a bed beside a tiny lounging area and stove. The back doors could open to a lake or state park. Where would her decorative clogs and pine cone collection go? She didn't say. But I wouldn't be surprised if one day she donated most of her belongings and, without warning, hit the road. She'd threatened to do as much once before in Florida, around 2015, after Molder passed. Newly untethered, she'd decided to retire early, move back to Seoul, take care of her parents. Old feelings of unfulfilled filial duty kept resurfacing. Halmoni and Harabeoji had entered their eighties. How odd it was to witness her embattled by warring selves: the daughter she aspired to be and the woman she was—a conundrum we shared in silence.

Umma quit her job, booked a one-way ticket, and then, at the last minute, changed her mind. Not Korea, not yet.

. . .

COINCIDENTALLY, TALK OF TULSA seemed to proliferate weeks before my relocation. The HBO series *Watchmen* had recently aired, catalyzing conversation around the 1921 Tulsa Race Massacre, when a white mob destroyed the Greenwood District's Black Wall Street—an epicenter of African American culture. Some considered the show a "predictive text" to the events in spring 2020, presaging the brutal outcome of unchecked police violence and racism. Black Lives Matter protests accelerated worldwide while Tulsa officials continued employing radar technology to unearth possible mass grave sites. I would be living a few streets over from Greenwood, my time overlapping with the centennial anniversary of the riots.

Additionally, the Supreme Court had begun hearing oral arguments via teleconference for McGirt v. Oklahoma. The case reignited discussions around the U.S. government's forced relocation of five major Native American tribes (the Cherokee, Choctaw, Chickasaw, Seminole, and Muscogee Nations) from their ancestral lands in the Southeastern United States. From 1830 to 1850 up to 100,000—including those enslaved by Indigenous peoples—marched the Trail of Tears to Oklahoma territory, leading to thousands of deaths. McGirt v. Oklahoma resulted in a landmark ruling: Crimes committed by Native Americans on land promised to the Muscogee in the 1830s would be subject to tribal law. The decision is seen as a recognition of the land's reservation status following centuries of broken promises.

Then, days before my arrival, during a local stay-at-home order, Trump held a rally at the Bank of Oklahoma Center—a 19,000-seat sports arena, also blocks away from my apartment. K-pop stans claimed to have goosed ticket sales, and updates of the underwhelming turnout peppered my social feeds. The synchronicity of events suggested this was a striking time to live in Tulsa, a place of tremendous loss, rehabilitation, spectacle, and long overdue reckonings.

My mother helped me move. I packed up the car with my cat and some mementos (photos of Halmoni and Harabeoji, knickknacks from my own travels), leaving the rest of my "worldly pojessions" at the Flintstones house. We drove across six states in two days. I didn't realize I set up my home the way Umma does: everything on the walls and in the cabinets within twenty-four hours, to feel nested for as long as we plan to stay.

After she returned to South Carolina, I popped into my mother's email to reset an account I helped her manage and found service quotes from several Columbia movers. I called her. "Are you moving again?" I asked. "No," she said cagily. "I already did."

In the two weeks since I'd last seen her, she'd purchased a well-maintained condo in a bedraggled complex at the edge of Forest Acres and had shuttled our shit there, seemingly under the cloak of night. She didn't say why she'd avoided telling me, but I knew. If she kept it to herself, no one could stop her.

* * *

MY TULSA APARTMENT looked like the set for a New York City loft on a CW television show: industrial top-hinge windows, exposed brick, aged concrete, high ceilings, and near-aggressive sunlight (requiring sunscreen indoors). At any hour, I could hear the meandering thunks of a drum kit. My place faced a building owned by Hanson that functioned as the band's studio and unofficial groupie hub. I hadn't spent a single minute thinking about those brothers since middle school, when I'd purchased a T-shirt from the 99 Cents Only Store for the sole purpose of drawing horns and mustaches on their screen-printed faces, to then display my objections at school. So firm was my distaste for their music.

Perhaps this was my debt to pay. Apparently, they had continued to record albums post-"MMMbop" fame. They'd been fertile in other ways, procreating something like fifteen children among them. They were old now, which meant *I* was old now—an unnerving revelation, given I was just beginning to figure my shit out. Sometimes I'd run into the youngest or the middle one or the tall one in the alley, where they averted their eyes, accustomed to the fervor of their heart-eyed disciples. HanFans frequently loitered around the alley, eager for an encounter. They snapped dozens of photos, holding awkward poses beside the band's logo, which was painted on a colorful beer-centric mural opposite my windows. Due to the pandemic, the annual Hanson Day festival—an illogically named, three-day affair drawing droves to downtown Tulsa—had been postponed. This did not deter the most ardent HanFans. Their tenacity had carried them through puberty and they'd emerged on the other side as adults, loyalty consecrated. They were almost always white women in their thirties and forties if I were to hazard a guess. Their giddy titterings leached into my apartment, where I observed from my perch with David Attenborough–esque fascination. The brothers hurriedly exited their studio, blasting down the alley in their gas guzzlers, on more than one occasion nearly mowing down my neighbor and his dog.

Other than these minor calamities, my studio was the nicest place I'd ever lived. I could finally keep a plant alive. Given the space's terrarium-like quality, my potted friends thrived there, and soon I was surrounded by the soft jungle I'd long desired. My life, the imagined one and the real one, were finally beginning to align.

The only problem was that it was all in Tulsa. Which is to say I was far away from the things that nourished me: the mountains, the sea, friends, family. And romance? Well, I was familiar by then with the reality of dating in a mid-sized American city. Locals typically got hitched in their early twenties to other locals and by their thirties had shacked up, banged out a couple kids, and were spending their days enjoying the adequate pleasures of suburban life. Wood-fired pizza at the wood-fired pizza place. Brunches at the indoor food hall. Jogs at the riverwalk. Weekend jaunts to the brewery to sip craft beer while the little ones ran riot on the AstroTurf.

That said, while in lockdown for the fellowship's two-week mandatory quarantine, I perused two dating apps—for anthropological reasons, of course. Every iteration available (women for anyone with a pulse) posed grim returns. The most promising within the maximum 1,000-mile search radius: a bi-curious, twenty-five-year-old mother of three and proponent of *It's Mom's Time to Wine*–type home decor and a God-fearing, flannel-swathed fifty-year-old man standing proudly beside a bull's backside.

I had already accepted the statistics were not in my favor. Even if I met someone, the issue of reciprocation presented another obstacle—I was an acquired taste. That was partially why I'd fled my own small town as a teenager. Now such places offered refuge for artmaking but depleted possibilities in the way of booty, let alone meaningful companionship.

Then, to my surprise, about five weeks into my stay, I met someone. It was the kind of narrative in which I never thought I'd find myself embroiled, like the improbable plot of a Hallmark movie: skeptical city transplant meets charming rural doctor. He was Choctaw and taught medical residents how to serve his community in pastoral Southeastern Oklahoma, where the only grocery store within a thirty-minute drive was a picked-over Dollar General. He possessed a biting sense of humor, was well traveled, appreciated Christopher Guest movies, *The Golden Girls*, poetry by Joy Harjo, and he spoke with a melodic Northwestern Arkansas drawl.

Our courtship was an unusual one, long-distance yet intensified by the terrors of a pre-vaccine pandemic; initially an epistolary flirtation. Getting-to-know-you texts gave way to deeper intimacies (family dynamics, past loves, heartbreaks, where we'd been and where we hoped to go—perhaps one day together). We were two realists cautiously embarking on the roseate stages of possibility. Like me he'd plowed toward a professional goal and had awoken at the cusp of forty to find himself achieving yet alone. What were the chances we'd find each other? It was strange, we agreed, to feel . . . what was the word he used . . . hopeful. I visited him two and a half hours away where he showed me his family's land he'd bought back, and the plot where he planned to build a home. He told me I smelled like fresh tilled soil (a compliment). We built fires, smoked joints, planted and tended a garden while his handsome dog basked beside us in the sun. And in the dark, we learned each other's pleasures and mysteries, sighed and touched and buckled from laughter, marveling at the absurdity of how right it was we'd met.

Come fall we drove to Zion National Park, camped in sub-freezing temperatures, and nearly ran out of water on the grueling trek back. At Christmas, we chopped down a tree from the Oklahoma hills and trimmed it with tinsel while granddaddy longlegs spiders scampered across his kitchen floor. He came to Tulsa, too, arriving to my elaborately planned meals (cioppino, Peruvian chicken, caviar service with tater tots, Detroit-style pizza with forty-eight-hour laminated dough, with wine pairings and a welcome cocktail ready the moment he walked through the door). I adored our style of domestic life. Ecstatic is hardly the word to describe how Umma felt. "Finally," she said, "you won't have to be like me."

Sure, there were cracks in the facade, I wasn't naive. On video calls, he and Umma bonded over their shared challenges as leaders in adjacent fields. But separately, my mother warned me of his specific limitations. "He will belong to his job four days of the week," she explained. "But you get the other three." I would never understand his work, what it required of him, but did we need to know everything to make room for each other? When Sundays rolled around, he returned to his home, or I returned to mine, and we relished our time apart. I imagined we could carry on this way, content, indefinitely.

I am not the hopeless romantic type. At thirty-six I had released the notion I might ever experience a traditional life or partnership. Yet he made it so easy to entertain. While I did not ask him to profess as much, certain promises were made, elaborate ones, about our combined future. A family. A home. Financial stability. Only after I allowed myself to envision such a life did our time together skitter to a halt. Some imperceptible tide shifted between Covid waves, when no reprieve from his nightmarish working conditions appeared to be in sight. I made my needs smaller and smaller because I had survived on less before. But eventually his fantasies no longer included me; he wanted to run away to a cabin in the woods to build fires and smoke joints and make pottery but with only the company of his dog. Could I really blame him? He told me patients were dying in his hospital's hallways, no free beds in neighboring states. After a 140-hour workweek, there wasn't much left to give himself, let alone another person. To love someone is easy, to share your life is another matter.

There had been one last gasp, when his spirits turned for about a week. I didn't know it, but Umma had found his email address online and sent him a letter. *I'm very resourceful,* she wrote. *Please do not tell my daughter I have contacted you. Jennifer would be mortified.* She explained how much I was crying, which made her upset, because when I hurt, she hurt (*a mother thing*). *I've come to really care about you,* she continued. *I haven't had much luck in love. I think what you have together is worth fighting for.*

In the end I held on a little longer than I should have. Who wouldn't want a good thing to last? Then I realized the rocky weeks outnumbered the blissful ones, the good thing worth fighting for, already lost. I did not get a satisfying goodbye, so I burned his underwear in a bonfire under a full moon and with time let that other life go. The experience did not leave me embittered or resentful (though he'd assured me it would). No. What I felt instead was something like wistfulness, for the other version of me—in whichever alternate timeline or universe she existed—who'd found a lasting way to love that, in this life, continued to elude me.

. . .

By February 2022, as I neared the end of my fellowship, friends had become accustomed to asking me two questions: *How are you? . . . Also* where *are you?* I never made any grand pronouncements regarding my various arrivals and departures, because then people expect you to have a plan. Oddly enough, I was beginning to better understand my mother in the process. Her sneakiness had been a way to elude what she could not or did not care to answer. And answering to no one for her, I think, represented the truest kind of freedom.

I didn't know what my mother's criteria for a forever home entailed anymore or what insoluble impulse kept her moving from place to place. Whatever that was, I didn't think I had it, because I did not approach my newest era effortlessly. To live this particular lifestyle, to be an artist, required a level of laxity. No one would ever describe me as "chill." I am a creature of sturdy preferences and beloved rituals. Though I was not thinking ahead for more than three months at a time, ideally I wanted to find somewhere I could stick around, in a home I could call my own. Where? That crucial detail, for the life of me, I could not figure. I had six months in Tulsa before I needed a plan. In the meantime, I luxuriated in what childless singledom can afford: unrestrained time to think and create— which some days felt too indulgent, like an unearned pre-retirement.

My mother, however, had reached that milestone in earnest: After forty years in the medical field, Umma hung up her scrubs, pilfered her last batch of surgical towels, and retired. She dyed her hair blond so she could smoothly transition into her natural silver color. No more root touch-ups. No more diva surgeons to coddle. No more on-call shifts or 5 a.m. alarms. We toasted her career with very good champagne while noshing on fried mandu and banchan. She could now do as she pleased, which entailed knitting endless pairs of mismatched socks while mainlining *American Greed* and *Buried in the Backyard.* But ten days after our celebration, guilt tolled its bell, beckoning her back to the motherland. Umma flew to Korea to care for my grandparents. The three-month stints, she'd decided, would be a compromise, part-timing her filial duties.

My grandma and grandpa were ninety-two and ninety-four respectively (our best guesses anyway). Since moving back from the States in 2006, they'd been living, without incident, in an apartment complex in Suwon, south of Seoul. Aside from a government-subsidized healthcare worker who stopped by three hours every weekday, they'd made do on their own. They could both cook rice, bathe, and wash clothes, but the efficacy of accomplishing these tasks had dwindled dramatically in recent years. Most importantly, though, they had each other—a fact Halmoni flaunted when she could still walk, strutting around the neighborhood in her carefully fashioned ensembles and red painted lips, arm-in-arm with Harabeoji, the other ajummas on the sidelines wilting with envy. The woman looked good, not a day over eighty, had her real teeth and fewer white hairs than my mother. She'd taken impeccable care of her skin, thanks to her American cosmetics (there was no convincing Halmoni of K-beauty's wonders), and she adhered to old school antiaging philosophies, like sleeping strictly on her back to prevent wrinkles or holding a soft smile while awake, no matter what wicked thoughts throttled her mind or spilled from her mouth.

Unlike my grandmother, my grandfather had subdued over the years. He was once an imposing figure known for never breaking his word. He'd grown up in a rural southern village, sleeping on a straw-filled mattress in a dirt-floor hut, the son of a craftsman who sold woven goods at open markets. He ran away to Seoul at fourteen, worked menial jobs, joined a military academy, and rose in the ranks of the Korean army until reaching artillery colonel. The harabeoji I knew tended to a hanging garden he built from scrap wood outside his Southern California apartment, pumped iron, and flexed his tennis ball–sized biceps, proclaiming himself, "Pop-eye! Pop-eye!" as I giggled at his feet. With my father in absentia, Harabeoji changed my diapers and raised me. How many lives in one life. The same man fought on the front lines of the Korean War. His firstborn, my Uncle Kai, was one month old when northern Korea officially invaded its southern half. Harabeoji decided to leave combat and check on Halmoni and the baby. Communist soldiers soon swarmed their village; if he had been found, the whole family would surely have perished. So, for four months, my grandfather hid in a hole in the backyard, large enough to store an oblong kimchi urn. Once North Korean soldiers vacated the area, my grandpa crawled out of the kimchi hole, returned to his troops, and, after a brief internal investigation, returned to battle.

Now Harabeoji's military awards hung above his lounging chair where he watched sumo wrestling and baduk tournaments whenever Halmoni permitted him control of the remote. Their place was equipped with electric-heated floors and multiple kimchi refrigerators, high-speed Wi-Fi they didn't know how to use, and cable television that blasted from the Samsung flat-screen sunrise to sunset. By 2022, they were getting on, both hard of hearing and forgetful. Moreover, neither of them accepted the consequence of time: that their bodies had aged much faster than their minds, stripping them slowly of basic autonomy. Ease and independence do not disappear at once but in small impactful frictions. Trimming toenails or opening jars become enervating digressions, blunting resolve in the course of one's final grand descent.

Aside from South Korea's strict Covid-19 parameters (requiring a seven-day off-site quarantine), Umma's trips seemed straightforward enough: take two planes, an airport "limojean" charter bus, then a taxi to my grandparents' apartment, wash hands immediately upon entering before even saying hello (to do otherwise would invoke Halmoni's germophobic wrath), abide by another code of living for ninety days, then head home. Umma had been twenty-three when she left Korea. It had been so long, perhaps she'd forgotten why. She could serve her parents lunches and dinners, run errands, manage their complex pill regimens, tidy the house. She would give them the very things she'd withheld for forty-seven years: her fealty and time.

She returned to Korea lugging, per usual, two enormous suitcases filled with their requests: Estée Lauder products and American clothes, prewashed, for Halmoni; Jif peanut butter and Coffee Mate powdered creamer for Harabeoji ("*Made in USA, numba one*," as he says); and enough Centrum Silver to last through the next century.

It was not the homecoming Umma had imagined. Based on her calls, things were not going well. My mother's mere presence had destabilized my grandparents' ecosystem. She ought to have known as much based on our own cohabitation. Umma blitzed into their world like a supercell, pitching Tupperware and Yuban coffee cans my grandfather had repurposed since the 1990s. To him, ever the child of poverty, nothing ought to be wasted. Bear-shaped honey bottles could be reused for fresh-pressed sesame oil, junk mail cut into scrap paper. Umma cleaned out the regular fridge and the banchan fridge and the kimchi fridges, rearranged the coffee cans and the honey bears, disrupting the organized chaos, catapulting Harabeoji into conniptions. "*What did you do?!*" he'd shout, confused.

Then there was Grandma. I had never been on the receiving end, but the woman was masterful in the art of verbal evisceration. We're talking sniper-like precision, from a little old lady not even five feet tall. Any affront, real or imagined, could warrant her fury. "She's not a drama queen," my mother said. "She's a drama *empress*." It seemed better, sometimes, that Halmoni and I didn't speak the same language.

So many rules under her roof, as totalitarian as Umma remembered. Wait three rings before answering the landline. Boil the floor rags for one hour—no more, no less. Put on a face mask half an hour before the healthcare worker arrives, just in case. No leaving the house but for Halmoni-sanctioned errands (which she would time, so no dilly-dallying). Umma could not even escape to her room for privacy. Halmoni would shuffle over via walker, swing the door open, and ask, suspiciously, "Why are you keeping this closed?" If the healthcare aid asked Umma a question, Halmoni answered: "*I'm* the lady of the house. Don't bother asking her—she's just a visitor." And since Grandma's body could no longer manage certain strenuous tasks, she instructed Umma to carry out her demands, like a puppet master. "This might be my last kimchi," she'd announce, before micromanaging Umma's every movement, down to how each green onion ought to be cut (into one-inch pieces) or how the cabbage leaves should be smothered with gochugaru (exactly so). Old memories shook to the surface:

First grade, 1959. My grandmother outside Umma's class, standing among the poplar trees, eight months pregnant. Whenever Umma got distracted, Halmoni took an umbrella, poked it through the classroom window, and batted her daughter on the head. At home, Grandma would quiz little Umma. "*I heard the answer*," she'd say. "*Why didn't you?*" Such vigilance. She wanted Umma to graduate at the top of her class, to enter an elite secondary school, to then be admitted to an elite university, so she could marry a man from a family well-to-do. All that for her only girl to run away and secretly elope with a grifter.

By week five, Umma wanted out. "I should be grateful they still alive," she confessed over the phone. "But this remind me how miserable I was growing up. It was unbearable. So painful. My life repeats itself." Then she'd fix her phone's camera onto Grandma. I saw a shrunken woman with a placid grin peeking out from beneath a mountain of blankets, innocent *who, me?* eyes glued to the television.

"She keep saying, 'It's gonna end when I die, but I'm not dying. I don't know why I've been cursed with a long life. I wanna die. I'm just waiting to die. I pray to God to take me every night, but I'm not dying,'" Umma spilled, exasperated. "She takes medication all day long. She ain't gonna die any time soon."

Plus, she was born with a lot of bok. According to Halmoni, that's why my grandparents have survived as well as they have, because of her good luck. It was preordained by her saju, an ancient Korean fortune-telling practice. Through a series of calculations factoring in birth time and the lunar calendar, a person's fate is determined through what is known as their four pillars of destiny.

Was it Halmoni's destiny to outlive her spouse? Not on her watch. "She won't even let Harabeoji nap," Umma recounted on one of our calls. Earlier, Grandma had stood by Grandpa's bedside, shouting: "You can't sleep! When people get old and sleep all the time, that means they're gonna die. You told me you were gonna watch *me* die. I gotta go first. Wake up!"

"I mean, what kind of life he has?" Umma said, breathless with laughter. "He can't even die on his own!" But Umma agreed; Halmoni had a point. "Once he's gone, she'll be cham-bap. And no one wants cold rice."

. . .

DESPITE A HARROWING first visit and vowing never to return again, Umma flew back for another three-month stretch in late 2022. A month into her stay, 158 people died in a Halloween crowd crush; news of the tragedy in Itaewon—a neighborhood in central Seoul—scattered far and wide. The last peacetime disaster had been in 2014, when the MV *Sewol* ferry sank. As I recall, Halmoni and Harabeoji mourned that loss acutely; 250 of the deceased were teenagers attending a class field trip. The nation grieved. A memorial at Gwanghwamun Square displayed the victims' school photos. Bouquets were tossed into the sea.

The crowd crush struck a different chord. Halloween is not a traditional Korean holiday, but especially since the 2010s, young people have been flocking to Itaewon for a night of incognito play. The South Korea government had installed strict Covid regulations that lasted longer than any of their Western counterparts, and the prolonged isolation, social distancing, and indoor–outdoor mask requirements had ramped up unprecedented excitement for the 2022 Halloween festivities. Due to its closeness to an American military base, Itaewon was once known as a destination for seedy pleasure-seekers. Over the last fifty years, the district has accumulated trendy boutiques, restaurants, and bars. It is home to South Korea's most visible queer community, a street dotted with saunas and bars called Homo Hill. It's also a haven to foreigners and young Koreans alike in search of letting loose from societal pressures in the form of binge drinking and club hopping along the neighborhood's iconic, narrow alleyways.

On October 29, some 130,000 people descended onto Itaewon, dressed as fairies, goblins, ghouls, and characters from *Squid Game*. By 10 P.M. a bottleneck amassed in a sloped lane beside the Hamilton Hotel. Those crammed into the eleven-foot-wide space formed a throng of panicked bodies, struggling to breathe and wriggle free. Some fell and entered cardiac arrest; others were smothered to death. It was an anomaly so monstrous I could hardly wrap my head around it.

It is within the realm of possibility that eight years after the MV *Sewol*, a surviving teen could have grown up and attended the festivities in Itaewon. There is an entire generation now in their early twenties, whose formative years have been bookended by freak accidents of an otherworldly, dystopian order. What was really happening in Korea?

When I called Umma, she and my grandparents appeared unfazed. Aside from a lack of crowd control and general organizational oversight, to them the events had been entirely preventable.

"It is sad," Umma said. "But these young people had a choice."

"It isn't a Korean holiday," Harabeoji shouted in the background. "Why would they go?"

If you survived what he had, then voluntarily attending a deadly party will seem like a preposterous life choice. I was not born in Korea, but if I had been, I'd belong to what is referred to as the MZ Generation: the Millennial and Z eras combined, those born between 1981 and 2005 into an industrial powerhouse, raised never knowing firsthand the country's most formative devastations. MZers are considered individualistic, environmentally conscious, and fluent in the digital world. The divide between young Koreans and their elders is tectonic. Neither group seems to understand the other, yet both hold existential disappointments about a changing national ethos toward work, family, and quality of life.

It occurred to me then how my knowledge of Koreanness had been filtered exclusively through the prism of my grandparents' and parents' experiences. I had yet to see Korea through the eyes of my generation. To understand on my own terms, I decided I would need to go and see for myself.

• • •

THE FIRST THREE TRIPS I took to South Korea are imperceptible now, superimposed into a triple exposure. I was twenty and twenty-six and twenty-seven but ever trapped in the language of a child. Goo-goo-ga-ga–level Korean, laden with that lumbering, unditchable American accent.

The first trip had been especially weird for Umma, who had not set foot on homeland soil since the early 1980s. The country she left behind was not the one she remembered. Shiny skyscrapers reflecting the city in infinite directions, bullet trains, digital billboards, K-everything everywhere, in a landscape rendered uncanny over time. Laurie spoke better Hangukmal than I could, but something happened to the three of us there, maybe on the plane ride over or in the crossing of seas and time zones. We arrived blinking and spacy, our words jumbling and untangling in a lingual no-man's-land somewhere between Korean and English.

Getting to central Seoul from Halmoni and Harabeoji's apartment required village bus and subway rides. Once there, we roamed the old districts' slender pathways, herding to and from landmarks with the haste of tourists. We ate corn dogs sheathed in crinkle-cut French fries, pillowy buns swaddling molten kimchi and minced pork, and squiggly fish cake skewers we washed down with hot salty broth. The taxi drivers sensed my mother had been gone a while, purely by her Korean—when she spoke it, anyway. Sometimes she slipped into English, the train tracks switching mid-course, mind and body meridians and decades apart.

This was clearest when we visited her alma mater, a women's university she described as the Korean equivalent to Wellesley ("You know, where Hillary Clinton went," she'd tout). When Umma was in college, everyone wore lanyards with photo IDs. As our mother, she stood on a street corner, stopped two students, and in frenzied English implored: "Where are your badges? Where are your badges!?"

"Hasn't it been twenty-six years?" Laurie asked. But Umma kept scanning the campus for a stabilizing clue. It was like watching Marty McFly's many discombobulations, his present self reckoning with his future self, yet all of him inconceivably ensnared in the past.

As for me, I'd traveled—not just the fourteen-hour flight, or the limo-jean bus ride to Halmoni and Harabeoji's town, or the two-hour commute into Seoul, but a much greater distance—to enter the actual place long abstracted in my mind. It was real now; I was in the country people insisted I "came from." But then a perfect thing happened. Every stranger I encountered in Korea spoke to me in Japanese. I didn't look like the women in Korea. I didn't dress like the women in Korea. I didn't speak like the women in Korea. Umma bartered for me at the open markets in her rusty mother tongue: "*Do you carry the* BIGGGGGGEST *shoe size?*" she beseeched the vendors. They each shook their heads in disbelief. Nothing could accommodate my enormous American feet. Quite literally, I did not fit in.

I took photos with a Canon point-and-shoot in an attempt to retain every detail for later review: the grisaille panorama of the Han River; steam billowing in helices from street food carts; the gamut of ssam lettuces (emerald, violet, curly, embossed) in which to wrap char-grilled meats; the way Grandpa tied trash wrappers into neat origami squares; Halmoni's contemplative face on our excursion to the outdoor folk village, how she looked up at the wing-tipped tiled rooftops and the open-fire kitchen replicas, as if plunged into a scene of her own past, to say, "*Yes, yes, this is exactly how it was.*" What a thing to witness, her memories enshrined into a waking history, as if petrified alive.

I left the camera in a PC bang while checking my email and blubbered over the loss for days. I wanted to hold on to every texture and hue, every relic and triviality, because everything felt equally consequential. It was the week I'd properly grown up. If home was a physical place where I was supposed to feel I belonged, maybe I wasn't "from" anywhere. This revelation was so overwhelming I blacked out at dinner with my family, trying to keep up with my uncles shot-for-shot of soju. Around the dinner table, we fussed over who would refill Harabeoji's glass, an honor to serve him with deferential hands as he talked-story of the old days. The last thing I remember was how my grandparents leaned toward each other and exchanged words in Japanese, when they wanted no one else to understand them.

On another trip, maybe my second, I'd returned amped with the energy of redemption. I'd taken a Korean class in New York and could, albeit very slowly, read Hangul. I made a solo day trip into Seoul, where signs and newspaper articles stirred to life around me, like a Magic Eye poster's secret image springing into view. Here was the language I'd ducked for years. At last, I could read! I could read!

Someone could have warned me. About 90 percent of what I translated turned out to be phonetically spelled English: tehdehbijeon; baeteoli; peullaespom; ohtohmehtik; gaseulaiting; moobuhmen-tuh; Netpeulligseu. Television; battery; platform; automatic; gaslighting; movement; Netflix.

On my fourth trip—when I went to meet Byron Kim, before my life imploded in New York—Umma, who happened to be visiting at the same time, drank too much soju and cried out for her dead dog, "*Moldaaaaaa, Moldayahhh, Moldaaaaaa.*" Halmoni, Harabeoji, and I, we just let her go there. What other way can that kind of heartache be assuaged? But was she really crying about the dog? The next morning, Umma awoke having no recollection, only to say, as if her actions belonged to someone else, "필름이 끈겼어." *The film cut to black.*

·　·　·

FOUR DAYS AFTER the Halloween crowd crush, on November 2, 2022, North Korea launched twenty-three short-range missiles—their highest count in a single day. One ballistic missile landed sixteen miles from South Korea's maritime border, a line North Korea does not formally acknowledge. The incident caused an air raid siren to sound on nearby Ulleung Island, located a mere seventy-five miles east of the South Korean mainland. Any significant military action from the United States or South Korea would lead to the "most horrible price in history," a North Korean official had warned.

South Korean president Yoon Suk-yeol considered the latest in the North's brinkmanship to be an "effective territorial encroachment" and countered with tit-for-tat air-to-surface missile launches, mirroring the exact target distances to those dispatched by North Korea. The provocations alarmed both Russian and Japanese governments, increasing fears of what might result from mounting tensions amid the Ukrainian conflict. North Korea had increased missile tests tenfold since 2021 and would, by 2022's end, reach a record of more than seventy launches.

Umma, Halmoni, and Harabeoji had been glued to the TV. News programs analyzed and predicted possible outcomes. "This is the closest to an outright escalation," Umma told me over the phone.

"*I guess I'm gonna die sitting down,*" Halmoni muttered in the background. My grandparents lived on the fourteenth floor. Should an emergency evacuation commence, Halmoni did not find it likely she'd make it to the garage for safe shelter.

"*You should go home,*" Grandpa advised Umma. "*There could be war any day now.*" This was the reason why they kept three months' worth of rice rations and bottled water, just in case. War and death, always on their minds.

Geopolitical tensions may be a constant concern for my grandparents' generation, but for those on the outside looking in, South Korea appears to be otherwise flourishing. To some, missile test headlines are muffled by the latest gossip revolving around K-pop stars. It can be easy to forget war never ended on the peninsula; it merely paused, by way of an armistice agreement. And in the decades since, the Republic of Korea has performed nothing short of a miracle, evolving from an economically ravaged developing nation into a pop culture juggernaut. By February 2020, when the movie *Parasite* swept the Palme d'Or at Cannes Film Festival and later took a Best Picture Oscar and three other major trophies at the ninety-second Academy Awards, it seemed like K-culture held a viselike grip on lifestyle and entertainment markets, from cosmetics (K-beauty) to food (K-cuisine), television (K-drama), film (K-movies), and music (K-pop). Unsettling statistics have dovetailed with this progress. For such a small country, South Korea boasts a startling number of cosmetic surgeries per capita. (In 2011, it was designated the plastic surgery capital of the world.) Korea also retains the highest suicide rate among wealthy nations, and it has maintained the lowest birth rate of any country for ten years. These matters are not prominently discussed, barring the one-off, voyeuristic deep dive that crops up in Western media every few years.

If you're like me, it may seem as if Korea's cultural influence has rocketed out of nowhere. But the Korean wave, also known as Hallyu, is not a situation of happenstance. Nor is it the result of sheer chutzpah (although Koreans have historically demonstrated plenty of that). As author Euny Hong notes in *The Birth of Korean Cool*, you can trace the K-phenomenon back to 1997 and the Asian financial crisis, which devastated three decades of South Korea's postwar economic progress. After a bailout from the International Monetary Fund (a request deemed the "Second National Disgrace" surpassed only by Japanese imperialism), the South Korean government initiated a series of investments in domestic entertainment industries. Treating music, animation, drama, and film with the same energy and industrial policy framework as their standard manufactured goods (cars, tech, and electronics) would hopefully inspire international demand for cultural assets only Korea could provide, leading to the country's monetary gain and in turn spurring national pride and global influence. In 1998, various departments and offices under President Kim Dae-jung aided in promoting K-culture commodities worldwide. Wiring every home with high-speed internet helped stoke intrigue through widely accessible and sharable media. Within a decade, Hallyu splashed its way across Asia, Europe, and the United States.

Not every Korean has benefited from the country's cultural cachet. The fiercely competitive environment that occasioned Korea's zombie-like rebirth has also produced a troubling sociological schism. The plot for *Parasite*, in which a poor family enters a rich family's employ (under false pretenses and to disastrous effect), stresses the vast dichotomy between Korea's haves and have-nots. The movie exaggerates some of these real-life dilemmas in a format of and by the very system that has cleaved the nation into decisive realms.

MZers came of age in South Korea's newly established era of wealth and were dropped into exceedingly competitive academic and professional gauntlets. Expenses are astronomical and opportunities are sparse, which has shaped their priorities. Older Koreans have called them the "giving up generation" because data suggests they're forgoing traditional milestones such as buying property, getting married, or having babies. Their Korea is unrecognizable to what their parents or grandparents know. I could relate. The rest, though, felt wildly extrinsic, if surreal, to my American mind.

Since I was a teenager, every now and then I have pictured what my life could have been like if I'd been born and raised in Korea. My mother wouldn't have married my father in these bizarro circumstances, so I'm aware I wouldn't be *me*. Yet I've still wondered: Who would I be there? A housewife, a K-drama actor, a writer. I let myself enter these alternate planes because, in them, my sharpest pain points vanish: I can speak Korean, look Korean, be Korean with an otherwise unknown ease.

Where you are shapes who you are, so I suppose that's why lately I couldn't seem to shake a constant sensation of unsettledness—and not about where I'd relocate next. The more I moved, the more I wondered who I was becoming and if I was getting farther from or closer to a kind of completeness. Learning about my MZ counterparts impelled a peculiar recalibration, as if a dislocated sensibility I could never really reconcile was snapping into place: If you can know who you aren't, could that somehow clarify who you are?

And so, about a month out, I decided to approach my trip from a different stance. I would stay in Seoul on my own for a couple nights. I would join K-culture excursions appealing strictly to outsiders enthralled by the great Korean wave. I would go as the foreigner I am, to look for whichever version of me I might find there, lying in relief.

HALMONI AND HARABEOJI'S HOUSE

"Sweet Dot Home" Apartments
3BR, 2BA

Via the *Korea Herald*:

Located 30 kilometers south of Seoul, Suwon is the largest metropolis of Gyeonggi Province.

Besides being home to a World Heritage site and some 1.1 million residents, it is also known as the "city of filial piety."

King Jeongjo, who reigned during the Joseon Dynasty from 1777 to 1800 as the 22nd king, wanted to build a "utopian city" to remember his ill-fated father Prince Sado—who was victimized in faction struggles in 1762—by constructing a fortress around his father's tomb at Haenggung Palace.

A Case of the Horses

I WAS TALKING TO A Korean friend in London in the winter of 2021 when the topic initially arose. "Sounds like your mom has yeokmasal," she said nonchalantly. "You know, the wanderer's curse."

No, I didn't know, had never heard of the word let alone its ominous connotations. From what I could acquire in English online, the meaning of yeokmasal derives from Chinese characters. Yeok: station, ma: horse, sal: not so directly translatable but, in this context, some amalgamation of aura, vibe, destiny, bad or negative energy/spirit/curse. The term may date as far back as the Silla dynasty. Koreans traveled then across great distances on horseback; in order to maintain efficient transportation speeds, riders would trade out their tired steeds at horse stations dotted across the country. When someone has yeokmasal, they will wander, station to station, stopping only long enough to refresh their horse before moving wherever the wind carries them. Such is the nomad's burden, itchy feet whisking you away from the family you are meant to honor and serve. The wanderer's curse is supposedly hereditary and a measurable disposition. To find out whether one is beset with yeokmasal, one must consult a fortune-teller (a common practice across all tiers of caste in ancient Korea). One's saju is deciphered from birth chart information; within specific astrological coordinates, one may discover, among other fates, whether one is plagued with the curse.

Today yeokmasal is not associated with the blemished implications of yore. Living abroad for vocational opportunities can be viewed as a boon. Confucian principles regarding familial duty still apply, so maybe it is understood that a person is destined to eventually go back home and settle down. These days the term can even be filtered through the high-gloss sheen of wanderlust, the globetrotter's longing for exploration that glorifies the romanticism—not the instability—of perpetual travel. Wandering is a familiar preoccupation for my generation in America—a time of constant in-betweenness, especially so for children of immigrants. It is no wonder, then, that Millennials have been drawn to "vanlife," a trend that gained popularity across the country around 2015, perhaps peaking post-2020 Coronavirus isolation. Even my mother could see the appeal. In a van, you could stay at home *and* move around. Why buy a house or pay rent when you could make anywhere your yard? Kitted-out vehicles afforded thrill-seekers with the open road's vanishing point, thrusting them toward a titillating, unseeable future.

Anyone who's been on the road for longer than a week understands there are pitfalls to what may seem like a derring-do flex of freedom. There are certainly ways to bathe and nest in a confined mobile space, but for how long? Wanderlust conveys an air of exhilaration, risk for the sake of stimulation and adventure. But to be a nomad is another matter, something more enduring, a state that shudders with existential restlessness. No end in sight. No thrill either.

Unless you are Buddhist, uncertainty can feel like a soulful affliction, holding both provocative and terrifying possibilities: fulfillment of purpose or the bottomless unknown. Wandering is perhaps a way to embrace uncertainty, making discovery feel constant and ripe with promise. Are those who possess the wanderer's curse galloping toward hope? Or are they ever averting stillness, so that whatever they may be escaping never gets the chance to catch up?

When I asked my mother about yeokmasal, she said, without hesitation, "Oh yea . . . I have that." At no point had Umma received a saju reading of her own, though it didn't take prescience to see the woman had a case of the horses. Her itinerant ways belonged to a bigger story. I was thirty when she unloaded the bombshell over dinner with two of my closest friends. She hadn't shared it with anyone—not my father nor my sister—before.

I'd assumed Umma's season of wandering started with Alaska, when she'd answered that listing in the nurses' journal. However, sometime around 1967, when my mother was fifteen, she spotted a help wanted ad in a Korean newspaper. A beer hall located outside of Seoul offered lucrative pay, uniforms, and lodging. Fed up with Halmoni's constant surveillance, Umma boarded a bus and walked into the beer hall, ready to work and live a life on her own. They hired her on the spot.

Yes, she was offered room, board, and uniforms, but the costs were directly deducted from her wages, leaving her in the red. She carried out waitress tasks during the day but was horrified to learn the beer hall functioned as a brothel at night. The details get hazy here. Coworkers helped hide Umma from the men who requested her company. After three months, she went home. "I was very lucky," she said.

Umma resumed her old life as if the other one had never happened. She went back to high school, graduated from the Wellesley equivalent. "I don't even know what I wanted," she confessed of that time. "And I still don't know what I want."

So Alaska hadn't been a fluke. She'd been that woman all along, who ran away to the beer hall in 1967, to America in 1976, to Ketchikan in 2007. "I'm still looking for something that it's not there," she told me on a recent call. "I don't know what it is I'm looking for." Almost anticipating what I had not spoken, she added: "You know, you don't have to be like me . . . "

There was a time I believed I couldn't possibly be anything like her. Now I wondered: Would I be as unsettled at seventy, too?

Did I even have a choice?

• • •

To FIND OUT if I was "officially" accursed, I'd have to get my saju read in Seoul. Did I believe in that kind of stuff? Kind of. I am not a woo-woo person; I like to say I am medium-woo, prone to occasional metaphysical rumination. I know my astrological signs, but I don't know when or which planet is in what house aligned in or out of my favor.

I asked my Korean Londoner friend for a recommendation. "I can tell you right now, you have yeokmasal," she told me, hardly containing her laughter. "You don't need to go to him to find out." But I wanted to hear what this soothsayer could glean about both Umma and me, so we made the appointment. Our guy was apparently quite legit, as far as fortune-tellers go. The plan: My mother would join me in Seoul for one day and translate our readings. I would pad out my itinerary with other activities prior to her arrival. In order to get the full immersion I was seeking, I decided to sample Airbnb's suggested Experiences—excursions led by local "experts." In Tuscany, there are truffle hunting expeditions. In Oaxaca, traditional cooking classes. In Seoul, options revolve around K-culture. Regardless of the focus, every host relays some essential notion of Koreanness in their overviews—whether in Korea's history, its treasures and trades, or its current ontological dilemmas.

"Are you Warmton or Coolton?" asks one host. K-beauty professionals can decipher your "personal color" within a one-hour session, because "knowing your own body color is helpful for making a good image." In another you can learn how to apply makeup like Korean idols and celebrities, "drawing eyebrows that can greatly influence your impression" and "shading to make your face look slimmer" during your stay in the "Beauty Kingdom."

You can also take K-pop vocal and dance lessons where you'll be endowed with "so much insider info, you may just make it in the industry yourself." Because Koreans love to drink, you can play drinking games, sharing fried chicken and clinking thimbles of soju with strangers, to "feel the culture of a real Korean college student." And for the more emo-minded, you can delve into young Korea's "sad cultures" on a walking tour through Gangnam District.

I was taken by one host named GJ. She offered a range of Experiences, from conversational Korean language courses to something called "Amazing toilet restroom tour," exploring, I presume, Seoul's most noteworthy water closets. I was charmed by her hustler's gusto and kooky "what you'll do" descriptions. For a seemingly unremarkable stroll around her outskirts neighborhood, participants can "dive into real Korean life" to "get to know what Parasite claims. Here is a chance to look around the local residences where we actually are. You may be able to smell them."

"Is it a waste of the commission that this platform takes?" she shares on her bio page. "I agree with that a little bit. But they made typical trip different. Isn't it? . . . The reason why I can continue to have positive personalities is that I don't make my living by those experiences. I am ready to show you my sincerity, and I want to feel your sincerity, too."

GJ happened to offer saju readings, branded as a form of "Oriental fortune-telling." She would follow it with something called K-tarot, an additional reading performed with a handmade deck of cards based on illustrated Korean divination texts known as "dangsaju." GJ explicitly states her services are *not* for native Koreans. I couldn't track down any other English-speaking saju readings, so I signed up. Because I would be paired with another American client, I decided I'd mostly observe, vérité style. "This experience has nothing to do with supernatural shamanism," GJ mentioned in a message. "Fortuneteller is not shaman. Two are different. I will talk about what is saju to you!"

GJ's K-tarot may be a clever marketing ploy, appealing to astrology enthusiasts, but it also gestures to a greater trend in Korea. The clairvoyance business has seen renewed interest, especially among Korean youth. According to *Korea Economic Daily*, as of 2018 the industry was on its way to becoming worth $3.7 billion in South Korea. Market research indicated two-thirds of all Koreans seek guidance from fortune-tellers at least once a year—a number that apparently increased post-pandemic.

In any Seoul neighborhood, you will likely come across fortune-teller tents set up on sidewalks, where seers offer tarot card, face, and palm readings at minimal cost. The most popular services, however, are saju readings. These days one can book online for sessions held at YouTube-famous fortune-telling cafés. In some of these establishments, rather confusingly, women present themselves as mudangs (Korean shamans) and augur via the landing patterns of tossed wooden sticks or ancient coins.

Like GJ mentioned, mudangs and fortune-tellers are not the same—but they can overlap, perhaps in the way a square is a rectangle but a rectangle is not a square. They are sometimes referred to interchangeably or without much distinction. These nebulous parameters likely present ample opportunities to profit off the ductile faith of others.

The busiest saju season is from December to February, after the completion of academic exams and before the lunar new year. Young Koreans ask questions about college admissions, which schools they ought to attend, whether the country will go to war, or if this year they'll fall in love. Couples visit to determine their matrimonial harmony in a reading called gunghap. Business tycoons and bureaucrats also request guidance with risky financial acquisitions and career moves. There are a number of controversies involving prominent South Korean leaders across conservative and progressive ideologies, who defer to the private counsel of personal fortune-tellers throughout pivotal political decisions.

One's pillars of destiny are fixed, so any fortune-teller ought to divine the same characters based on birth information. For Koreans, though, one's lot in life is not set in stone. Saju is like a cosmic blueprint. Ultimately an individual wields the power to alter their fate through intentional choices or sometimes with the help of expensive talismans. And that's the kind of enterprising spirit Koreans can get behind.

Janet Shin, a professor of the Oriental Science Department at Wonkwang Digital University and the *Korea Times*'s resident fortune-telling columnist, believes saju ought to be treated with academic interest rather than brushed off as woo-woo hooey given how its storied past is woven into Korea's philosophical history. There are centuries-old dang saju texts displayed in the National Museum of Korea and the Museum of Folk History. Sources differ on the exact origins, though many believe saju is based on Chinese philosophies. According to Shin, saju's historical background is indeterminable, due to competing political interests and ideologies that have fluctuated across multiple dynasties throughout East Asia.

Wherever it started, saju has become as Korean as kimchi. And, like any metaphysical belief system, it functions as a way of making sense of the unknowable, to better comprehend one's place in the world.

But how does saju work? The word, which translates to "four pillars," resembles the Chinese astrological tradition of Ba Zi. While Ba Zi readings are influenced by elements from the *I-ching*, or *The Book of Changes*, to interpret readings Koreans rely on their sacred tome known as *Tojeong Bigyeol* or *Secrets of Tojeong*, written by Lee Ji-ham, a scholar of the Joseon dynasty.

The process itself involves an explosion of numbers, beginning with those pillars, based on birth year, month, date, and hour. Each pillar is divided into two rows (one of "celestial stems" and another of "earthly branches") for a total of eight characters. Every character corresponds to one of five elements—earth, wood, fire, water, and metal—and is attributed with yin or yang (dual forces sometimes simplified as positive or negative energies). Additionally, each pillar represents a stage of life, read from right to left (birth to childhood, adolescence to young adulthood, and so forth until death).

With so many factors at play, it may seem as if one's personal saju permutations are rare. In actuality, there are only 518,400 possible variations in a sexagenary cycle. Uniqueness arises not through the numbers themselves but in how and by whom those numbers are interpreted. Prognostications are dependent on the diviner's personal proclivities and beliefs. One fortune-teller may infuse elements of quantum theory into their readings, or psychoanalysis, while another may prioritize their client's reactions and body language to shape the bricolage. Some might not believe in fate or destiny at all, valuing the social or performative aspects of the transaction instead. In other words, there is no single way of practicing saju. It is a tradition dependent upon subjectivity and its very own lore.

Nowadays folks can skip a face-to-face encounter altogether by entering their info into an app for speedy results. But for my purposes, I would need to interact with humans attuned with divination skills. Which is one reason why I decided to meet with GJ. Saju schematics are dizzying and resources are written in Korean or Chinese, so there are limits to what I could research in English. GJ had been studying saju for a mere two years. Even though her approach was marketed for foreigners, I needed to beef up on basics before the legit, second appointment. I also wasn't confident Umma would convey necessary nuance—or if she'd even show up. Hours before my departure, she got wishy-washy on me. Maybe she wouldn't even make it to the saju appointment. "It's against my religion," she joked. And with that, I boarded my flight.

*   *   *

THERE ARE TWO KOREAN adages that have melded in my mind, the contours of where one begins and the other ends coiling into an eternal knot: An eighty-year-old mother worries about her sixty-year-old daughter, as if she isn't grown but still a baby playing dangerously close to the ocean. Despite my jumbling, the message is clear: No matter the life events that have come to pass between birth and going long in the tooth, a mother never stops being a mother. She is forever inclined to fret over her child's safety, as if they are always on the brink of being washed away to sea.

The flip side, imbued with less sentimentality, is to say in some ways a mother and child's dynamic is endlessly entwined, roles locked, however fraught. This doomed rendition is what I fear plagues Umma and Halmoni. Under her mother's rule, Umma was a child again paying, so it seemed, for infractions of the past. Sixty days in captivity and Umma had deflated. The old "in theory versus in practice" trap. Halmoni micromanaged every detail in her three-bedroom fiefdom. If a dish clanked in the sink, Halmoni accused Umma of breaking her fine American Corelle "china." If the mesh laundry bag tore she'd claim no one else understood how to correctly zip the zippers. No going outside, either, unless permitted by Halmoni because of "*Oh-mi-koo-ron, Oh-mi-koo-ron,*" the Covid variant lurking everywhere like the boogeyman.

There are boutique nursing homes in South Korea called Silvertowns equipped with saunas and gourmet kitchens paralleling four-star hotels. But in no way would my grandma and grandpa agree to relocate to an assisted living facility. Or maybe they'd kick Halmoni out. Lately Umma had taken to calling Grandma "El Diablo." I have rarely seen that side of my grandmother. She was particular; I could relate. Was she really *that* bad?

To be fair, the woman has endured extraordinary loss. By my age, she'd already given birth to five children, though only four survived. During the war, after Harabeoji left the kimchi hole, Halmoni headed south by foot, walking the 200 miles to Busan with her firstborn swaddled on her back. On the journey, Communist soldiers stopped to interrogate her. When they asked her a question, she pinched her baby under his bundled blanket. He shrieked until the sound became so insufferable, the soldiers let them go. Around that time, her own father was murdered—in an ordinary, public, tragic way, is how my mother describes it: "Probably village people saw him killed. You know, there are a lot of sad stories. That's how everybody went through in her generation." No one talks about trauma, perhaps because there was so much of it to go around. "Horrible stories, everywhere," Umma said. "Now they a dying breed."

For reasons beyond my understanding, Halmoni has loved me fiercely since the moment I was born. She'd ridden in the car with Harabeoji, when Umma drove herself to the hospital while in labor. And she was there, hours later, when my four pillars aligned. I grew up knowing only who she was in America, the woman with a perfect trapezoidal perm who took Jazzercise at a fitness studio in Arcadia; who mixed up "Thank you" and "You welcome" at the Ralphs checkout; who once lovingly made me thirteen potato pancakes I ate in one sitting. I was now unmarried, childless, and perpetually broke—metrics that, if I were any other person, would qualify me as an abject failure. None of this mattered in Halmoni's eyes. There were things I would not understand about her, and things she would not understand about me. But in ways I felt known by her on a molecular level. Even where language faltered, I came from my mother, who came from her, and somehow that was enough for her to love me.

My mother and her mother's relationship, this I could not grasp. Affectionless. Conditional. Broken. I'd never seen them touch. It was eye-opening, then, to reconsider my adolescence and the rockier periods between Umma and me. How shocked I used to be, by her antagonism: "Oh, you want me to be one of those white moms? *Awww sweetie! It's gonna be okay?!*" she'd mock. "Well, I'm not." We'd managed to foster an uncommon reciprocity anyway. On the maternal sliding scale, this was a staggering improvement. There was no place of tenderness she'd known, in between.

*   *   *

AT THE LAST MINUTE, Umma decided my uncle Yong, whom I hadn't seen in twenty-five years, would be picking me up at Incheon Airport. There were around fifty masked Koreans at the Arrivals hall. Any one of them could have been him. I called out in English, "Uncle? Uncle?" until, sufficiently humiliated, I aimlessly paced the same patch of terrazzo for half an hour. I called my mother, who was livid (she didn't believe me when I told her multiple exits existed in the terminal). Finally my uncle and I reunited, and we headed off.

Day one, Halmoni was her usual doting self, offering to make galbi jjim, saving the best kimchi bites at lunch for me. She humored my requests, like when I asked to take a photo of our hands side-by-side; Umma, Grandma, and me, our features long, slender, elegant—extensions of one lineage—a kind of progression through time in our aging replications.

There were glimpses of Halmoni's mulish ways, like when she nagged Harabeoji about the correct way to make rice, both of them sans hearing aids screaming back and forth until Halmoni won out. But it didn't seem diablo-ish. "She's set in her ways," I said, like a dummy. "You're new to this whole dynamic," my mother snapped. "I been here almost *three* month."

It began the next afternoon. First, a hunger strike. Umma presented Halmoni with a tray of food at 12:30 P.M. on the dot. The empress rebuffed her. "I did something," Umma said. "I don't know what yet, but she's mad."

Next, a rejected peace offering. Umma had handed Halmoni a box of her favorite choux buns from Paris Baguette and she turned away, spurning them like a picky child. Moments later Grandma propped herself up onto her walker handles and announced: "Who bought these? If it was Yong, okay. If *she* bought them, I won't have any."

A convoluted yarn unspooled over dinner, while singers on a competition TV program belted out old country songs in the background. Korean Columbo had pieced it together: Earlier that day, Halmoni wanted to give me a baggie of old barrettes. I thought I'd communicated how I didn't need them or maybe I'd take them later or maybe I smiled a stupid smile, thanked her, and walked away. Halmoni believed my mother had been standing behind me, urging me to refuse the gift. I returned to the guest bedroom to work on my laptop (as I always do—lying down), while Umma played a coloring game on her phone. But Grandma misconstrued this scene as a conspiratorial debrief. In her own house, the nerve! The treason!

"I saw you," Halmoni concluded. Soju was flowing, and we hadn't even served the rice yet when Umma erupted—seventy days or maybe seventy years of stifled lament. "*When you treat me this way, I might as well be dead*," she screamed in Korean. "*I want to die! I want to die! I want to die!*" The outburst was not well received. Halmoni doubled down. Harabeoji ordered Umma to stop ("*Just apologize to your mother and eat.*"). "Did that happen, Jennifer?" Umma shouted. "Did that happen?" My puerile, desperate Korean only making things worse, my awkward gesticulations, pantomiming laptop-typing in recline, to fill in the blanks: "*No Halmoni, I . . . computer. Umma didn't. I sorry. Me! I did!*" But there was no convincing her.

Umma stood up, yell-crying, the words too quick and complex for me to keep up. Eventually Halmoni demurred, unconvincingly: "So be it. Must have made a mistake." And because the food was getting cold, she commanded us to drop the thing pronto. Which prompted Umma to stumble off to the veranda, where she wept and huffed guttural animal sounds that merged with the operatic performances blaring from the television. I found her tucked into a ball beneath the hanging laundry. And I watched as Umma's mind slipped, the way it does sometimes for new English speakers, the past tense mixing with the present. "It's just like when I was a little girl," she whimpered. "Always different for my brothers. So controlling. I never get to go out. She never give me any spending money. I can't go out with my friend. Everyone else gets spending money but me." Between sobs, she instructed me to go back inside. "If you stay too long, she will become suspicious."

After eight minutes of losing her shit out on the veranda, Umma returned to the table and apologized. "That was a real meltdown," she admitted in English, suddenly clear as day.

Later we lay on the unforgiving, stone-like mattress we shared. Umma asked to play tunes on YouTube. "Faithfully" by Journey. "I Started a Joke" by the Bee Gees. "Morning Has Broken" by Cat Stevens. "Bridge Over Troubled Water" by Simon and Garfunkel. This was the music she'd heard at a teahouse back at university, when she'd strode up the stairs, greeted by a photo of Rod Stewart with his trademark shaggy do. "I was so young," she said. She sang along with girlish zeal, completing the adolescent reversion of her homecoming. For the finale, she asked me to make a promise: "At my funeral, I want you to play this song."

We watched the video together. The Bee Gees wrote "Immortality" specifically for Celine Dion to sing, and this behind-the-scenes clip captured their studio recording session. To tell you the truth it brought me to tears. More importantly, it brought the Gibbs to tears. There is leonine Barry, clutching a tissue, listening with his eyes closed as Celine's voice flitters up and down the scales. "So this is who I am. And this is all I know . . ." Maurice is standing in his cowboy hat, beside Robin with his purple-tinted glasses. Candles flicker in the foreground, the camera pans, soft focus; a story unfolds—a child's destiny fulfilled, never-ending storms, fate up in the wind. One Gibb reaches an arm out to Celine; she reaches back. In come the brothers for the chorus, on breathy falsetto wings. "We don't say goodbye . . ."

The whole while Umma was singing too, her voice quivering with a practiced, tempered longing. And now I was the one doing the guttural weeping. I was thinking about before the blow-up, when she'd recounted again how miserable and controlling Halmoni had been throughout her childhood, how she'd vowed to never be like her, *ever*. Umma may not have hit me on the head with an umbrella at school, but she had also been quite miserable and controlling in her own way. Didn't she remember? She roused from wherever in the past she'd floated to, looked at me as if shaken awake only to return betrayed. How could I? Or . . . how could she? And when she retreated again, perhaps she was thinking: No matter how she'd tried, she still turned out like her mother. I thought about that too—what we can't get away from, what we wish we could—as I turned over, lulled by the Gibbs' feather light harmonies, and pretended to fall asleep.

. . .

BEFORE VENTURING INTO SEOUL for four nights, I prepare my usual, embarrassingly exhaustive document for traveling somewhere new, listing where I want to eat and drink (best mandu, sundubu, third wave coffee, Korean rotisserie chicken) along with several phonetically spelled-out common phrases I can refer to when stage fright short-circuits my brain. **Can I take this to-go?** / Ee-guh po-jang dweh-yo? / 이거 포장 돼요? **I'm sorry (formal)** / Joesonghabnida / 죄송합니다.

Grandpa is worried about me getting around, because my Korean is so shitty. Grandma says thieves abound in the big city, so I need to wear my purse front and center. Umma has not informed Halmoni about how she'll stay with me in Seoul for one day, but we're proceeding as planned. She waves me off when I depart, morose but acceptant, like one of the string quartet musicians who resolves to play one last song on a capsizing *Titanic*.

I've chosen to stay in a hanok—a traditional Korean house with tiled rooftops and rice paper doors. This one offers classic Korean breakfasts, heated wooden floors, an interior courtyard with an Oriental garden, and a private sauna and spa tub. It is located a short walk from Gyeongbokgung—the primary palace of the Joseon dynasty—where I spend a sunny but bitterly cold afternoon touring the grounds and nearby folk museum.

Visitors donning hanboks receive free admission to any of the city's palaces. It's a popular activity, and one I'd seen advertised in many Airbnb Experiences. For about seventy dollars, you can spend two hours cosplaying Korean royalty while a multilingual professional photographer documents your every move. The fee includes "VIP treatment": borrowing Korean outfits with the help of a "Personal Hanbok assistant" and optional hairstyling or accessories at additional cost. The host will then snap faux candid shots of you and your partner or friends beneath Gwanghwamun—Gyeongbokgung's towering gate—or beneath the vibrant rainbow-like dancheong paintings adorning the eaves, or while sauntering by the royal banquet hall's tree-lined lake. Tourists of varying backgrounds find the pastime alluring, as seen in one host's photo gallery: a lesbian couple smiling in complete regalia mid-stroll; a woman in a hijab pinching up her carnation-pink chima, curtsy-ready; a Fu Manchu–mustachioed man wielding a fake sword.

On my visit, I weave around a dozen of these simultaneous photo shoots. I see a gaggle of Chinese women posing in choreographed group formations. There are several white dudes, begrudgingly outfitted in full court dress, including coronet headgear, trailing their Asian girlfriends from balustrade to balustrade, recording the inanities on their smartphones. Some rent their outfits directly from one of the many boutiques in the surrounding neighborhood and the costumed families, couples, and teens waltz around the ancient streets in their sneakers, clutching selfie sticks, posing together at tea shops or nearby Bukchon Hanok Village. The epitome of Korea can be found in these transactional displays, antiquity clashing with modernity—specifically jarring at Gyeongbokgung. The palace was first constructed in 1395; 93 percent of its original 500 buildings were obliterated during occupation, when the Japanese empire sought to destroy any signifiers of Korean legacy. Now there's an entire cottage industry for larping olden-day Korea in the twenty-first century.

That evening, I participate in something more my speed: a Korean youth generation tour that promises to peel back Korea's shiny veneer, exposing the country's "sad cultures." As a former Morrissey fan, I suspect I'm the ideal participant for a sad cultures tour. I meet June, our docent, at the Gangnam Style "horse dance" stage. Our cohort consists of a couple from Singapore, a young Kiwi doctor, and a finance guy in a Union Square Donuts beanie.

Fifty years ago, Gangnam, meaning "south of the river," teemed with rice paddies and agricultural landscape. Today it is a district reputed for its uber wealthy residents—synonymous with a Beverly Hills lavishness available to only a sliver of the population. June is a handsome Korean guy in his twenties with the prototypical em-dash eyebrows, Spock sideburns, and a hint of edge (a tragus piercing). He says by the end of our time together, we will know Korea's dark side and why his peers in the MZ generation frequently describe their predicament as "living in hell."

Hell Joseon is the dystopia MZers were born into and cannot escape. Beginning in the 1960s, government resources and funding had been funneled almost entirely to central Seoul. Park Chung-hee seized power via military coup in 1961, served as president from 1963 until his assassination in 1979, and many of his economic reforms led to Korea's meteoric transformation, often referred to as the Miracle of the Han River. Some see Park as a despot, others as a complicated leader who rectified the nation through stringent, if dictatorial, control. He enforced rapid development, including the implementation of key infrastructure (bridges and roads) and an emphasis on exportation of domestic goods to kickstart the country's industrial growth. Further expedited by Seoul's bid to host the 1988 Summer Olympics, soon high-rises sprouted from the land. Furious productivity established untenable momentum. It seems MZers now feel trapped by many of the systems that hoisted the country from financial collapse. They are encumbered by impossible-to-maintain ideals, manifested in appearance, career, and social demands, in an ongoing climate of state-led media censorship and political oppression. But, June assures us, this will be "not whining tour . . . I love my people."

Due to the inequity of postwar development, areas outside the city have lagged behind Seoul's progress. Rural towns do not provide adequate opportunities, jobs, and healthcare for young people and have become largely occupied by Korea's elderly. According to June, 92 percent of the Korean population resides in urbanized, metropolitan areas, which constitute only 16.7 percent of the entire country's usable land. Buying a home in Seoul, the nation's capital city, is inconceivable for most; the going rate for an apartment—not a house—hovers around one million U.S. dollars, while the average monthly salary clocks in around $2,800. As a result, the life of Korea's youth generation is rife with ceaseless, gladiatorial competition. In a time when family-run conglomerates (known as chaebols) dominate contemporary Korean society, Golden Spoons (those born into wealth) can easily skip the line to ascend quickly in the corporate world, while those from more humble upbringings toil in the muck indefinitely.

We walk by hagwons, the cutthroat after-school academies so intense the government had to install a 10 P.M. curfew to regulate children's excessive study hours. Next are the pylon signs filled with the names of plastic surgery clinics that accommodate Korea's obsession with "lookism." There is even a Korean web toon called Lookism (that has since been adapted into a Netflix anime series of the same name) in which Park Hyung Seok, an unattractive, self-loathing high school teenager, assumes a strapping body by day, but must return to his shlub self at night. In that form he is treated with stereotypical derision by bullies prior to his metamorphosis and has zero friends; no women will give him the time of day; and he's so depressed he wants to die. When he's living as his hotter self, his life improves. Women swoon at the sight of his K-pop-idol physique, and he becomes a social media influencer and a model. The moral is ambiguous. Perhaps the point is that Park Hyungseok must confront how good-looking people experience life differently, which directly affects how one sees oneself. In psychological terms, this can be referred to as the Looking Glass theory, in which a person interprets their identity based on how others perceive them. Meaning that self-image is not conceived in isolation but among others, through social dynamics, because individuals and society work in concert, one entity informing the other. Each social encounter is a mirror in which one's reflection varies. And ultimately the individual must weigh and assess this feedback to find a kind of equilibrium.

Balance is not so simple in Korea. According to June, it is common for companies to require headshots with job applications. "It doesn't matter who you are on the inside, only how you look on the outside," he states, expressionless. With regard to plastic surgery's ubiquity, he asks, "Have we gone too far? Maybe."

By some estimates, one in three women between the ages of nineteen and twenty-nine have undergone procedures. With the incremental tweaks, everyone has begun to look the same—white skin, rounder eyes, V-line chins, button noses, upturned smiles, slimmer calves, bigger breasts, smaller faces—but also farther and farther away from looking Korean. When June's friend moved abroad, she told him, "I feel free. I don't have to care about how I look finally."

Korea's triumphant comeback narrative has spawned these hellish preoccupations. "Earlier generation struggled and worked so hard," June says. "Their screams were covered by development and successes. [They said] let's give those successes to our next generation." But those children now feel trapped. "We can't develop faster. They had hope, older generation, but we can't develop like old days," June continues. "Younger generation sees there's no hope."

Suicide is arguably the saddest of the sad cultures we broach on our two-hour doom-and-gloom cruise. Before inviting us to eat Korean fried chicken—perhaps the most depressing post-mortem drinks hang invite I've ever received—June concludes his spiel on the banks of the Han River. We could spot nearby Mapo Bridge, a disturbingly frequent suicide destination. In 2012, Samsung Life Insurance posted uplifting messages along the railings to deter potential victims from leaping to their deaths. "Doesn't it feel good to be outside walking on a bridge?" one sign said. "Worries are nothing," said another. The topic is so common within cultural discourse, there's even a suicide jumping joke among young Koreans. "What temperature is the Han River today?" one will ask. And to any answer they'll retort, "Nevermind, too cold!" It's an eerie evolution. In the span of fifty years, the Han River has come to symbolize new beginnings for one generation and definitive ends for another.

* * *

AFTER A LIGHT BREAKFAST of marinated fish and fermented soybean soup, I meet GJ outside Bulgwang Station for my first saju reading. She's in her forties, lean and springy, with an almost twitchy alertness, like a cricket. She's pacing, checking the time, waiting for our second participant. Sandra, a Black woman also in her forties, from San Diego, finally arrives in a taxi, apologetic for the delay. She's wearing a beret. Despite having been in Seoul for two weeks on vacation, she hasn't taken the subway yet. I ask what brought her to South Korea in the dead of winter. Her answer has something to do with working in the health sector, a visit for ideas to share back home. As for this Westerner-centric fortune-telling event? "Oh, curiosity," she says, then adds coquettishly, "I have my reasons."

We trail GJ's brisk pace and our guide chatters away about the busy day, her teenage daughter's exams, and the park we pass, recently revamped to serve the community. Elderly Koreans are seated at the benches, embanked in bristly dead grass.

We de-layer and order drinks at a spacious bookstore–café. GJ can't seem to catch her breath. She's starting a new sentence before finishing the last one, her mind moving faster than her body can handle. Through the course of the session, she will refill her black coffee three times. At the moment, she's losing track of her belongings, touching pens and loose papers, looking under the table, into her bag, monologuing a continuous, nervous ramble until handing us gifts: tangerines and long-twist donuts called kkwabaegi.

Sandra appears unbothered by our host's frenetic state. "Coffee and carbs!" she sings.

Though the answer is rather obvious, I ask GJ anyway: "Are you okay?"

"I'm okay," she says, then immediately reneges. "Actually, I'm not okay." She's awaiting text updates about her daughter's exam results. We learn her kid skips class and doesn't care much about school which, in Korea, is a very bad, very big deal. GJ interrupts her own tangent.

"This is my personal history. I'm so sorry. Just give me your birth day and time." She hands us an informational printout along with pages she's ripped from her notebook so we can write down our birth information, then leaves to retrieve our coffees.

It occurs to me that I've never seen a fortune-teller stressed. "She seems frazzled," I whisper to Sandra. "It's freaking me out a little bit." Sandra shrugs as classical music, like the ambient soundtrack at a shopping mall, tinkles in the background. I stare at the printout, which is covered with boxes, charts, and phoneticized Korean-to-English words, including the ten celestial stems and twelve earthly branches. There's a pentagram too, each point representing one of the five elements, +/- signs marked throughout a list of characters. The four pillars are represented by eight squares, one marked "social mask," another "success."

Sandra asks me where I'm from, and I tell her Brooklyn because nowhere else feels right. I haven't returned to California since my mother left seventeen years ago. Even though I've lived in Tulsa for two and a half years, it isn't home. New York isn't anymore either, but it's as close as I've gotten so far. "You don't have an accent," Sandra notices. "Cheater!" I smile and let out a nervous warble, because obviously I've lied and both of us know it.

GJ returns and begins punching numbers into an app on her phone. It will calculate our eight characters and correlating energies she'll interpret. GJ takes a swig of her java, slams the mug on the table, and continues mumbling and scribbling into her notebook. I notice Sandra's birth date and fill the gap of silence: "Ah, you were almost a New Year's baby!"

"All the women in my family are basically Capricorns," she says, swirling her latte. "It's really scary. We have nothing but earth signs."

"WOW. Wow," GJ exclaims. Apparently, out of eight characters, I only have two elements: tree and water. "I . . . I met the first person to have only two . . ." she says. "I so curious. It's very simple. But you are not a simple person." She switches over to Sandra's numbers, pleased. "As you see, you have ALL of five element."

Noticing my disappointment (is two bad?), Sandra whispers to me, generously, "Just means I'm complicated."

After more coffee chugging and notebook scribbling and mug slamming, GJ is ready to explain Sandra's pillars. She's pointing with her
pen tip to characters and boxes on our printouts. I have been listening
to Korean people talk in accents my entire life, but I cannot seem to
keep up with GJ. Yet Sandra is "mm"ing and "hmm"ing, gasping and
concurring with "One hundred percent" or "That's so true." At one
point they share a giggle about a third-pillar revelation and Sandra's
propensity toward secret-keeping ("*so* Capricorn"), which prompts her
to say: "It's like Diana Ross. I'm coming out!"

Why? How??

GJ agrees. She's chewing loudly on her donut as she continues:
"You are medium fire, candle. Not big flame. Yea? It's not the danger-
ous! People know you. Earth and fire. Negative earth. This is a conti-
nent. Maybe hollow, is very wide. . . . And then this fire, fighting fire,
big fire . . . So this is really good. Negative earth is . . . *guard*, they,
everybody know what is your potential . . . If earth character have big
energy, earth need tree, be control. Fire . . . "

"It's opposite," Sandra finishes.

"Yea, opposite. We say, kill. Literally means kill. Tree kill earth. But
it is not correct word in English so . . . earth need tree. And fire *hurt*.
Fire melt metal."

I'm thinking, *Is Sandra killing earth? How does a medium fire melt
metal?* when GJ turns to me, laughing a little too hard, and says: "*You*
don't have fire!" Which feels like a dig, but seeing as how I don't know
what's happening, I release an unconvincing "Ahhh." And while I don't
know how she arrived at such a conclusion, Sandra summarizes with an
analogy having to do with how forests need a good scorching every now
and then to kill off diseases so new saplings can grow.

"Can you understand?" GJ asks me.

I cannot. How did Sandra *get* all that? I can understand GJ is speaking English but the words sound randomly strung together as if pulled
from a bingo tumbler. She turns to my chart. "You have all tree. Tree is
a start," she says, pointing to the top of the pentagram. "*You* start a lot.
You have energy to start. But there was no finish-y." It's a good and bad

thing, I'm guessing. Some people are too afraid to start anything new, but starting too often can also be a weakness.

Sandra mmhmms. "You're lacking something in experience," she says. "There's something missing. . . . You fall short in a sense."

"How do you know??" GJ asks, impressed.

"Just listening to you," Sandra replies. "When you think about yin and yang, you think about positive and negative. To be a well-balanced individual . . . you shouldn't have all negative, and you shouldn't have all positive. You should have a good, equal balance."

"That's right," GJ says.

"What this is saying is basically *when* in your life span it's going to happen," Sandra goes on, gesturing to the pillars. "Or it's trying to point out what happened in your life."

"That's right," GJ says.

One tree is giant (me). One character hides and never answers (my father). One has energy to survive (my mother). Then we start getting into the good stuff. "Tree never stay in one place. I think you're still here," GJ says, of my second pillar. "This is very important period in your life. You . . . make some achievement. Or you try something very hard things? Because it's really nice timing here . . . OR? Or somebody, somebody inspiration, inspired by you. Or your work or . . . your art-work is about you."

I tell her I'm writing a book. She digresses, sharing how she's written and self-published six books. She has concerns about South Korea's hier-archical collective society and how the disparity has affected recorded history. For example, Bukchon Hanok Village, with its in-tact tradi-tional Korean homes, is a common tourist attraction. I'd chosen to stay in a hanok because as gross as it is to admit, doing so felt "authen-tic." However, GJ gripes, most of what remains of Korea's past upholds royal-family, upper-class culture. There is no lasting evidence of how commoners lived. Thatched homes, the domiciles for 90 percent of the population, were destroyed or collapsed half a century ago. She laments how the rich have all the power, how the poor, younger generation is never meant to complain. Her books offer young people advice. "I want

to show this about alternative," she says, laughing strangely. "Don't suicide. Just call somebody. Just call somebody. Yea."

By the time we get to my fourth pillar, it appears that around age
seventy or eighty I will need some grounding. Children, maybe, to balance all my treeness. "Or! Or a very precious thing in your life. Like a
children or like a pet or maybe your book! You need this background,
earth, because you are a giant tree. Giant tree need earth. Be positive.
Earth. It is only background? Or your family?" she sums up, sucking her
teeth. "Or . . . very precious things what it is in your life."

"She's saying you're stuck in the past," Sandra translates.

"I cannot say, I don't want to say it is too late," GJ admits, hesitantly.
"There is nothing to be late . . ." Which sounds like she's saying it's too
late. To remedy that, I'll need an earth character. I ask her what that
would look like.

"Just try to think about it. I don't have the process. So you have to
step by step," she says, bursting into incredulous laughter, "to reach
your future." In her opinion, I'll achieve far more than writing. Traveling, art, branching out like the tree I am. As for Sandra, GJ has other
ideas: "I think you should be fortune-teller. I think you have some ability." Sandra gets a touch bashful, as it seems this is not the first time
she's heard the suggestion. "What do you do?" GJ asks.

"Real estate."

"Really??" GJ says, baffled. And for once I can understand exactly
what she means.

We wrap up with her K-tarot. Each card in her deck (which bears
no relation to European divination tarot) depicts a Korean word and its
meaning. "This is about . . . your true character," GJ elaborates. Then
she counts tally marks on a scratch paper based on our birth coordinates, searches for the corresponding cards, and fans out four per person. "You have the best," she says to Sandra, pointing to "long life." She
also has two luck cards. "Two luck is best," GJ dotes.

As for me, I'm shocked to find I have two "wander" cards, 역, trans-
literated as "yeok" and "yeog," positioned in the time frames of near
future and future. This prompts me to ask about yeokmasal. GJ is taken

aback, as if she hasn't heard the word in ages. It means something different now, she explains. Today yeokmasal is more about travel, and the fortune to explore the world beyond home. If you have a partner or children, it's not possible to leave. "Old people insist yeokmasal and travel life is not good. . . . But I think yeokmasal is good. You are live *now*."

"How do you know if you have yeokmasal?"

"We have to calculate," she says. "Jen . . ." she trails off, tapping away at another app on her phone. After a minute, the results are in. "Ahhhh," she says. "You have yeokmasal." She shows me the screen, which depicts an unambiguous 70 percent. "Anyway . . . you should focus not about travel," she deduces. "Why you don't feel about your home. It means, you think you don't have a home. Because you are Korean, but Korean American. Yea. This is your identity."

I could have let that sink in, but I pivot to another two points she's mentioned. Something about separating from my partner but that we'll meet again. And, supposedly, I'm meant to be famous in Korea. These things will happen before I'm sixty. "Cool," I say, relieved. "I have some time."

GJ finds this hilarious. "You worry about you don't have enough time!"

Again apt, but I deflect. Me? Famous in Korea? "Yea. Why not?" GJ says. "Korean American. Korean American. We need them!"

"But you get there," Sandra affirms. "On your own time . . . Which is the right time."

역 • Yeog: Wander

If you stay for a long time, it will be
ominous, so you will move often!
It's good to move often if you don't
stay in one place for a long time.

Permutations

PERFECT HOME

Sq. ft.: Unknown; 3BR, 2BA

B Y THE TIME I got the second, more traditional saju reading translated and transcribed, I'd been back in Tulsa for three months. It's
a peculiar thing, living in a place temporarily for almost three years.
The housing market in Tulsa was a relatively favorable one, and I could
afford a fixer-upper in town if I wanted—though I had no intention to
buy. Tulsa was the happy hour bar that turned into "I'll have another if
you will" or "one more round?" until suddenly it was last call and the
old barkeep was shouting, "You don't have to go home, but you can't
stay here!" Except I didn't know where home was supposed to be either.
Nothing against Tulsa; just wasn't a place I intended on staying long-
term. After my fellowship ended, I'd extended my lease through the following summer, at which time I'd return to my mother's South Carolina
condo, house-sit while she visited Korea, then spend the other six months
of the year testing out new cities, to see where I'd land more permanently
next. Even so, I'd spent the better part of my time in Oklahoma perusing
real estate websites, casually collecting a list of ideals: original built-ins,
decorative stained-glass, wood stoves, skylights, igloo-like glass-block
walls, a Florida room for my indoor tropicals, a small backyard with
space for a fire pit and a garden. And Umma, being Umma, would text
me no-context links to listings for homes outside of Knoxville, Tennessee, and Birmingham, Alabama. To see what was out there, she'd say.

While I waited for the translation, I reviewed my session notes.
There were constellation points that, even in Umma's dubious retelling,
sounded promising. For example, the second fortune-teller told me I
needed to live somewhere warm. While I wasn't heeding his word as
scripture, I'd be lying if I said I didn't keep his advice in mind. He'd certainly made an impression from the moment Umma and I arrived for
our appointment, stepping through his hanok's ancient wooden gate.
The door opened like a portal to another century. A rock garden and

wind chimes greeted us. We heard a soft voice, enshrouded by a rice paper wall, beckon: "*Come in . . .*"

Our guru was sitting cross-legged on the floor behind a plexiglass partition (a Covid measure) perched atop a low-lying table. He was wearing a white quilted ensemble, very chic, very sharp, accented by his crop of salt-and-pepper hair and minimalist spectacles that seemed to float from his face. A bookcase containing several of his published books loomed in the background—so my mother, playing the role of reluctant interpreter, told me.

"He's kind of a big deal, he says."

I asked about his white outfit. He explained that normally, when you live at a monastery, you wear gray clothes. After prospering as an architect for many years, he quit, walked into a forest, and became a monk. Then he returned to Seoul, where he has been reading saju for the last thirty-three years. "It's good for me to wear gray clothes too, but the white clothes look clean," he said.

Though a weathered copy of a saju tome lay open on his desk, he used an enormous desktop computer to enter our four pillars data, then printed out the results for reference. He would refer to me by Jennipur but also a Korean name my grandfather had bestowed upon me at birth that no one has ever called me.

"Why did you come here today?" he asked me, via Umma.

She spoke for minutes. Something something Jesus. Something something yeokmasal. He nodded, smiling, as if he already knew.

"It's not like he's gonna say definitely this or that. But he's gonna tell you *why*," she said.

"Which why?"

They discussed. Something something past, present. Tree, metal, earth, fire, water. Eight characters, eight destinies. "Whatever it is," she reiterated vaguely.

After a spell of suspenseful deliberation, it was time for him to begin. My mother and I leaned toward the plexiglass to better hear his serene voice, which he maintained in an elevated whisper. They conversed for a moment until Umma strongly concurred with an ohhhhhh. What? What *oh*?

"You look like a big tree," she said.

"Oh."

A tide of words rushed out of him, until Umma interjected in English: "What does that mean?" More discussion. "Ah. You're like tree, but you not rooted," she elaborated. "So if you are rooted, they can't move. But because you're like a big . . . trunk."

(Later, when I get the translation, the transcript reads: "But Hyesung's energy is not in a state of rootedness . . . but rather like . . . a log. A log does not have roots in the earth." So actually, I am a log.)

"That way you can move wherever you want," Umma added.

He went on. Something about being a leader.

"Did you hear that?" she asked. "Because you have leader quality, you have to live like a leader, which means you have to gather people, groom people, nurture people. That's your destiny. Does that make sense?"

"I guess?" I said. The grooming part sounded a bit cult-y but he continued.

"You have a lot of trees," she said. Just like GJ had relayed.

I heard him say the Korean word for metal, then English ("pulp-uh"). Something about a book. Education. Teaching. Namja chingu (boyfriend). My mother huffed in agreement. I heard "boypuhdenduh." "Husbunduh." More boyfriend talk. A husband.

"You don't like to be tied down. You have a lot of friends, but you don't have any BOYFRIEND," she said, the last word emphasized loudly.

Then a poetic monologue of sorts, even though I couldn't catch everything, the sounds hummed, potent with meaning.

"Your prince charming is coming," Umma said.

Her editorializing, I surmised.

Umma's eyes widened as dates flew around. In two years, I'd make a big achievement. I'd experience a change of mind. In four more, I'd settle down in one place. I'd be moving around until my fifties. But not forever.

Then Umma snuck in her own question that surprised me. "*Will she ever speak to her father again?*" she asked in Korean. I had been wondering this myself.

As the fortune-teller answered, I thought about Ecuador. According to Laurie, after his alleged trailer and boardinghouse stints, our father wanted to live abroad, speaking Spanish every day. Maybe his money could stretch farther there; maybe he could at last retire. Maybe I would fly out, to Quito or Mindo or Tena, as if something about crossing the equatorial line could fundamentally alter him, or me, wiping the slate clean, resetting us to zero. Maybe I'd drive up to his home, and maybe upon seeing me, he'd step outside, still young, hair still combed and parted, his expression borne of incredulity—as if he'd been waiting, all this time.

Laurie says he's finally starting to show his age. His once flush, square-ish countenance would probably shock me now, the way an old dog's does, when it's suddenly gone gray in the muzzle. Certain creatures you forget can grow old, until you realize they do, even if you're not ready and it's almost time to say goodbye.

Umma mulled over the fortune-teller's answer for a beat. "You are gonna be able to meet your dad, when you are successful," she told me. "And I said I don't know if he's gonna be alive or not, but I'm *pretty* sure he will. He's healthy." As soon as two years, supposedly I'd be ready.

"*Any more questions?*" the fortune-teller asked.

"*She wants to know if she has yeokmasal,*" Umma said.

He replied immediately. "Aigoo, A LOT he says!" which got Umma laughing. Then she suggested I ought to write about my travels, like Rick Steves.

"Is it a curse?" I asked

"It's not a curse," she interpreted. "It's the life you live."

He ended by telling me I need to be smiling, even when I sleep. As for Umma's reading, she gave me the Cliff's Notes rendition. He said she's strong. "Absolutely," she agreed. She has two of everything: two jobs, two nationalities, two husbands.

"Two husbands?" I asked. But they'd moved on. Something will change in two years. A new hobby, a new namja chingu maybe. And she will experience success as well. That's when she turned to me and drudged up a promise I couldn't remember making: "You said when you make a lot of money you're gonna buy house in south of France, and I'm gonna live with you."

And he nodded to this. We are to live in a warm country, with bright sunlight and plenty of color, a glorious, passionate place. Northern Spain. French Riviera. Miami. Anywhere but England (too much rain). Somewhere warm, somewhere peaceful. And as I smile in my sleep, Umma is to walk in the sun every day.

"Fancy places where we need to live."

"We need to live somewhere fancy?" I said surprised.

"South of France he said is good. We need to go to warm weather. Both of us. Same."

Did she have yeokmasal too?

"I have *more*," Umma confirmed, chuckling. "He's right! I'm just like flowing water. Never stand still. Isn't that the something?"

As we finished up, I hesitantly asked one more question: "Will . . . I ever have a child?"

He deliberated for a good minute, which I took as a no.

"Yea, you will," Umma said. "Not now because you were born in the winter. Your body is cold. But soon . . . You're gonna be so fertile. If you want child it's gonna happen naturally. If you don't want, you need to take birth control."

The fertile part was a little weird, but *okay* . . . it was my destiny.

"*We're similar, aren't we?*" Umma asked in Korean.

He appeared amused.

"But," Umma added, smiling, "I have more yeokmasal than you."

RATHER OBVIOUSLY, a wandering curse is not based in science. Not exactly. Researchers have investigated whether chemical or genetic reasons motivate our need to explore uncharted terrains, and they've turned to the human genome for answers. In 2016, a burst of online articles published around the concept of a "wanderlust gene." Those bearing the polymorphic DRD4-7R gene variant are said to share a lower sensitivity to dopamine—a neurotransmitter often called a "feel-good chemical"—and as a result actively pursue pleasure-seeking stimuli. High dopamine release is frequently associated with increased impulsiveness and risk-taking behaviors; it's the thing that gets us to seek out novel experiences and repeat those circumstances, discoveries, and thrills. Allegedly 20 percent of the population carries the 7R variant.

Some researchers think the gene is connected to a collective sensibility. A significant study conducted in 1999 by the University of California examined a time frame between 1,000 and 30,000 years ago and concluded that 7R appeared with higher frequency among those who descended from migratory cultures. A study in 2011 also supported these findings. In other words, those who travel are perhaps predisposed to continue traveling, driven by an intrinsic restlessness. But as any expert will tell you, innumerable factors contribute to our complex neurological pathways, so even though the wanderlust gene is a catchy name, there's no such thing as a singular, causal science-based determinant that shapes an individual's itinerant tendencies. Wanderlust is likely the wrong word for it anyway; its German roots connote desire—to hike or roam about in pleasure and delight. Is there pleasure or delight in restlessness? One study published in 2008 examined the differences among recently settled and nomadic groups of North Kenyan pastoralists called the Ariaal. Statistics showed 7R appeared more advantageous for the nomadic group, who were stronger and better nourished than if they'd resided as settled villagers. This suggests the gene is better adapted by those who live a mobile life. Restlessness is dependent on a number of changeable conditions, and whether ancestors of the Ariaal possessed that disposition can never be known. We will never know what the settled Ariaal experienced either, and to what extent their livelihood diminished while staying in place. What if, for some of us, a sedentary lifestyle could lead to a kind of physical distress? Such an affliction would seem almost folkloric—one might say even a curse.

• • •

WHEN I GOT BACK from Seoul, I realized I'd been circling the work of two Korean wanderers, riders on separate horses galloping station to station in parallel expanses.

Author and artist Theresa Hak Kyung Cha was born in 1951, to a Korea at war. She came from nomadic lineage; her mother was born in Manchuria to Korean parents exiled during Japanese occupation. Cha moved with her family to Hawaii in 1962, uprooting two years later to settle in the Bay Area in 1964. As an adult, Cha relocated again to New York City, where her life was tragically cut short in 1982.

My mother was born one year after Cha. As twentysomethings, they both lived in northern California, but when Umma was changing bed pans at a nursing home, Cha was generating bold experimental film, performance, and written conceptual artworks. She was fluent in English, Korean, and French and had lived in Paris while studying avant-garde cinema. She published her book *Dictee*—an amalgam of poetry, collage, and memoir—a week before her death.

Cha was raped and murdered by a security guard at the iconic Puck Building on Lafayette and Houston Streets in Manhattan. I did not know of Cha's story when I saw the building's exterior establishing shots in episodes of *Will & Grace* in the late 1990s. I did not know of her story when, freshman year of college, my arts department held a mixer on the penthouse floor. I did not know of her story until reading Cathy Park Hong's *Minor Feelings*, which prompted me to read *Dictee*.

Cha's visual and written creations revolved around dislocation, the ache of expatriation suffusing her projects with a palpable sense of not longing but loss. One might speculate that she, like my mother, like me, had been saddled with yeokmasal. My mother, while creative, is not an artist. *Dictee* is not something Umma will ever read. Once, I recited to her a few lines; for a time, she and Cha shared somewhat synchronous epicycles, so I wanted to get her opinion:

"It murmurs inside. It murmurs. Inside is the pain of speech the pain to say. Larger still. Greater than is the pain not to say. To not say. Says nothing against the pain to speak. It festers inside. The wound, liquid, dust. Must break. Must void."

After a lengthy pause, Umma said, "This woman is not well," and that was the end of that. I have said the same thing about my mother, possibly at her most despairing phases in the not-so-distant past. Incredibly, I now see her differently because of Cha's impermeability.

Though Cha's writing has been described as slippery, uncompromisingly difficult, and feral, it has sustained an enigmatic ascent in the decades since the author's passing. Academics and the literary firmament have praised *Dictee* for its daring obfuscation, anointing Cha as a canonical figure in Asian American and feminist letters. Its 2022 restoration, as well as the publication of Cha's unfinished works, *Exilée and Temps Morts*, spurred a number of laudatory responses. Admirers have hosted live *Dictee* marathon readings and a comprehensive collection of her visual artwork was featured in the 2022 Whitney Biennial.

Dictee's inaccessibility is its most compelling attribute. The book is split into nine sections, each named after Greek muses, real and imagined. It's a patchwork of anguish via multiple protagonists—from Joan of Arc and revolutionary activist Yu Guan-Sun to Cha's own mother. Perhaps most tortured of them all is the narrator, in thrall to the vacillating limitations of language and identity. There is no plot. Rather, through repetitions and echoes built from a kinetic vernacular, she plumbs the enduring impact of Korean national traumas, where a homeland and mother tongue are reachable only in memory. The text itself is the point—a shattering of conventional syntax, pieced back into an unrecognizable form that intentionally skirts traditional meaning-making.

On my first attempt reading the book, I stopped after ten pages and scanned the jacket copy for any clue as to what I'd encountered. "The element that unites these women is suffering and the transcendence of suffering," it said. In the forty-plus years *Dictee* has existed, extensive critical analyses have attempted to decode and construe the book's contents. Some say the broken intermingling of English and French is a way of challenging our notions of grammar and communication. But I see her intentional opaqueness, within oppression and freedom, fluency and the ineffable, literature and conceptual art, as existing in a nowhere space, in between. That is *Dictee*'s power. In Cha's constructed world, words stack until the mounting progression transforms into something extralinguistic, resulting not so much in meaning as in psychic and physical distress. Where no one language suffices, she invents her own. You're not supposed to "get" it, you're supposed to "feel" it.

When I went to the 2022 Whitney Biennial, I made a beeline to Cha's section—a white tented structure erected to house her body of visual and textual work. I stayed in the room for an hour. There was one video of a mouth emerging in and out of static, attempting to speak. There were photographs of a performance art piece in which Cha is dressed in all-white, like a Korean shaman performing a ritual, holding a banner imprinted with the phrase: *Words / fail / me*. A video projection called *Permutations* depicted stills of Cha's sister's face, the back of her head, and at the end of the reel a single frame of Cha herself intercut in a barely perceptible blip, as if to imply that in our kin lies a sliver of our own selves. Although who could say. I left having no idea what I'd watched, only that in the process of looking, some mechanism in my brain had unlatched. Cha rejected the notion of finite interpretation. What an extraordinary risk, something like valor, to express alienation without fear of alienation, to thrust a bit of yourself into the world, in a flurry of questions with no answers, refusing to be easily understood.

I'd spent most of my life trying to understand my mother, as if anyone can ever be fully known. What was behind this desire? Perhaps the illusion of what clarity can provide. If I could be fully known, maybe by extension I could be fully accepted, fully forgiven, fully loved. A facile, closed loop. But you don't have to understand a person to love them. Which reminded me of my mother and my mother's mother, a bloodline of women who never cared to be understood nor had ever sought to understand anyone else intently. Something basic, almost primal, necessary, having nothing to do with comprehension, sustained us. They gave me life and showed me how to live it. What else did I need?

• • •

"Once, my fortune-teller told me that I have five horses:
five horses in my fortune, in my life. That means that I travel a lot.
I'm destined to leave home and live somewhere else and travel to many
places: that's a story."
—Do Ho Suh in an interview with PBS, 2003

I know a fellow horse curse compatriot when I see one. Do Ho Suh is often described as a nomadic artist by critics and acolytes alike, but his preoccupation deserves some refinement. Like Cha, there's a sense of dislocation threaded throughout Suh's body of work. The fabric sculptures for which he is most renowned embody the psychic longing a wanderer might carry with them, even if they leave everything else familiar behind.

Suh grew up the son of an accomplished, classical Korean painter, had attended prestigious Seoul National University, and, after receiving both fine arts bachelor's and master's degrees, moved to the States to repeat the process again at Rhode Island School of Design and Yale School of Art. During his initial American years, he'd experienced a kind of homesickness for his childhood residence. He grew up in an architectural masterpiece—a replica of a nineteenth-century scholar's hanok located originally within King Sunjo's Changdeokgung Palace. The conflict of memory and space threaded throughout Suh's work owes its provenance to this childhood home, an idyll ensconced in modernizing, postwar, urban Seoul. He has described the incongruence, exiting the hanok's grand wooden gate and heading to school, as if emerging from a secret garden suspended in time. He would soon find himself yearning for the comfort of this place once he relocated to America, which later motivated his most recognizable works.

The first was *Seoul Home/L.A. Home/New York Home/Baltimore Home/London Home/Seattle Home* (1999), a full-scale recreation of his family's hanok, made of translucent, hand-sewn silk panels. Photos depict a monochromatic structure that, when in situ, hangs from ceiling wires, levitating like a ghost. The textile is a traditional Korean fabric custom-made in a celadon hue; the hard-edged lines, tile grooves, and lattice-worked screens, though rendered with painstaking detail, appear oddly transient, projecting not so much an exact duplicate but the home caught in spiritual limbo, memorialized in wavering patina. It reminded me of a snake's molted skin, bearing the uncanny silhouette of a once-living thing. While monumental in dimension, the piece is soft enough to be stored in hand luggage, transported and reconstructed anywhere in the world. One might categorize such a conceit—"carrying a space in a suitcase," as Suh puts it—as commentary on cultural displacement. But perhaps these resurrections, when considered in sum, are more aptly expressions of grief, each structure an attempt to make the ephemeral persist beyond natural constraints of time.

This is clearest in his ongoing series shown under the title *Perfect Home.* The artworks are wide-ranging: a theoretical simulated bridge designed to connect Seoul and New York with a hanok perched at its center (*A Perfect Home: The Bridge Project*, 2010); his compactable Seoul home in its varied reimaginings (*Do Ho Suh: Perfect Home*, 2012); and a fabric architectural clone of his Manhattan studio apartment (*Perfect Home II*, 2003).

Suh lived on the bottom floor of a brownstone in Chelsea for nearly two decades. The building was owned by a genial man, whom Suh befriended over the course of his tenancy. The artist measured the hallways, staircases, and every millimeter of his apartment to fashion the space, like his hanok, as a to-scale fabric recreation. Around 2016, the landlord's health appeared in sharp decline, the property's sale, remodeling, and demolition imminent. So, Suh coated his studio with paper and shaded the entire surface with graphite, pastels, and colored pencils for a final ode. The project, *Rubbing / Loving*, he once described as a spiritual quest. The phonetic spelling of "rubbing" in Korean can also be read as "loving," and Suh's work of frottage is precisely that: a tribute to a built environment's every crack and crevice, every surface touched and ritualized one last time. Or was it? The artist recounted in one interview how he'd visited a wise man who claimed that in a past life, Suh had been a Buddhist monk who'd stopped to polish rocks while hiking the Himalayas. "I realized I was doing the exact same thing," he said, amazed. Life after life, a repetition.

Home, for Suh and his movable constructions, can be infinitely repeatable—we're the ones who change. I considered this when I went to New York to see an exhibition of his work in 2018. My friends happened to be out of town, so I got to stay in their apartment and briefly step into a life I have never personally inhabited in Manhattan. They owned grown-up things signifying comfort and permanence, like a proper eight-person dining table handmade from sturdy reclaimed wood, a real-deal womb chair, quality linens and pricy kitchen gadgets, a surround-sound system, manicured bonsais, and a lithe bird of paradise potted in a 100-pound cement planter shipped from Vietnam. The apartment came with a skylight, and there was enough room to do two cartwheels across the hardwood floor if you pleased.

Suh's perfect home (Chelsea edition) had been packed, shipped, and installed in many galleries over its illustrious fifteen years. At the Brooklyn Museum, it appeared unchanged by its age—still a phantasm of intricately stitched diaphanous panels, shaded in cerulean, celadon, lavender, and rose, upheld by a stainless-steel armature. I walked down the hall, through the doorways, as if touring a freeze-frame of someone's dream. The built-in shelves above the fireplace sagged like little hammocks. The radiator drooped. The doorknobs hung like wilted buds. Stovetop burners sat sunken in a lugubrious kitchen, and the toilet seat looked crumpled as if accidentally crushed and reformed. There were no signs of personal ephemera or human presence. The echo of murmurings from the museum's Beaux-Arts rotunda filtered through the nylon walls, as if mimicking the voices and countless conversations held in the apartment over the course of its own life. We couldn't touch what surrounded us but the panels fluttered as I exited, reminding me of the space's liminality, static and mobile, dead and undead, alive so long as we remembered it.

Suh resides now in London with his wife and children. He isn't much of a nomad anymore. Maybe he never was. To my mind, nomads don't look back. *Perfect Home* is about the frailty of nostalgia, holding in reverence a preserved ideal possible only in the tomb of memory. And even then it lingers askew, for the briefness during which we behold it. Maybe instead of wandering, what he continues to feel is the placelessness Cha knew, his borne of longing, not loss. And maybe the longing has something to do with who he was, not where he was—a wistfulness for a time that cannot be fully resurrected or experienced, in this life, ever again.

Before leaving the city, I visited my former apartment block. There was no stench lurking around the corner. Dozens of restaurants and shops had opened and shut since I'd left, though Congee Village, with its Cher-like stamina, continued to glow its fluorescent signage. I'd stumbled home across the street after too many rounds of five-dollar lychee martinis how many times? Who could count.

There was the apartment on Allen and Broome, same hulking brick facade, though the entrance had received a facelift: a glass entry, a fancy silver-leaf building number, and management had wised up by placing the trash cans outside. As I stood there no one came or went but I could still hear the heavy thud of the old metal door slamming shut behind me. I could smell the lobby dankness wafting up in a sour gust too. And my god, what was I/she wearing, black Reebok high-tops, too-long skinny jeans, a skull necklace draped below her shaggy cut and red-tinged bangs; the tiny metal key jimmying open the mailbox, Umma's postcard shoved there between the Con Ed bill and junk fliers; the way she held her breath and trudged up the stairs, wondering who the sender had become, not knowing the beginning could be an end and the end a beginning, neither one good nor bad, just movement along an ambiguous orbit. I left her there in that one morsel of time, stretched it out, savoring all the angles on the walk back toward someone else's home, every street I crossed both unquestioningly familiar and far away.

*   *   *

PEOPLE ASK ME all the time now if I miss New York. My answer is always the same: I miss being young in New York. When uncertainty held untold possibilities. I guess at a certain age, wherever you are, hopefulness dulls in favor of practicality. Maybe that's why I don't mind dabbling in saju, to reinvigorate the prospect of potential. This is what the practice has reiterated over centuries, while also speaking to a basic human preoccupation: the desire to know the unknowable. Korea has been invaded some 400 times in the course of its turbulent history; its own redemption narratives, of a nearly supranatural sort, gesture to a kind of unrelenting faith. Perfect isn't possible, but we try anyway. Destiny gives a person purpose, implies the existence of order or control in the mist of otherwise uncertain futures. Saju is one of the elaborate structures we create to exercise hope.

Maybe this is why my mother keeps moving. A thing doesn't have to last to be meaningful. Every house she's passed through contains the same objects, resurrected and restaged in permutations—Molder's box of ashes and sweaters; the toucan-painted feather from Costa Rica; the photo of her bouffant wind-socking off Copa Cabana beach. She has thrust herself into the world, in a flurry of questions with no answers. Wherever she goes, I find her.

. . .

Jen Saju Translation

FORTUNE-TELLER: Why did you come today?

UMMA: To tell the story would be long . . . I went to the US and married a Jesus-believing person, and believe in Jesus. Still now, but my children, they went to church up until high school and stop going after they went to college. So then she wanted have her saju read. . . . I think she has yeokmasal. Since she travels so much. But she thinks she has yeokmasal too, and said she wants to know those things about herself. (laughs)

FORTUNE-TELLER: Because she is a writer, I believe her ability to associate or formulate is very good. If I say in dictionary terms, you are like this, or like this, you won't understand it. The point is not what you are, but why. So I will explain why you are the way that you are . . .

Everyone has their own energy. Of those, Hye-sung's energy is that of a large tree. She does many things at once. . . . And so this takes shape as a second house, another house, and in this way you live in many places and make connections with many places, but you feel comfortable with this. But the tree has a quality that branches up. You say a tree goes up, up towards the sky. So Jennifer has big desires and ambitions. Big dreams . . .

To cut a tree, you would need a saw. But Jennifer is a tree that is already cut. It is refined and tempered. So you don't need a saw. The energy, to Jennifer, is also the realm of men, husband, work. You don't like to be restrained. You are an eternally free person. Thus those friends, boyfriends, are not one, but because you are a free person, you live with many people that you meet, like friends. Jennifer's name will be known to the world. With that, the world will see Jennifer differently. And because they see you differently, then a stylish man will come . . .

Marriage is a choice. You can think about it then. That's not important now. . . . This is what you can know: The energy ahead should be about forgetting the past, and letting go, only thinking about what you run into.

The yeokmasal is a lot. Endless. At least about ten, twenty years from now, the yeokmasal will fade a little. Take it slowly.

You are nomadic . . . You can make it your specialty. With that you can go to India, or Korea, or South America . . . Think about it. The philosophy within it.

In the old days they said for a woman to have yeokmasal was to beg, or make cheap money, but now people who have yeokmasal are more active and dynamic. It's a good thing, in modern times.

UMMA: Do I have yeokmasal?

FORTUNE-TELLER: Yes, quite a lot. In your case, since you are like flowing water, you must continue to flow. Endlessly flow. If you become stagnant, you are bound to rot. Move constantly.

UMMA: Are there a lot of similarities between us?

FORTUNE-TELLER: Very similar. The disposition is different but still similar. That is why when your daughter becomes happier, your condition improves as well.

. . .

AFTER I SPLIT from the rural doctor, I did something a younger me would have found exceedingly loserish. I immersed myself in the world of self-help books. Had I checked these titles out at the library, the desk clerk would have noticed I was really going through something: *When Things Fall Apart: Heart Advice for Difficult Times; The Gifts of Imperfection; Letting Go: The Pathway to Surrender; The Magic; You Can Heal Your Life; Braving the Wilderness: The Quest for True Belonging and the Courage to Stand Alone; The Universe Has Your Back: Transform Fear to Faith; The Four Agreements: A Practical Guide to Personal Freedom*; and, perhaps the most tragic of them all, *May Cause Miracles: A 40-Day Guidebook of Subtle Shifts for Radical Change and Unlimited Happiness*. Knowing better, I bought them used online or downloaded audio versions, so as to keep the mortification level as private as possible.

I turned to these texts because torturing myself with unanswerable questions didn't seem to be getting me anywhere. Unless you want to stay wallowing in isolation for eternity, when you're at the bottom of a well, there is no other place to go but up—even if that means summoning the cheesiest of affirmations you, in a level-headed state, might reactively swat aside. As one friend put it, when I'd hit an unbearable-to-be-around, self-pitying nadir: "What's the alternative? To be miserable the rest of your life?" For a cynic, this sounded like a livable scenario though not a particularly fulfilling one. Solitude (a choice) I could get behind, but the prospect of being alone in longing's unending mysteries resounded loudest. Even skeptics crave assurances—those rare spaces of relief in the morass of time.

The schlock factor in many of these books was, as one might imagine, off the fucking charts. It was easier to dismiss when the writing—mostly published in the 1980s through the early 2010s—teemed with clichés and cringey, saccharine manifestos. The harder part had to do with sitting in the discomfort of earnestness. Being earnest gets a bad rap, maybe because wanting something so sincerely can make a person feel exposed. It is not the same as self-seriousness (and I wanted nothing to do with that anymore). In earnest, I had to face the truth of myself, which felt both indulgent and dreadful—but necessary for moving on.

So I read and listened. I did not metamorphose into an instant optimist. I find it deeply fishy when someone, seemingly overnight, transforms into a manifesting, meditating wellness-as-life-brand type. Those charades are thinly glued in place. I just hoped the overcorrection might get me somewhere softer than before. Less cynical. What was the word . . . hopeful. Not everything stuck. (One book claimed you could cure cancer with the power of positive thinking.) I sifted out the worthwhile bits and dumped the rest. Weeks passed until I reached a clearing, where one worthy question lingered: If I could randomly meet someone in rural Oklahoma, who knew what could happen next? Nothing is certain. Nothing. But did that have to be such a bad thing?

If you had asked my punk ass back in 2006 whether I'd ever live in Tulsa, if you had told me that's where I'd figure my shit out and become a settled person, not in this town but in whoever it is I've become, I would have laughed and laughed, because life is so unknowable yet the human condition is such that we try to solve for the variables anyway. I thought I'd been flailing my whole adult life, as if I'd scammed my way into half the opportunities afforded to me. But then a friend of mine pointed out I wasn't faking anything. Being an artist means posing plans and then seeing them through, however they unfold. I would leave Tulsa knowing one thing for sure: To be an artist means to live in constant residence with uncertainty. This doesn't mean you like it. This doesn't mean you're good at the topsy-turvyness either. It just means you accept that there are things you can control and things you can't—and that the latter might lead you to somewhere better than imagined.

I do like to imagine. When I was still dating the doctor, I attended a New Year's Day virtual intention-setting workshop hosted by a poet friend. I know, I know, but it's not as annoying as it sounds. The two-hour session involved mostly journal writing, so you could reflect on the past year, what you wanted to keep, what you wanted to usher out, what you wanted to welcome. It culminated with a visualization exercise. I had never done one before and since I was loved up at the time, I was feeling especially optimistic and open to fantasizing about future possibilities. My poet friend has a supremely soothing voice. We closed our eyes, and she walked us through the scenario.

It is the year 2031. Morning.

Does the sun wake you up? Do you rise naturally or by an alarm? What do your feet touch first when you get out of bed? What does your home look like? What colors and textures do you see? Who is with you?

The day goes on like this, and we walk the halls and porches and lawns and city streets populating our futures, through pleasant minutiae and meals with loved ones until night falls and we end the exercise in silence.

One year later, after breaking up with the doctor, I attended the workshop again.

It is the year 2032. Morning.

I awake in the same exact place as I did in 2031, same crisp white bed linens, except the doctor is neatly snipped out of the picture. My feet swivel onto the rug I've placed atop the Spanish terra-cotta tile, too cool to the touch first thing in the morning. I make coffee in the sun-drenched kitchen, put my boots on, and traipse across the long grasses to my A-frame studio heated by its wood stove. I work much of the day, pausing for a light lunch and peeking out the window to see Umma, as ever, pulling weeds in the garden. Later, when the kid comes home from school, the three of us head to the sauna (because Koreans love saunas). It's scorching inside, just the way Umma likes it. We are nude, the little one's blueness hidden against the cedar planks, and we're panting with such satisfaction, pleased by the pain of the heat, as if that means the medicine is working. We eat dinner, and Umma promptly floods her dish with kimchi juice, which gets the kid doubling over, laughing (my me). We go for a night walk, and the kid pulls Umma along by the arm to inspect this bug and that star, her limbs slack like a marionette. When it's bedtime, Umma retreats to her tiny home out back, to nod off to the cold-case recitations on her screen she's heard a million times before. So for a while it's just the little one and me. Reading stories. Me cleaning her ears, her cleaning mine, the two of us nestled like monkeys. She's babbling about some made-up yarn of gibberish, so gleeful in the world of her own creation I can hardly comprehend, but I listen along until she's out, mid-sentence. Then in my bed, as I enter the most delicious sleep, I'm wondering if she'll grow up to have my hands, which look exactly like Umma's hands, and Halmoni's hands—all of us the same.

Author's Note

A WORK LARGELY DRAWN FROM MEMORY IS A SOFT creation, subject to the malleability of time and the frailty of recollection. *The Wanderer's Curse* is a nonfiction book that contains significant swathes reimagined from my memories as well as my mother's, the latter of which frequently change from telling to telling. I have done my best to honor the truth, so far as I (and she) remember it. Some scenes may be composited, as is often the case when any of us recall the past. Certain names have been changed, as have potentially identifying characteristics.

Though it is not incumbent on authors to do so, I put the manuscript through an assiduous fact-check to ensure information has been relayed as accurately as possible. There is one intentional divergence from technical accuracy. Many children of immigrants, myself included, consider themselves "first-generation," meaning they are the first in their family to be born stateside. The dominant phrasing employed by institutions, such as the U.S. Census Bureau, is "second-generation." I have opted instead for language that best reflects my lived experience.

Acknowledgments

I genuinely wasn't sure I'd ever finish writing this thing, so if you encountered me over the last fifteen years, listened to the ideas banging around in my head, and offered any bit of interest: Thank you. Additionally, if I was your bartender between 2015 and 2017 and I was a crabby lil B—I am *very* sorry. I was really going through something, as evidenced in these pages. Next drink is on me.

To my agent, Claudia Ballard, your unwavering faith in this story and my voice has pulled me through some of the darkest moments, when I simply did not see a way forward in artmaking or life. I am indebted to you.

Melanie Tortoroli, you have been a dream editor, guiding me with a steady hand. Thank you for taking the leap when I didn't have an ending, sitting under that condensation drip at Bar Pisellino, and reminding me time and again to trust the process.

Flowers of gratitude to the many folks who ushered me through the gauntlet to get to this stage: Camille Morgan and Oma Nairine at WME; Janet McDonald for her insightful copy edits; Annabel Brazaitis and Huneeya Siddiqui at Norton, along with Ingsu Liu and Grace Han for making the book a beautiful, real-life object.

Early support and encouragement from Bonnie Friedman, Henry Hu, Lisa Hennessey, Nancy Roach, Kendra MacLeod, Winifred MacLeod,

David Fitzgerald, and the Deems helped me believe I was on to something. Thank you.

I consider myself a late bloomer. There are scant opportunities out there for "emerging writers" seeking structured mentorship over the age of thirty. Saeed Jones, I'm grateful you created a place for people like me to bloom at all, and for saying my work belonged in the world. To you and the BuzzFeed Reader team—Karolina Waclawiak, Rachel Sanders, and Tomi Obaro—thank you for changing my life.

When it comes to a writing family, I won the jumbo check. The only way I stayed on track, week to week, page by page, is because of Aurvi Sharma—my sister throughout the terrifying, often deluded, ever exhilarating ride that is writing a book. Aurvi, you next.

Jaquira Díaz, you showed me how to keep going. You and Lars Horn (best swimmer I know) have pushed me to see storytelling and life from new vistas, and when I belly flopped on the way down, you also offered a soft place to land.

Tiana Clark, the sparkle dust, long silly phone calls, tight tens, and full woo got me here. I would carry your absurdly heavy suitcase anywhere.

Friendship, advice, secrets, gossip, laughing fits, and assurances from Aja Gabel, Amy Kurzweil, Mike Scalise, T Kira Madden, Jean Garnett, Erin Adair-Hodges, Jenny Croft, and Boris Dralyuk ferried me through the long, choppy stretches of uncertainty.

I have been damn lucky to collect loved ones in my wanderings, from New York to London, Portland to Pittsburgh. I am never alone because of these wonderful people: Carrie Lukasiewicz, Nicolas Carr, Kat Deem, Gaz Morgan, Christina Chaey, Justin Ross, Lauren Fleming, Addoley Dzegede, Lyndon Barrois Jr., Dana Balch, Ángel Diaz, Jessica Harvey, Cynthia Wong, John David Harmon, Monesh Punjabi, Corrie Wang, Shuai Wang, Julie Alpert, Andy Arkley, Yoanna Tang, James London, and Frances Badalamenti. I have subjected many of you to cozy nights of marathon-watching *House Hunters International* and other mindless delights which, as we all know, are essential to my "process."

Ryan Fitzgibbon, every hug, impromptu hang, or adventure replenished my reserves so I could return to writing, feeling human again.

I want to live near you always. Fireside Manhattans and Christmas lasagnas forever.

Erin Roberts, our sessions buoyed me across three challenging years. Thank you for teaching me to slow down, and for using the perfect wine metaphor to convey the importance of gentle pressure. The cork hasn't broken quite yet because of you.

Artists Byron Kim, Michael Joo, Nikki S. Lee, Theresa Hak Kyung Cha, and Do Ho Suh I consider patron saints for this book and in life; their work showed me what is possible from what is not known.

Thank you to Wheatley's dedicated, benevolent staff who welcomed me with grace and noble tolerance. To Richland Library, we are fortunate for the abundance you provide the community. To librarians everywhere, thank you.

Time, space, and care from the Virginia Center for the Creative Arts, the Carson McCullers Center for Writers and Musicians, Tulsa Artist Fellowship, and Loghaven Artist Residency allowed me to create and think freely while surrounded by brilliant people.

Special thanks to *The American Scholar*, BuzzFeed News, Catapult, and Hub City Press for publishing the earliest expressions of this project. Thank you to Wolhee Choe, who dedicated her life to championing artists from the Korean diaspora, and the AHL Foundation for generously extending an opportunity for me to write in her honor. Thank you Laura Graziano and The Berkeley Art Museum and Pacific Film Archive, who permitted me to excerpt Theresa Hak Kyung Cha's poem and continue to advocate for Cha's illustrious body of work. Authors Euny Hong and Ai Ra Kim have written expertly about modern Korean history; I would be lost without their contributions. Dr. Tark Ji-il graciously Skyped in English at the very start of my Korean church research, and I am humbled by his continued kindness. Song-soo Kim, GJ, and 이상인 were invaluable during my yeokmasal inquiry, as was Cecilia Kim with her skillful translation. Fact-checker Kadal Jesuthasan's nuance and perspicacity took me to the finish line when I needed the clarity most.

Fiona, my sweet soul, by my side when I was just a dirtbag twentysomething in New York and a sad sap in South Carolina. I am lucky to be loved by you.

To our original family archivist 박두연, and the indomitable 조금하, 사랑해요. You are with me always. Lastly, I love you Umma, Laurie, and Nari—our next generation, who was born like us: with a blue butt.